SHAKESPEARE'S PLAYS IN PERFORMANCE

New and Revised

John Russell Brown

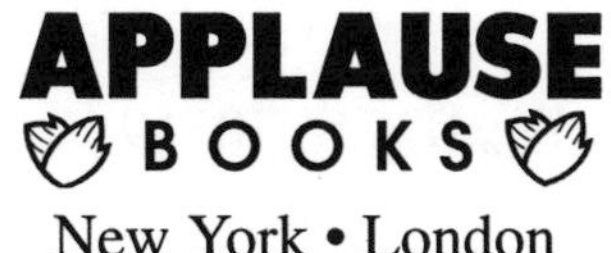
APPLAUSE BOOKS
New York • London

SHAKESPEARE'S PLAYS IN PERFORMANCE

New and Revised

ISBN: 1-55783-136-X

Library of Congress Cataloging-in-Publication Data

Brown, John Russell
Shakespeare's Plays in Performance / John Russell Brown.
New and rev.
p. cm.
Includes bibliographic references and index.
ISBN 1-55783-136-X (pbk.) : $15.95
1. Shakespeare, William, 1564-1616 -- Dramatic production.
2. Shakespeare, William, 1564-1616 -- Stage history. 3. Theater --History. I. Title.
PR3091.B73 1992
822.3'3 -- dc20 92-25205
CIP

Applause Theatre Books
211 West 71st Street
New York, NY 10023
Phone: 212-595-4735 Fax: 212-721-2856

406 Vale Road
Tonbridge Kent TN9 1XR
Phone 0732 357755 Fax 0732 770219

CONTENTS

PART ONE: THE TEXT AND THE ACTORS

PART TWO: ACTION AND THE STAGE

PART THREE: THE PLAY AND THE AUDIENCE

APPENDICES

List of Plates

Cover Photo from Theatre for a New Audience's
Jeffrey Horowitz, Artistic/Producting Director,
Production of THE TEMPEST by William Shakespeare
Direction, Masks and Puppetry by Julie Taymor
Sets and Costumes by G.W. Mercier
Lighting by Frances Aronson

ROBERT STATTEL: Prospero
LOUISE SMITH: Ariel
AVERY BROOKS: Caliban
KELLY WALTERS: Trinculo
ERNEST PERRY, Jr.: Stephano
RENEE BUCCIARELLI, MELISSA FORD, RICHARD HESTER: Puppeteers

Photo by Richard Feldman
Presented by the American Shakespeare Theatre April 27-May 16, 1987

ACKNOWLEDGEMENTS

THE author gratefully acknowledges permission to publish in revised form material that has appeared elsewhere: Edward Arnold (Publishers) Ltd, publishers of *Stratford-upon-Avon Studies*, for Chapters 6, 7 and 10; the Speech Association of America, publishers of the *Quarterly Journal of Speech*, for part of Chapter 2; Chapter 4 is a complete reworking of ideas first expressed in two articles in *Tulane Drama Review*; Columbia University Press for Appendix I, which first appeared in *Reinterpretations of Elizabethan Drama*, ed. Norman Rabkin; and to the University of Delaware Press for Appendix II, which first appeared in *Shakespeare and the Sense of Performance*, ed. Marvin and Ruth Thompson.

A passage from *Lichtenberg's Visits to England*, translated by Margaret L. Mare and W. H. Quarrell (1938), is reprinted by courtesy of the Clarendon Press; one from Bernard Shaw's theatre criticism by permission of the Public Trustee and the Society of Authors; one from M. Saint-Denis, *Theatre: the Rediscovery of Style* (1960), by courtesy of the author; and one from T. S. Eliot's 'Seneca in Elizabethan Translation', published in *Elizabethan Dramatists* and *Selected Essays of T. S. Eliot*, by permission of Faber and Faber Ltd and Harcourt, Brace and World, Inc.

Unless otherwise stated, quotations are taken from Peter Alexander's edition of the *Complete Works* (1951).

Illustrations are reproduced by courtesy of the late Mr Gordon Craig (Plates 5-8), the Harvard Theatre Collection (Plate 4), the Trustees of the National Portrait Gallery (Plate 1), Joe Cocks Studio (Plate 3) Lanny Nagler (Plate 9) and G.W. Mercier (Plates 10-12).

A NOTE ON THE THIRD EDITION

The opportunity to publish a revised and enlarged edition of Shakespeare's Play in Performance has allowed me to make some corrections and refinements, and to extend and reinforce my argument.

Several chapters and an appendix referring to British productions of the nineteen-sixties have been removed, but they are replace with two entirely new chapters and two new appendices. Chapter 8 considers how characters engage with each other in performance and offers a new way of assessing their stage-life. Chapter 11 examines Shakespeare's use of stage properties, costumes and scenic devices, especially in the later plays.

Together the articles reprinted in the new appendices offer an appraisal of what is now called "performance criticism." Both were written after the original publication of my book and are in some ways a response to its reception. Appendix i argues that a concern for the practicalities of theatre must modify both the methods and intentions of literary critics. Appendix ii contrasts an actor's exploration of Shakespeare's text with the work of critics and semioticians; it also shows what can be learnt from attendance at performances and from the study of theatre history.

In its new form, my book is offered as an up-to-date means of understanding Shakespeare's plays and of enjoying the theatrical life for which they were intended.

John Russell Brown.
Ann Arbor, March 1993

WHY are Shakespeare's plays so actable? How do they draw and hold their audiences? How can we gain an impression of performance from reading a text? How should the plays be staged in our theatres to reflect the fullness of Shakespeare's imagination? These are some of the questions that led me to write this book, to try one approach and then another, to experiment in stage-productions and in research and argument. A knowledge of what precisely can and should happen when a play is performed is, for me, the essential first step towards an understanding of Shakespeare, and perhaps the most difficult and fascinating of all.

I start with the text and the actor, which is the closest point of contact between Shakespeare and those who perform his plays. Problems of style and interpretation are at once encountered, and confusions due to changes in taste and conditions of performance. While general considerations prepare for the more particular, every chapter in the first part of the book is basically concerned with how an actor must respond to the text and what revaluations of that text are accomplished by his performance. I have tried to look and listen, as well as read, to respond to entire characterizations as well as momentary and immediate effects, and to remember the excitement of great and original performances.

Many of my examples are taken from the 'early middle' period — from *Romeo and Juliet*, *Richard II*, *The Merchant of Venice* and *Much Ado About Nothing*, from *Julius Caesar* and *Hamlet*. I do not avoid the challenge of later plays, but the comparative clarity of those I have chosen for most sustained comment permits a bolder handling; and yet their artistry is so assured that debate about the extent of Shakespeare's achievement is unnecessary. They are also free from authorship problems, and were first printed from manuscripts close to Shakespeare's own.

After actors, I consider the stage and stage-action — again in conjunction with a close study of texts. Here it is necessary to treat plays individually and to find appropriate terms for complex and continually changing phenomena. We are considering the 'form and pressure' of a dramatic image in which poetry, ambiguities, moral concepts and characterizations are inextricably involved with visual and temporal effects — compositions in form, color and rhythm, devices of scale, contrast, repetition, sequence, tension and tempo. Gordon Craig's *On the Art of the Theatre* has this advice for a director of Shakespeare's tragedies:

> Let me tell you at the commencement that it is the large and sweeping impression produced by means of scene and the movement of the figures which is undoubtedly the most valuable means at your disposal.

There is so much else that asks for immediate attention in Shakespeare's texts that Craig explains:

> I say this only after very many doubts and after much experience.[1]

In this part of my book I try to show the power of the 'large and sweeping impressions' of setting and movement, and to indicate what stage effects are required by the dialogue in addition to those described in the brief and often unreliable stage-directions.

In a third section I proceed to the audience and very briefly discuss the nature of its response.

There are several other books I could have written on my theme. Each chapter might have been a disputation with established literary opinion. Or I could have recorded contemporary productions and shown the range of their achievement, or collected evidence from theatre history; either way I would have written about effects that can certainly be achieved in performance. More technically, I could have documented my own experiments in production and what I lost in width of reference offset by precision of detail. Or I might have been entirely speculative, considering ideal productions in theatres from the Elizabethan or any other age; but so the actors' complete embodiment of Shakespeare's roles would have been forgotten.

The book I have chosen to write is both speculative and practical. I have tried to use the practical achievements of others and, by repeated recourse to the text of the plays, to seek more clues to the stage reality that lies there waiting to be awakened. I have seldom argued about specific interpretations but the whole book advocates a decisive movement away from literary criticism towards theatrical study.

PART ONE

The Text and the Actors

ONE

Verbal Drama

OPENING Shakespeare's *Works* every reader is liable to attend to the words only; they are cunning and wonderful, and absorb immediate interest. Our minds can be pleasurably entangled, at any point, in a subtle net of ambiguities, complexities and levels of meaning, of word-music and allusiveness; and having caught us in one segment, the whole play, or several plays, can be animated by our efforts to understand. Shakespeare's verbal art is, in fact, a trap; it can prevent us from inquiring further.

Perhaps rhetorical passages are the strongest barriers. Figurative argument marching vigorously within a metrical form towards some culminating statement both convinces and arrests as we read: so in *Henry V*:

> Therefore doth heaven divide
> The state of man in divers functions,
> Setting endeavour in continual motion;
> To which is fixed as an aim or butt
> Obedience; for so work the honey bees,
> Creatures that by a rule in nature teach
> The act of order to a peopled kingdom.
> They have a king, and officers of sorts,
> Where some like magistrates correct at home;
> Others like merchants venture trade abroad;
> Others like soldiers, armed in their stings,
> Make boot upon the summer's velvet buds,
> Which pillage they with merry march bring home
> To the tent-royal of their emperor....
>
> I.2.183-96

And further traps are hidden even here, for we must keep alert if we are to remember the whole argument when the next two lines catch us with their euphony, allusiveness, and completeness:

> Who, busied in his majesty, surveys
> The singing masons building roofs of gold...

The 'singing masons...' draws our attention away from neighboring lines, becoming independent of the immediate context; our imagination feeds fully, and other business seems impertinent.

Or a conceit can dominate our thoughts by its mere elaboration; so in *Much Ado*, Hero sends Margaret to Beatrice:

> ...say that thou overheard'st us;
> And bid her steal into the pleached bower,
> Where honeysuckles, ripened by the sun,
> Forbid the sun to enter — like favorites,
> Made proud by princes, that advance their pride
> Against that power that bred it. There will she hide her
> To listen our propose.
>
> III.1.6-12

At first we may be puzzled by unnecessary decoration — 'Why not identify the bower simply?' we ask; but then the words claim our further consideration, and literary criticism and historical research occupy our thoughts. Yes: *steal* and *honeysuckles* are appropriate to the close, sweet yet familiar entanglement that will follow. *Ripened by the sun* is a contrast to Beatrice's earlier, 'Thus goes every one to the world but I, and I am sunburnt' (II.1.286-7).

The *honeysuckles* on the pleached bower are also *proud*; and so Hero, again contrasting natural growth, will soon arraign Beatrice:

> But nature never fram'd a woman's heart
> Of prouder stuff than that of Beatrice.
> Disdain and scorn ride sparkling in her eyes,
> Misprising what they look on; and her wit
> Values itself so highly that to her
> All matter else seems weak. She cannot love....
>
> III.1.49-54

The *honeysuckles, ripened by the sun*, are like Beatrice in denying the full nature of the power that made them *favorites*. Nor must we miss the topicality of this decorative conceit: favorites *were* powerful at the court of Elizabeth I in 1598-9 when *Much Ado* was written.[1] The great Lord Burghley died on 13 September 1598, and for some years his son, Robert, had been rising to influence challenged by the more military and handsome Earl of Essex. Francis Bacon warned the Earl not to force the issue:

> My Lord, these courses be like to hot waters, they will help at a pang: but if you use them, you shall spoil the stomach, and you shall be fain still to make them stronger and stronger, and yet in the end they will lose their operation.

And there were lesser favorites like Sir Christopher Hatton — 'a mere vegetable of the Court, that sprung up at night' — Sir Walter Raleigh, or the Queen's godson, Sir John Harington. Power could suddenly be lost: when Harington returned from Ireland knighted by Essex, the Queen exclaimed, 'By God's Son! I am no Queen; that man is above me' and banished the comparatively innocent godson from Court. When Hero likens honeysuckles to proud favorites her words draw our attention until we observe the whole play in little: pride *versus* nature, in Beatrice, Benedick, Don John and Dogberry ('I am a wise fellow; and, which is more, as pretty a piece of flesh as any is in Messina...'); a reminder of the impermanence of pride, and honeysuckles and favorites.

One decorative passage can send us to more words, to the course of the play's action, and back again to words; we stay fascinated in the verbal contrivance and have little leisure to ask how important this steeplechase is for the comedy as a whole. Books have been filled with accounts of these pursuits: Shakespeare's use of language and his imagery, his themes perceived in the 'poetic texture' of the dialogue. While none of these studies would claim to be inclusive or final, all suggest that a careful study of words reveals a coherent 'attitude to life' which is a hidden, unifying influence on the structure and substance of the plays.

In the eighteenth century, before literary criticism grew subtle and hardworking, a fascination with Shakespeare's words led to numerous collections of the 'beauties of Shakespeare'. So when the poet, Pope, prepared an edition of the plays, he helped his readers and showed his own discrimination by marking with asterisks the finest passages. Now that we no longer quote a splendid passage and leave its wings unmeasured by criticism, we are still liable to be held by the words and pride ourselves on showing the relevance and complexity of any highly wrought passage.

*

But there are many other elements in a drama that must be appreciated — those which are not so easily reached through the printed page — and the very words themselves can be fully known only if they are considered in their dramatic context. They must be heard in sequence, supported by actors' impersonations, related to the physical and visual elements of performance; and so, perhaps, revalued.

For example, theatre history reminds us of numerous lines that would yield a lean harvest to literary investigation, but have inspired successive audiences to wonder and applause. Notable in the earlier plays is Richard III's 'A horse! a horse! my kingdom for a horse!' (V.5.7), or Petruchio's response to the Shrew's last speech, 'Why, there's a wench! Come on, and kiss me, Kate' (V.2.180); dramatic considerations of physical action and bearing, intonation and emphasis, a new simplicity and weight of utterance, carry these moments. In *II Henry IV* the crucial moment in the last long interview between the dying king and Prince Hal is the simple, incomplete verse-line, 'O my son' (IV.4.178), which every actor of the role in my experience has made more affecting than the other hundred and fifty lines of the duologue. Hamlet has many such lines: 'Go on; I'll follow thee' to the Ghost, and 'O God!', 'Murder!', 'My uncle!' (I.4.79 and 86, and I.5.24 and 40, etc.). When Hamlet first calls the Ghost 'father' many actors have found that the text asks for particular emphasis:

> Kean, we are told, was no longer frightened. Booth 'dropped on one knee... and bowed his head, not in terror, but in awe and love.' At the sight of the spirit, Salvini's face was 'illumined with an awe-struck joy'; and his Hamlet, 'spontaneously, and one would almost say unconsciously, uncovers his head'.[2]

The theatrical fact of the silent Ghost meeting Hamlet is large and, in ways that the reader might never guess, the text grows in performance to answer it. Later, Hamlet's first words in his mother's closet, 'Now, mother, what's the matter?' and, near the end of the same scene, his repeated 'Good night, mother'(III.4.8 and 4.159-77) are powerful beyond literary analysis. Such uncomplicated, forceful lines are in the comedies too, in Rosalind's 'And so am I for no woman' (*As You Like It*, V.2.81-95) or Benedick's 'This can be no trick' (*Much Ado*, II.3.201). All these live only in their dramatic context, nourished by timing, surprise, repetition, change of dramatic idiom, physical performance, mood, grouping.

In the greatest tragedies Shakespeare seems especially concerned to build theatrical intensity and revelation with the barest verbal material. Obviously, Lady Macbeth's sleep walking scene verbally echoes important themes and introduces staggering images and juxtapositions of ideas, but its full power is not easily revealed by literary analysis. According to the Doctor and Gentlewoman her 'Oh, oh, oh!' (V.1.49) is the emotional climax revealing a heart 'sorely charg'd': her fullest suffering lies beneath the words that somnambulism releases. For a literary analyst, Macbeth's last couplet:

> Lay on Macduff;
> And damn'd be him that first cries 'Hold, enough!'
>
> V.8.33-4

has a metrical obviousness and traces of fustian; it gains stature and meaning only in enactment, by a physical resurgence and concentration. Here is a report of Irving's Macbeth in *The Academy* of 2 October 1875:

> What one finds so good in his Fifth Act, is not only the gradations of abjectness and horror, as evil news follow on evil news, but the self-control that has long deserted him, gathered together at last; and the end, whatever the end may be, accepted with some return of the old courage, only more reckless and wild; for it is the last chance and a poor one....
>
> Mr Irving's fight with Macduff illustrates quite perfectly, in its savage and hopeless wildness, the last temper of Macbeth.

These are effects that are supported by the text but can be realized only in performance.

King Lear alone could provide weighty evidence of the need to pass beyond literary analysis: 'Come, boy' and 'I shall go mad! (I.5.47; II.4.285) to the fool — the 'tone in which Garrick uttered' these last words 'absolutely thrilled' his audience;[3] and:

> I will say nothing.
>
> Didst thou give all to thy daughters?
>
> Come, unbutton here.
>
> Give me thy arm;
> Poor Tom shall lead thee.
>
> Then kill, kill, kill, kill, kill, kill!

    Come, come; I am a king,
My masters, know you that.

Then there's life in't. Nay, an you get it, you shall
get it by running. Sa, sa, sa, sa.

    Do not laugh at me;
For, as I am a man, I think this lady
To be my child Cordelia.
                —And so I am, I am.

    Thou'lt come no more,
Never, never, never, never, never.
Pray you undo this button. Thank you, sir.
Do you see this? Look on her. Look, her lips.
Look there, look there!

III.2.38; III.4.48 and 108; IV.1.79-80; IV.6.188 and 201-5; IV.7.68-70; V.3.307-11.

Words like *laugh* and *man*, *my child* and *I am*, or *never*, *see* and *look* and even *button* will yield to literary analysis and show something of the relevance of these passages; and so will their syntax and metre. But Cordelia's 'And so I am, I am' or Lear's 'Look there, look there!' demand theatrical criticism to explain the rightness, delicacy and overwhelming intensity of feeling that accompanies the monosyllables in performance. These are the moments that stay with the audience long after the play is finished.

*

A dramatic text is spoken and heard; some words may be, as it were, in capital letters, some may be written very small indeed, some almost illegible — quite different from the uniform scale of a printed page. In non-dramatic forms of writing such effects may sometimes be managed, but for a play in performance they are necessary, and greatly magnified. Listen to anyone's speech: the words 'I will' spoken very quickly have a different meaning and are almost opposite in aural effect compared with the same words spoken very slowly and quietly. Or coming after a long sentence and complicated interplay of syntax and metre, they will sound differently and mean differently from the same words in a nimble prose exchange; alterations of pitch or stress, or of tone and texture, also modify them. In such ways the literary meaning and metrical effect of a printed text develop through performance into something far more complicated.

The first rule for reading the text of a play is to remember that dramatic energy is dynamic not static, that the dramatist has tried to control the tempo of performance in the smallest detail, to prepare, sustain and release moments of large emotion and alternately lead forward and hold back the audience's attention. The second rule is to remember the actor, whose sensibility and physical performance support the words, and the other actors on stage with him.

Short but sustained speech will illustrate the dynamic qualities of theatrical writing; for example, Oberon's reply to Puck just before day comes to the wood outside Athens in *A Midsummer Night's Dream*:

> But we are spirits of another sort:
> I with the Morning's love have oft made sport;
> And, like a forester, the groves may tread
> Even till the eastern gate, all fiery red,
> Opening on Neptune with fair blessed beams,
> Turns into yellow gold his salt green streams.
> But, notwithstanding, haste, make no delay;
> We may effect this business yet ere day.
>
> III.2.388-95

The plot is scarcely forwarded by the information of the first six lines, but much else is accomplished. Time and the general situation are established with talk of the 'eastern gate, all fiery red'. And the gold and fiery light of the sun in opposition to cold water, repeats an important theme in the play, echoing earlier references to a 'cold fruitless moon', 'salt tears', 'the moon, the governess of floods, Pale in her anger', or the sea's 'contagious fogs'. But to understand its theatrical effect enactment must be considered as well: these ideas are not neatly defined, but placed and imaged so that the warmth and yellow radiance transfigure the salt and green sea; the sun overpowers the sea with the long, tidal reach of syntax, so making the green one gold. When the actor speaks the lines this metrical effect is inescapable; rhythm, pitch, stress and phrase ensure its communication. So, too, the character Oberon grows, the long, controlled sound of his speech giving him an authority which he has no need to claim — often a main consideration in the balance of an acted scene. The control is astonishing: after the quick descriptive clause of 'like a forester', another adverbial clause follows and within that yet another with 'Opening on Neptune with fair blessed beams'; he has leisure, even, for the double epithet of 'fair blessed' at its close, before the strong and simple verb of the main clause is supplied in 'Turns'. The impression of controlled power in Oberon depends largely on temporal and musical means and on the clarity of performance; and because these are usually unrecognized in operation by the audience, they work with seeming inevitability — this, again, is part of their effect, giving an impression of reserved power.

The influence of these six lines extends beyond the time in which they are spoken. They accentuate, by contrast, the renewed speed of Oberon's concluding couplet when he leaves without doubting Puck's response, and the energy, compactness and outspokenness of Puck left alone on the stage:

> Up and down, up and down,
> I will lead them up and down...

Their reverberations continue when the lovers enter, for the young men's unsustained rhythms in asserting power, by contrast with both Puck and Oberon, will sound shallow and insecure:

> Where art thou, proud Demetrius? Speak thou now...

Out of dramatic context, both rhythm and vocabulary might be called direct and efficient, but theatrical enactment must revalue this.

When we progress beyond the meaning of words, and our own appreciation of rhythm and texture, to their enactment, we move quickly from the printed page to the whole stage, from variations of tempo and emphasis to physical movement, silence, posture, grouping, the potential surprise of an entrance or exit, from argument and statement to lively and emotional performances. We must continue to ask 'What is the effect?' in preference to 'What is the meaning?' When at last we ask the second question we have to account for impressions which quotation of the text alone can never represent.

*

The dynamic nature of theatrical energy ensures that a dramatist must be specially concerned with metre and prose rhythms. (The lameness of translated plays is some indication of the importance of an author's time-control through speech.) Someone who did not understand a word of English could hear Cordelia's answer to Lear in performance and gain some impression of her physical involvement and the extremity, purity and strength of her feeling. The rhythms of her short speech must answer and satisfy the rhythms of his longer speech:

> Do not laugh at me;
> For, as I am a man, I think this lady
> To be my child Cordelia.
> —— And so I am, I am.

To manage the proper rhythmic balance, the two impersonators of these roles must be closely and silently attuned to each other's performance and, therefore, they will communicate a shared, delicate and intuitive sympathy; how this reaches the audience is not easily explained, but it is an effect good actors can command in such a context. Metre and syntax instigate, and release, the physical and emotive elements of performance.

In Shakespeare's day this generative power of words in a theatrical context could be controlled surely by virtue of the firm metrical base of blank verse. When he began to write, the iambic beat was over-assertive; in his preface to *Menaphon* (1589), Thomas Nashe criticized dramatists who indulged the 'spacious volubility of a drumming decasyllabon'. But other writers besides William Webbe, in his *Discourse of English Poetry* (1586), judged that the 'natural course of most English verses seemeth to run upon the old iambic stroke',[4] and most sought to refine rather than replace its 'measure' or 'certain frame'.

By accepting a far more regular metre than would be tolerated today, the Elizabethans discovered a manner of speech that was both forcible and subtle. As Sir Philip Sidney put it, each syllable could be 'peysed', or weighed:

> The Senate of Poets hath chosen verse as their fittest raiment... not speaking (table-talk fashion or like men in a dream) words as they chanceably fall from the mouth, but peysing each syllable of each word by just proportion according to the dignity of the subject.[5]

For play-writing, metre was almost universal: Hamlet asks the players for 'temperance' and 'smoothness' even in the 'very torrent, tempest, and, as I may say, whirlwind of your passion' (III.2.6-8) and this implies rigorous verbal accomplishment for both actor and author. Joseph Hall's *Virgidemiarum* (1598) pictures some dramatists watching a play and following the actors in a manuscript as if it were a musical score:

> Meanwhile our poets in high parliament,
> Sit watching every word, and gesturement,
> Like curious censors of some doughty gear,
> Whispering their verdict in their fellow's ear.
> Woe to the word whose margent in their scroll
> Is noted with a black condemning coal.
> But if each period might the synod please —
> Ho! bring the ivy boughs, and bands of bays.

I.3.45-53

Blank verse gives the necessary control, power, and coherence for physical enactment to grow out of the speaking of the text. The control comes by 'peysing' each syllable and varying the interplay of syntax and metre. Impressions of emotion grow by breaking a regular confinement, or by extending over many lines a single unit of rhythmic design. And coherence derives from the regularity sustained beneath all manner of irregularities, the now discreet and scarcely heard 'drumming' of the iambic pentameters. Metre enables a dramatic poet to influence the dynamics of production and the actors' performances.

In *Romeo and Juliet*, Friar Lawrence enters the play alone, carrying a basket:

> The gray-ey'd morn smiles on the frowning night,
> Check'ring the eastern clouds with streaks of light;
> And fleckèd darkness like a drunkard reels
> From forth day's path and Titan's fiery wheels.
> Now, ere the sun advance his burning eye
> The day to cheer and night's dank dew to dry,
> I must up-fill this osier cage of ours
> With baleful weeds and precious-juiced flowers.

II.3.1-8

Thematically the soliloquy is significant. In the previous scene the sun had been associated with Juliet as Romeo exclaims:

> What light through yonder window breaks?
> It is the east, and Juliet is the sun.

II.2.2-3

Later Juliet is to call Romeo 'thou day in night', a light so fine that it will draw worship away from the 'garish sun' (III.2.17-25). At the end of the play, the Prince also speaks of the dawn:

> A glooming peace this morning with it brings,
> The sun for sorrow will not show his head.
>
> V.3.304-5

The night, too, recurs as an image throughout the play, in Romeo's foreboding and Juliet's invocation of 'gentle night' and 'loving black-brow'd night', and repeatedly in Romeo's dying speech in the 'palace of dim night' when Juliet's

> beauty makes
> This vault a feasting presence full of light.
>
> V.3.74-120

Here then, with his first entry, the Friar is presented verbally, as if he willingly accepts the alternation of night and day and of good and evil: thematically a position of strength. But by temporal effects his soliloquy means much more. Its antitheses fit neatly into the metrical line-units, and the rhyme. The iambics of the first couplet are regular except for the easy reversal in the first foot of the second line — 'Check'ring' — and the stronger reversal in the first line: 'The gray-ey'd morn *smiles* on the frowning night'. Notice how well-contained the 'frowning night' is, at the metrically regular end of the line; and how the potential threat is then dispersed in the belittling 'Check'ring' placed strongly in the first reversed foot of the next line. By all these means, the couplet is a stage-direction: Friar Lawrence's movements have a regular pace; he is neat; he is smoothly and pleasantly optimistic; he is gentle. The next line gives more power to darkness by comparing it with a 'drunkard' reeling, but still this reaction is not developed; here the notion is reduced in scale by 'fleckèd' and quenched by the overwhelming metrical strength of 'From forth day's path' at the beginning of the next line, and by the additional description in 'Titan's fiery wheels'. The image of a drunkard being almost run over by a chariot is potentially brutal; but the 'drunkard' is lost from consciousness in considering the course of the sun, and the Friar immediately veers to another aspect of his concerns, introduced with a regular pentameter without the trace of a caesura which earlier had contributed to an impression of neatness: 'Now ere the sun advance his burning eye'. 'Burning eye' suggests some danger but this is turned to favor and to prettiness in the double antitheses and early caesura of the next line: 'The day to cheer and night's dank dew to dry.' Here is an indication of thought and feeling that must suggest physical bearing; the Friar's temperament is nervous but habitually controlled by an easy intellectual optimism; he recognizes danger but dismisses it from his consideration by thoughts of the good. His posture, facial expressions, tone of voice expressing all this will add to the theatrical effect, especially as he is a new character alone on the large open stage, an object of intense scrutiny. So in performance, the Friar's acceptance of the 'alternation of night and day, and of good and evil' is not the position of strength the printed text might suggest: he is, also, somewhat shallow and petty.

In the Ball Scene of *Romeo and Juliet*, Act I Scene 5, metrical variety indicates the individual bearing of the actors and also major elements in stage-management. It starts with grumbling and emphatic prose for the servants suggesting a Breughel-like detail and scale. Then comes the more sustained but short-phrased, almost puffing, emphasis of Capulet managing his guests; he is largely monosyllabic, directly physical in detail, repetitive and, for a time, alliterative:

> Welcome, gentlemen! Ladies that have their toes
> Unplagu'd with corns will have a bout with you.
> Ah ha, my mistresses! which of you all
> Will now deny to dance? She that makes dainty,
> She I'll swear hath corns; am I come near ye now?
> Welcome, gentlemen!

and then he retires into the longer phrases of personal reminiscence. Romeo's question to a nameless servant:

> What lady's that which doth enrich the hand
> Of yonder knight?

is smoothly sustained in image and rhythm; the simple reply, 'I know not, sir', does not deflect him; he modifies his image, and rhymes with his own last word:

> O, she doth teach the torches to burn bright!

Metrical regularity is emphasized by alliteration and then a more powerful irregularity with 'burn bright!' at the end of the line. His imagery changes again, but in sustained response and guided by the rhymed couplets. Tybalt interjects in another rhythm, sharp and athletic:

> This, by his voice, should be a Montague.
> Fetch me my rapier, boy, What, dares the slave....

He changes from soliloquy to dialogue without embarrassment, and his speech builds quickly in emphatic statement. When he is questioned by Capulet his anger is sustained largely by repetition; he then becomes more brief and leaves with new, incisive threats.

The following dialogue between Romeo and Juliet is in complete contrast: they share a sonnet, its rhymes, form and images. The two lovers are strangely singled out from the other dancers and the sonnet, with its dominant image of worship, is their own predestined dance — impelled, gentle, mutual and awed; it requires a separation from the scene's ordinary pace — its blank verse and couplets — which they alone know. Through its verbal exchanges they move towards their kisses, first palm-to-palm and then lip-to-lip. Without such a presentation these intimate actions would have been lost in the crowded, animated scene, or might have been exaggerated by the actors in an effort to give them dramatic forcefulness; as Shakespeare directs through his metrical dialogue, the kisses have their own silence because our attention waits upon them for the completion of the sonnet. Even the words are revalued by their metrical setting: if the lovers did not have to share the rhythms and form of the sonnet, their conceits might ring too keenly; but, secure in the privacy of the sonnet, the wit can sound tender and contented as, perhaps, off-stage only, intimate love-talk can be.

*

Similes, metaphors and other figures of speech, when read in conjunction with the rhythm and tempo of speech, can indicate physical performance. The Friar's changing imagery suggests a timorous nature, Romeo's sustained imagery an absorption in a single feeling. But, perhaps more powerfully, images also display a general, overall excitement, a state of being in which fantasy becomes real.

When we read a printed text we pick our way slowly through the conceits — as we have attended to Hero's talk of honeysuckles. But the actor has assimilated all this — or should have done — so that in speaking the difficulties disappear and excitement takes their place.

Hero is a young girl in love, about to talk of love and to give thoughts of love to her cousin, who has derided love; lightly spoken her speech is alive with feeling as well as thought. The metre helps, too; notice the way in which 'like favorites' starts its new, energetic development at the end of a line after the period had seemed to be complete. In Anthony Mundy's *Zelauto* (1580), a novel which Shakespeare almost certainly read while preparing to write *The Merchant of Venice*, a young man becomes satisfied that his lady is concerned for him; he is said to look 'smug' and then:

> his conceits began to come so nimbly together, that he now rolled in his rhetoric, like a flea in a blanket.
>
> Sig. P3

However complex Shakespeare's imagery can seem, and however long a reader may pore over the words, from the stage it is often a widespreading vigour and enjoyment that is the dominant impression communicated to the audience.

Two testimonies are useful here. First Bernard Shaw inveighing against academic critics and elocution teachers:

> Powerful among the enemies of Shakespear are the commentator and the elocutionist: the commentator because, not knowing Shakespear's language, he sharpens his reasoning faculty... instead of sensitizing his artistic faculty to receive the impression of moods and inflexions of feeling conveyed by word-music; the elocutionist because... he devotes his life to the art of breaking up verse in such a way as to make it sound like insanely pompous prose. The effect of this on Shakespear's earlier verse, which is full of the naive delight of pure oscillation, to be enjoyed as an Italian enjoys a barcarolle, or a child a swing, or a baby a rocking-cradle, is destructively stupid.
>
> Review of *All's Well that Ends Well*, *Saturday Review*, 2 February 1895[6]

The second is from the publishers of the first edition of *Troilus and Cressida* in 1609 who wrote in their preface that Shakespeare had:

> such a dexterity, and power of wit, that the most displeased with plays are pleas'd with his comedies. And all such dull and heavy-witted worldlings, as were never capable of the wit of a comedy, coming by report of them to his representations have found that wit there, that they never found in themselves, and have parted better witted than they came; feeling an edge of

> wit set upon them, more than ever they dream'd they had brain to grind it on. So much and such savoured salt of wit is in his comedies, that they seem (for their height of pleasure) to be born in that sea that brought forth Venus.

Alive in performance, Shakespeare's most conceited and obscure passages can represent enjoyment or vigour or confidence or sexual excitement — all powerful over an audience; they may also suggest sensitivity, gentleness, deep involvement — the kind of feelings which do not startle an audience but affect them slowly. The reader misses all this because he does not assimilate the conceits and rhetoric as an actor does, nor hear them as one part of the actor's performance.

The remainder of the first part of this book offers some ways of defining and measuring the actors' necessary contribution.

TWO

Acting

THIS chapter is a digression. I have already made assumptions about an actor's response to Shakespeare's text that some scholars would challenge by reference to Elizabethan conditions of performance and so I want to examine these assumptions before proceeding further.

It used to be possible to quote Hamlet's advice to the players, point out that no extravagances were to be used, and leave the rest to the actor to interpret in the tradition of his art, but today many scholars believe that actors must rediscover a lost technique in order to present Shakespeare's plays. Many would say that Elizabethan acting was 'fundamentally formal' and only 'shaded by naturalism from time to time.'[1] 'Formal acting' has not been properly defined but is assumed to be the opposite of 'natural', and to make no attempt to give an impression of real life. It gives first place to literary qualities: 'poetry and its decent delivery' are considered 'the only real essentials of Elizabethan drama'.[2]

The quest for a historically correct acting style for Shakespeare is comparatively new, and an authoritative, complete and balanced treatise is yet to be published. But in the meantime, what guidance can scholarship give to actors, producers and readers of Shakespeare's plays?

It seems to me that the subject has been approached from an unfortunate angle and that, in consequence, the evidence has been distorted and misapplied. Briefly, I believe that 'formalism', as it is generally understood in this context, was fast dying out in Shakespeare's age, and that a new naturalism was the kindling spirit in his theatre. This was not what we understand by naturalism today, but it did aim at an illusion of real life. I want to reverse the statement which I have quoted above, and to say that Elizabethan acting aimed at an illusion of life, although vestiges of an old formalism remained. If I am right, actors today have a better chance of interpreting Shakespeare than those who were his contemporaries, for modern traditions are based on a thorough-going naturalism unknown to Elizabethans. If the relics of formalism are properly respected, we can realize the illusion of life with a new delicacy and completeness.

*

To prove my point, I would have to examine in detail, and in chronological sequence, the whole *corpus* of Elizabethan drama. All I can do here is to counter some of the arguments which might be brought against my statement, and present some evidence which I do not think has been sufficiently discussed.

The earliest advocates of formal acting based their statements on Elizabethan stage-conditions; for example, after describing the circled audience and the gallants sitting on the stage, S. L. Bethell maintained that

> ...even with the abundance of make-up, scenery, and properties in use today, it would have been impossible for actors so closely beset with audience, to create and sustain an illusion of actual life, especially as they performed in broad daylight.[3]

Obviously these conditions made it difficult to sustain an illusion of real life, but nevertheless it was certainly attempted and achieved. Thomas Heywood in his *An Apology for Actors* (1612) writes,

> ... turn to our domestic histories: what English blood, seeing the person of any bold Englishman presented, and doth not hug his fame, and honey at his valour, pursuing him in his enterprise with his best wishes and, as being wrapt in contemplation, offers to him in his heart all prosperous performance, *as if the personator were the man personated*? [4]

John Webster, in the Character of 'An Excellent Actor' (1615), uses almost the same words: 'what we see him personate, we think truly done before us.'[5] John Fletcher was praised for giving opportunity for a similar illusion:

> How didst thou sway the theatre! make us feel
> The players' wounds were true, and their swords, steel!
> Nay, stranger yet, how often did I know
> When the spectators ran to save the blow?
> Frozen with grief we could not stir away
> Until the Epilogue told us 'twas a play.[6]

Prolonged death speeches must have made the simulation of real life very difficult — *The Knight of the Burning Pestle* ridicules their excesses — but Burbage evidently could achieve it; not only did the audience think he actually died, but the dramatic illusion extended to the other actors in the scene with him:

> Oft have I seen him play this part in jest,
> So lively, that spectators and the rest
> Of his sad crew, whilst he but seem'd to bleed,
> Amazed, thought even then he died in deed.[7]

From such descriptions, we must assume that Elizabethan actors aimed at an illusion of real life and that the best of them achieved it.

Even when scholars accept such a statement, they still write down the acting as 'formal'. So Professor Harbage maintained that

> we are told what the actor did (in the estimation of the spectator), but not how he did it. Since the conventions of formal acting will be accepted as just while formal acting prevails, testimony like the above is nugatory.[8]

This argument satisfies the evidence if, on other grounds, the acting is known to have been 'formal'. But even if this is granted, the fact remains that an illusion of life was attempted; if our actors are more thorough in this respect, may they not be interpreting the plays in the new spirit in which they were written?

Arguments for formal acting which are based on the plays themselves are difficult to answer directly without a detailed, chronological study. But one may notice, in general, that much of the evidence is taken from early plays, the famous Towton scene in *III Henry VI* (II.5) being always to the fore. The formal, didactic arrangement of such scenes died out as the Morality plays, on which they seem to be based, disappeared also; it is not representative of the first decade of the seventeenth century. Direct address to the audience is another feature of Elizabethan plays which has been adduced in support of formal acting; such speeches have been thought to shatter 'all possibility of dramatic illusion'[9]. Here it is admitted that Shakespeare's plays do not provide any strikingly clear example, yet even if such were found it would not be an insurmountable obstacle to the simulation of real life on the stage. There was no gap between audience and stage in the Elizabethan theatre, so actors did not address the audience as if it were in another world. There was a reciprocal relationship; the audience could participate in the drama as easily as the actors could share a joke or enlist sympathy. The very fact that it is difficult to distinguish direct address from soliloquy, and soliloquy from true dialogue, shows that contact with the audience was quite unembarrassed. They shared a sturdy illusion of life.

The use of verse in Elizabethan drama has also been taken for a sign that acting was formal; for instance, it has been said of the sonnet embedded in the dialogue of *Romeo and Juliet* (I.5.91-104):

> Shakespeare's purpose can only be achieved if his audience is allowed to respond to the figures, the images, and the metrical pattern of these fourteen lines. There is no need to imitate dialogue realistically.[10]

But once more the development of new styles in writing and acting must be taken into account. When Jonson wrote *Timber*, the style of Marlowe already belonged to another age:

> The true artificer will not run away from nature, as he were afraid of her; or depart from life, and the likeness of truth; but speak to the capacity of his hearers. And though his language differ from the vulgar somewhat; it shall not fly from all humanity, with the *Tamerlanes*, and *Tamer-Chams* of the late age.[11]

Once the idea of development is accepted, the debatable question about Elizabethan acting ceases to be 'Was it formal or natural?'; it is rather, 'Which was the new, dominant style, the fashionable mode in which they would strive to produce even old plays or recalcitrant material?' I believe that the comparison between the style of Marlowe's age and that of Jonson's points in one direction only. It had become possible to speak the verse as if it were meant — as if, at that instant, it sprang from the mind of the speaker. Shakespeare's mature style has the best of two worlds: there is the eloquence, precision, structural strength and melody of verse, but there is also the immediacy and movement of actual speech. The dramatist has achieved the ideal which Puttenham sought in the courtly poet; he is now

> a dissembler only in the subtleties of his art; that is, when he is most artificial, so to disguise and cloak it as it may not appear, nor seem to proceed from him, by any study or trade of rules, but to be his natural.[12]

'Artificial' language must seem a 'natural' idiom. This new dialogue needed a new style of acting; as the verse became less obviously formal and declamatory, so did the acting. Both aimed at an illusion of 'natural' life.

•

One piece of external evidence has been generally accepted as an indication of formal acting. This is the Elizabethan comparison between the actor and the orator. The *locus classicus* is the Character of 'An Excellent Actor':

> Whatsoever is commendable in the grave orator, is most exquisitely perfect in him; for by a full and significant action of body, he charms our attention.[13]

A later statement is Richard Flecknoe's *A Short Discourse of the English Stage* (1664) which says that Richard Burbage

> had all the parts of an excellent orator (animating his words with speaking, and speech with action).[14]

The use of the word *action* to describe the bodily movements of both orator and actor shows how accepted was the comparison between the two kinds of artist.

From this evidence several deductions might be made: first, the actor used a declamatory voice as distinct from a conversational; secondly, he observed the phrasing, figures, and literary quality of his lines in the manner laid down for the orator; and thirdly, he used 'action' to enforce the meaning of his lines rather than to represent the emotion of a character or an involvement in business appropriate to the imagined situation. It has been suggested that John Bulwer's *Chirologia* and *Chironomia*, two books of manual signs for the use of orators, published in 1644 and written by a specialist in the teaching of the deaf, might represent the 'actions' used on the Elizabethan stage.[15] But the deductions can go further, and the actor is sometimes endowed with the intentions of the orator; it is thought that he excited the emotions of his audience rather than expressed those of the character he was representing. Under such conditions a play would be a number of speeches, rather than an image of actual life. It has even been suggested that, in Dr Johnson's words, an Elizabethan went to the theatre in order to

> hear a certain number of lines recited with just gesture and elegant modulation.[16]

Obviously one cannot deny the comparison between actor and orator, but this does not imply that the comparison held at all points; both artists spoke before an audience and used gestures — and there the comparison might rest. Distinctions between the two were clearly recognized by Elizabethans. So Abraham Fraunce, speaking of the orator, says that gesture should change with the voice,

> yet not parasitically as stage players use, but gravely and decently as becometh men of greater calling.[17]

The distinction may not be flattering to the actor but it is plain enough. Thomas Wright's *The Passions of the Mind* (1604) makes another distinction; here the orator is said to act 'really' to 'stir up all sorts of passions according to the exigency of the matter', whereas the player acts 'feignedly' in the performance of a fiction 'only to delight' (p. 179).

Rhetoric was taught in Elizabethan schools and universities where 'pronunciation' — or delivery — received its due attention. Indeed, Heywood in his *Apology* shows that acting was used as a means of training the young orator. If the arts of acting and oratory were truly similar, here would be an excellent 'school' for actors; but clearly it was not: scholars learned a style of acting for oratory that was condemned on the public stage. So, in *II The Return from Parnassus* (c. 1602), Kempe, the professional actor, criticizes the scholar-players as those who

> never speak in their walk, but at the end of the stage, just as though in walking... we should never speak but at a style, a gate, or a ditch, where a man can go no further.
>
> IV.3

Kempe criticizes them because they did not act as men do in real life. Richard Brome makes a similar distinction against scholar-players in *The Antipodes* (1640):

> Let me not see you act now,
> In your scholastic way, you brought to town wi' ye,
> ...I'll none of these absurdities in my house.
>
> II.2

The gestures described in Bulwer's books for orators could be among the scholastic absurdities which Brome inveighs against. In Campion's *Book of Airs* (1601), criticism is precise:

> But there are some, who to appear the more deep and singular in their

> judgement, will admit no music but that which is long, intricate, bated with fugue, chain'd with syncopation, and where the nature of every word is precisely express'd in the note, like the old exploded action in comedies, when if they did pronounce *Memini*, they would point to the hinder part of their heads, if *Video* put their finger in their eye.[18]

Here, rhetorical gestures are considered both scholastic ('deep and singular') and old-fashioned; clearly Campion thought they were not in use in the up-to-date theatres of London.

Perhaps the distinction between actor and orator is most clearly stated in Flecknoe's praise of Burbage which has already been quoted:

> He had all the parts of an excellent orator..., yet even then, he was an excellent actor still, never falling in his part when he had done speaking; but with his looks and gesture, maintaining it still unto the height....

Flecknoe says, in effect, that though Burbage had the graces of an orator, *yet even then he was an excellent actor* — in spite of some likeness of his art to oratory.

Earlier in the same passage, Flecknoe had claimed that Burbage

> was a delightful Proteus, so wholly transforming himself into his part, and putting off himself with his clothes, as he never (not so much as in the tyring-house) assum'd himself again until the play was done.

Such absorption in a role has nothing to do with oratory; it is closer to the acting techniques of Stanislavski. The actor obliterated his whole consciousness and outward bearing in those of his part, and did not merely declaim his lines with formal effectiveness. The Prologue to *Antonio and Mellida* (first performed in 1599) gives a similar impression where actors are shown preparing for their parts and speaking extempore in the appropriate 'veins'. An incidental image in *Coriolanus* implies the same technique:

> You have put me now to such a part which never
> I shall discharge to th' life.
>
> III.2.105-6

In the event, Coriolanus was unable to do as Burbage did and wholly transform himself into his assumed character.

*

There are many extant descriptions of Elizabethan acting but the value of this evidence is commonly belittled because it is written in the same technical language as the criticism of rhetoric and oratory. So Hamlet's advice to the players is dismissed as 'a cliché from classical criticism, equally applicable to all the arts'.[19] Or again, it is claimed that

> the poet has put into the mouth of his Prince nothing that conflicts with the directions normally provided by the teachers of rhetorical delivery.[20]

But the fact that the same language was used to describe acting and oratory does not mean that those arts were identical. The language of criticism was in its infancy and it was perhaps inevitable that acting should be dependent on the technical vocabulary of a more systematic art.

Descriptions of acting use many words and phrases from the criticism of oratory, but the new context may give new pertinency. The phrase *imitation of life* is an example. It is basic to the concept of poetry as an art of imitation, a concept which was not generally understood by Elizabethans — except for Sir Philip Sidney — as referring to the poet's revelation of ideal and universal truth. The usual interpretation is seen in Sir Thomas Elyot's description of comedy as 'a picture or as it were a mirror of man's life'[21] or in Ascham's idea that drama was a 'perfect *imitation*, or fair lively painted picture of the life of every degree of man'.[22] The phrase is constantly repeated; Lodge, Jonson, and Heywood all claimed on Cicero's authority that Comedy was '*imitatio vitae, speculum consuetudinis, et imago veritatis*'.[23]

The idea of drama as a picture of life suggests a parallel in criticism of the art of painting, and here the meaning of imitation is much clearer. For instance it is implicit throughout the description of the pictures offered to Christopher Sly in the Induction of *The Taming of the Shrew*:

—Dost thou love pictures? we will fetch thee straight
 Adonis painted by a running brook,
 And Cytherea all in sedges hid,
 Which seem to move and wanton with her breath
 Even as the waving sedges play wi' th' wind.
—We'll show thee Io as she was a maid
 And how she was beguiled and surpris'd,
 As lively painted as the deed was done.
—Or Daphne roaming through a thorny wood,
 Scratching her legs, that one shall swear she bleeds

And at that sight shall sad Apollo weep,
So workmanly the blood and tears are drawn.

I.2.47-58

'As lively painted as the deed was done' is the key to this description, and 'life-likeness' or the 'imitation of life' were constantly used in the criticism of the visual arts. So in *The Merchant of Venice*, Bassanio exclaims when he finds Portia's picture in the leaden casket, 'What demi-god Hath come so near creation?' (III.2.115-16), or Paulina in *The Winter's Tale* claims that her 'statue' can show life 'Lively mock'd' (V.3.19). For an example outside Shakespeare, we may take Thomas Nashe's description of the floor of an Italian summer house; it was

> painted with the beautifullest flowers that ever man's eye admired; which so lineally were delineated that he that view'd them afar off, and had not directly stood poringly over them, would have sworn they had lived indeed.[24]

Imitation of life was not the whole concern of renaissance artists, but their experiments in perspective and light were at first designed to deceive the external eye; their paintings were meant to look like real life.

When the phrase is used of acting, of performing in the 'picture' that was the drama, it seems to carry the same implications of deception and appearance of reality. So Webster praises the Queen's Men at the Red Bull for their acting in *The White Devil* (1612 or 1613):

> For the action of the play, 'twas generally well, and I dare affirm, with the joint testimony of some of their own quality, (for the true imitation of life, without striving to make nature a monster) the best that ever became them.

So also, an imitation of life is praised in *The Second Maiden's Tragedy* performed in 1611:

Thou shalt see my lady
Play her part naturally, more to the life
Than she's aware on.[25]

Shakespeare implies the same standards in *The Two Gentlemen of Verona*:

For I did play a lamentable part....
Which I so lively acted with my tears

> That my poor mistress, moved therewithal,
> Wept bitterly.
>
> IV.4.162-7

The idea of a play as a 'lively' picture may be seen in Rowley's verses on *The Duchess of Malfi* (1623):

> I never saw thy Duchess, till the day
> That she was lively bodied in thy play.

Most importantly the 'imitation of life' is implicit in Hamlet's advice to the players; he says that the end of playing is:

> to hold, as 'twere, the mirror up to nature; to show virtue her own feature, scorn her own image, and the very age and body of the time his form and pressure.
>
> III.2.20-4

When he criticizes actors who strut and bellow, he invokes the same standard:

> I have thought some of Nature's journeymen had made men, and had not made them well, they imitated humanity so abominably.
>
> III.2.31-4

Hamlet applies the same criterion to acting as Bassanio did to Portia's picture — how near is it to creation?

The concept of acting as an imitation of life agrees with the other evidence I have quoted, and suggests that Elizabethan actors aimed at an illusion of real life. It does not explain *all* in the best renaissance painting or the best Elizabethan acting, but it has an important place in the artists' intentions. To describe the resultant art as formal is to deny this intention; *natural* seems a more appropriate word.

*

There is probably some reluctance among scholars to admit that naturalism was a keynote of Elizabethan acting. Some critics would obviously wish the plays to be acted in a formal manner. For instance it is said that a person in a play may be

> first a symbol, second a human being;... [and the play itself can be] primarily an argument or parable, only secondarily forced, as it best may, to assume some correspondence with the forms and events of human affairs.[26]

This is an extreme case, but there are other hints of a fear that naturalism would make Shakespeare's plays smaller, that they would lose the meaning and richness that has been found in the study. Formal acting, on the other hand, seems to offer a declamation through which technical accomplishment could be appreciated and the argument or pattern of the drama, together with its literary finesse, could stand revealed. But there is more than one kind of naturalism; there is one for the plays set in a drawing-room, and another for plays dealing with kings and soldiers, inspired prophets and accomplished courtiers. A naturalism that was true to the poetic qualities of Shakespeare's text would not disguise the high themes of tragedy or the idealism of comedy, or the subtleties of versification.

I have said that Elizabethan dramatists and actors imitated life, but this does not mean that they tried to make their plays exactly the same as real life; they did not labor, in Marston's words, to 'relate any thing as an historian but to enlarge every thing as a poet'.[27] Their plays were more exciting and colorful, more full of meaning, than real life; indeed compared with them, 'Nature never set forth... so rich [a] tapestry'.[28] The important fact is that the audience was encouraged to take all this as real while the performance was in progress. Within the charmed circle of the theatre, a new world might be accepted and what they saw personated could seem to be truly done before them.

George Chapman once wrote a preface to a play which had never been performed, in which he tried to analyze what his writing had lost by this misfortune. Unlike some critics, he believed that

> scenical representation is so far from giving just cause of any least diminution, that the personal and exact life it gives to any history, or other such delineation of human actions, adds to them lustre, spirit, and apprehension.[29]

A 'personal and exact life' was what Chapman expected the actors to give to his play, and these words may serve to describe the naturalism which I believe to be the new power of Elizabethan acting. If actors in today's theatre wish to present Shakespeare's plays in the spirit in which they were written, they should respect and enjoy the magniloquence and music of the language, enter into the greatness of conception, and play all the time for an illusion of real life. They must constantly expect a miracle — that the verse shall be enfranchised as the natural idiom of human beings and that all of Shakespeare's strange creation shall become real and 'lively' on the stage. Because the Elizabethan actor was capable of this, Shakespeare, like others of his contemporaries, dared to 'repose eternity in the mouth of a player.'[30]

*

Several chapters that follow will be concerned, by the way, with the relative importance of the formal (or consciously artificial) elements of acting, and the naturalistic, as called forth by the text of Shakespeare's plays. But some further characteristics of Elizabethan actors should also be noted here as indications of the kind of presentation that is appropriate.

First, the plays were written to be boldly visual. Traces of an earlier iconographic style of acting and stage-management are found in Shakespeare's time. For example, in *Richard III*, III.2, when Hastings is about to go to London for the last time and so walk into the trap that Gloucester has laid for him, two characters, newly introduced into the play, appear: a pursuivant and a priest, representing the affairs of the world and the affairs of heaven. They are barely identified in words because their costumes and their general bearing represent their natures; they are meaningful as soon as they are *seen*. In the same tradition are the stage-directions at the end of the 1616 version of Marlowe's *Faustus*:

> *Enter the Good Angel and the Bad Angel at several doors.... Music while the throne descends.... Hell is discovered.*

Such iconographic staging was linked with new naturalism so that the stage-picture had a double standard similar to the actors' performances. On the one hand, the canopy over the open-air stage of the public theatres remained painted like a sky with stars, a 'heaven' over the stage. Ceremonies, feasts, processions and scenes of state continued to give a general meaning to the stage-action. In Henslowe's 'diary', which accounts for the back-stage efforts of several of the more popular companies at the turn of the century, lists of scenic properties include: a rock, a tomb, a Hell-mouth, the city of Rome, 'the cloth of the sun and moon', 'iii Imperial crowns; i plain crown'.[31] On the other hand, there was a pursuit of verisimilitude, such as the stage-direction in Heywood's *A Woman Killed with Kindness* (1603), mounted for one of

Henslowe's companies:

> *Enter* 3 *or* 4 *Servingmen, one with a voider and a wooden knife to take away all, another the salt and bread, another the tablecloth and napkins, another the carpet.* Jenkin *with two lights after them.*
>
> (Scene 8)

or the scene in *Much Ado* (II.4) in which the young ladies of Leonato's household prepare the bride for church, sending necessary messages and exchanging fashion-talk.

The most exact realism was, it is important to note, in the dress of the actors. One foreign visitor, Richard Platter, reported that, when noble lords died, their clothes were given to the servants who then sold them to actors for theatrical costumes. Certainly Henslowe's accounts show that his companies had a vast stock of costumes made of expensive 'real' material, including lace of gold, silver and copper. For Mrs Frankford in *A Woman Killed* he bought a special black velour dress for £6 3s.; a single ceremonial robe cost him £19. Typical entries in the Diary are:

> Lent unto Thomas dowton the 31 of Janewary 1598 to bye tafetie for ii womones gownes for the ii angrey wemen of abengton [a play by H. Porter] the some of... ix^{l}
>
> Layd owt for the company the 1 of febreyare 1598 to bye A blacke velluet gercken layed thick wth black sylke lace & A payer of Rownd hosse of paynes of sylke layd wth sylver lace & caneyanes of clothe of sylver at the Requeste of Robart shawe the some of... iiii^{ll}x^{s}

According to one calculation Henslowe's costumes cost more money than the theatres in which they were used and stored. Such expense would be justified in his competitive world only if the maintenance of high fashion and verisimilitude were considered necessary for the actors' performances.

*

Shakespeare's own company of actors, first known as the Chamberlain's Men and then, on the accession of James I, as the King's Men, differed in one respect from their rivals: they proved to be a more permanent organization. They stayed together for fifty years, until the closing of the theatres for the Civil War. A large number of old and new plays appeared in their repertory: in the spring of 1613, for instance, they were responsible for the 'fourteen several plays' that were performed at Court in celebration of a royal marriage. Such experience meant that the actors would have to play 'together', and 'to each other'. Early quick-moving and ingenious comedies, like *The Taming of the Shrew* and *Comedy of Errors*, obviously depend on team-work for properly sharp performance. And some tragedies, especially *Romeo and Juliet*, *King Lear* and *Coriolanus*, have concluding scenes where dramatic interest is carried as much by the characters encircling the stage as by the protagonists. More than this, many moments in every play that Shakespeare wrote repay subtle timing and interplay between characters: Orsino's silent involvement with the boy Cesario; Ophelia's taut reactions to Hamlet's passionate denunciations which indicate feelings that she does not express fully until after he has left the stage; the shifting extremes of belief and disbelief as Benedick and Beatrice learn to trust each other's hidden love. The original company of actors, knowing each other's methods — tricks of pitch, timing and tempo — may well have encouraged the writing of such corporate scenes.

The King's Men also had their undoubted 'stars', actors who drew all attention to themselves. According to Richard Flecknoe, Richard Burbage, the leading actor in Shakespeare's company, had the reputation of never leaving the stage without a round of applause — a skill that today is more common in Opera Houses than in Shakespearian theatres. The Duke of York in *Richard II* testifies that:

> in a theatre, the eyes of men
> After a well-grac'd actor leaves the stage
> Are idly bent on him that enters next,
> Thinking his prattle to be tedious.
>
> V.2.23-6

Burbage, Lowin, Tarlton and Kempe were widely known and had their equivalents of fans: as Hamlet welcomes his 'old friend' among the 'Tragedians of the City', so Richard Burbage was the 'old acquaintance' of the Earl of Pembroke. One dramatist likened the hero of his tragedy, *Barnavelt*, to a leading player:

> with such murmurs as glad spectators in a theatre grace their best actors with, they ever heard him, when to have had a sight of him, was held a prosperous omen; when no eye gazed on him that was not filled with admiration.
>
> ll.2475-82

Clearly the major roles of Elizabethan drama supported performances that held attention by exploiting a mixture of virtuoso skills, physical attractiveness and individual personality.

*

In one respect the Elizabethan actors will continue to baffle our understanding: their use of boy-actors for female roles. The main obstacle here is that the conditions in which they worked can never be reproduced: the absence of actresses for comparison; the rhetorical training in schools; a system of apprenticeship to senior actors; continual work in one company for as long as eight years, graduating slowly to the heroines.

But trying to judge their performances, we should remember that contemporary accounts make no concessions — Cleopatra's jibe at the 'squeaking' boy is a special case, and remarkable as such. The evidence suggests that the boys, like their elders, aimed at an 'imitation of life'. The puritan critics of the theatre complained of their 'lewd' gestures as positive incitements to lust. In Jonson's *The Devil is an Ass* (1616), the story is told of the boy-actor, Dick Robinson, masquerading in real life as a lawyer's wife and getting away with the impersonation:

> to see him behave it;
> And lay the law; and carve; and drink unto 'em;
> And then talk bawdy: and send frolics! O!
>
> II.3

The boys were helped, of course, by the dramatist, and in this Shakespeare was particularly careful. Many small roles, like Phebe or Audrey in *As You Like It*, or Octavia in *Antony and Cleopatra*, derive much of their effect from stylistic contrast with the rest of the play. Even more obviously demanding roles, like Ophelia, are often given few appearances, and some of those with secondary characters or for a solo-like scene that could be intensively rehearsed on its own; Ophelia is alone with Hamlet only once, and the same is true of Gertrude. A Rosalind has to sustain long scenes, but her speeches are so witty and energetic that the audience has little leisure for idle inquisition. When, near the close, she has to show 'strange powers' Shakespeare allowed her to be self-consciously theatrical and contrived an echoing and contrasting chorus on stage. For her reappearance in female clothes he brought on three other couples so that her happiness with Orlando is supported and defined by that of others, and seen as part of a full stage-picture.

But Shakespeare used more than expert tact: he accepted the limitations of boy-actors without confining his imagination. This is shown by the many generations of actresses who have inherited the boys' roles; they may cut or underplay some of the verbal wit and refuse some of the 'formal' restrictions, but still there has been more than sufficient material in the text of the plays to awaken their full talents. These roles, like others, can sustain formalism and naturalism; they can be part of an ensemble effect and support all the star-like attractions of talented and unique performers.

*

Bernard Beckerman has tried to define by a single word the style of the Elizabethans and of other actors who wish to respond fully to Shakespeare's text. Having quoted Hamlet's description of the player who

> in a dream of passion,
> Could force his soul so to his own conceit
> That from her working all his visage wann'd;
> Tears in his eyes, distraction in's aspect,
> A broken voice, and his whole function suiting
> With forms to his conceit ..
>
> II.2.545-50

he suggests that the mixture of 'ceremonious acting' and 'overwhelming passion intensively portrayed' should be called 'romantic acting'.[32] But this phrase does not sufficiently represent the formal or representative elements of the style nor the ensemble effects and realistically observed details of business. I would suggest 'heroic naturalism'; this catches the opposed inspirations, but it is still inadequate. A Polonius is needed to invent a definition. Let 'epic' stand for the ensemble and socially realistic elements, and 'romantic' for the passionate, imaginative and individual; then, perhaps, the phrase 'Epic-natural-romantic-virtuoso-formal' may be adequate.

THREE

Gestures and Business

THE end of Macbeth's role, as a reference to Irving has already shown, is not a speech but a wordless combat that in performance can express the last temper of the hero, his hopeless courage, pride and pain. The fight will need more time than any of his speeches in this Act and will hold the audience with its obvious excitement and danger: the tragedy is sustained at last by a piece of wordless stage business.

At the end of *Antony and Cleopatra* there are many words, but here physical enactment is a continual accompaniment, modifying and extending the verbal impression given to the audience. First the heroine is clothed in royal robe and a crown placed on her head, so that by her actions she can be seen preparing for what she calls the 'noble act' of suicide. The text suggests that the robing is effected too slowly for Cleopatra and so the glowing impression of her words mingles with physical haste and, perhaps, fumbling. She must wait for the business to be completed, until 'So, have you done?' (V.2.288) and then she kisses Charmian and Iras. This new business will again take some time to effect, for Cleopatra speaks punningly of a 'long farewell'. In performance both Queen and maids will share some moments of silence. Then, with no warning, Iras '*falls and dies*': this surprise movement at one and the same time alerts the audience, shows Cleopatra's composure, and suggests that her actions and words are all part of a process beyond her complete control. The thought of Antony kissing Iras reawakens Cleopatra's preparations so that now she reaches for an asp and places it at her own breast; and again she must wait, held physically still, as she calls upon the 'poor venomous fool' to 'be angry and dispatch'. Only when she feels it bite does she cry, 'Peace, peace!' For a moment she may again be still in her royal robes, but the pose is broken with another gesture as she takes another asp. She quickly completes this and begins to speak again. 'What should I stay…'; but then, quite suddenly, she is dead. There must be some compulsive movement at this point, for her crown is jerked 'awry'. When she is again quite still Charmian reaches up to rearrange the crown and so marks unmistakably that Cleopatra is now like a stage-property which must be 'put right'.

For all the splendor and passion of her words, Cleopatra is presented in the final scene partly by her pose, her gestures and stage-business, and those of her attendants: these add haste, impatience, lack of full control; they accentuate the dressing-up for a royal 'act', extend the moment of shared affection between the Queen and her attendants, and express (as words do not) the pain of death; they also ensure that the audience realizes quickly, before Caesar's entry, that the Queen has become a corpse.

*

Had Shakespeare been content to communicate by words, the actor's speaking of them and his movements in sympathy with them, he would have cut off one of two hands. He would have lost the wholly physical language which is the chief means of expression in primitive theatres and has been at the service of dramatists every time an actor steps on to a stage; he would have ignored traditions of visual excitement that, as we have seen, were strong in the Elizabethan theatre. His means of expression would have lost something of its power, for physical movement is a language to which an audience responds before it can be aware of doing so, the rapid and almost unresistable communication of color, visual form and contrast, sexual attraction or repulsion; its rhythm and changes of tempo link easily with the musical elements of verbal performance. Moreover gesture and movement form an instinctive language and are therefore capable of showing many of the psychological, physical or sociological realities that lie behind, and not infrequently enrich or deny, the more conscious interchanges of speech. Without this kind of communication Shakespeare could have named his imaginative vision but not given it tangible habitation, outlined the form of what he saw in the world around and within him, but not transmitted its pressures.

In short, if we are to understand Shakespeare's plays in performance we must proceed through the text and through the physical performance that is sustained and controlled by the words, towards movement, gestures and business which can become independent of the text, limiting, denying or extending the more textual effects.

Of course it is not possible to refer to any one stage production to learn about this physical language, for plays are often distorted by irrelevant and trivial stage-business. We must look, first, for the gestures and business that can be definitely implied from the text, like Macbeth's last fight or the stage management of Cleopatra's death. This will not supply all the necessary business (as we shall see), but enough to render this the best start.

Some help will come readily from stage-directions. When Coriolanus has stood listening to Volumnia's plea for Rome and watches her kneel and rise, there is an unusually precise direction (V.3): '*He holds her by the hand, silent.*' The text of this play was probably first printed from a manuscript prepared by Shakespeare himself,[1] but even without this reassurance we may believe that the gesture is intended to show that the hero's change of mind is instinctive rather than considered and verbalized. Earlier he had risen from his seat and had remained silent while Volumnia appealed to him, so these larger physical reactions have prepared the audience's attention for the small, but deeply significant, hand movement. Or in the last Act of *Much Ado*, when a stage-direction insists that four ladies are brought forward masked, it is clear that the drama depends momentarily on stage-business. This provides a repetition of the masking for dances in Act II, the origin of many of the complications of the plot, and so the audience is suddenly faced at the end of the comedy with a visual reminder that a new succession of mistakes could take place. Words could scarcely make the point lightly enough by themselves; but, with identical visors disguising individual identities, Claudio's 'Which is the lady I must seize upon?' and Benedick's 'Which is Beatrice?' once more accentuate the importance and hazards of a choice in love; for all Benedick's new assurance he is at the ladies' mercy.

Entrances are often immediately significant in a visual way. So, for example, Granville-Barker testified that when he thought he 'knew *King Lear* well enough' through study of the text, he still had not realized an effect, all words apart, that he discovered in rehearsal, when an entry very slowly brought about the meeting of 'blind Gloucester and mad Lear'.[2] Coriolanus entering in IV.4, after being banished from Rome, is directed to appear '*in mean apparel, disguis'd and muffled*'; this is a startling change from patrician's clothes that registers at once a humiliation and shame that he had not foreseen in Rome and which his words in the ensuing soliloquy do not directly express. Costume again helps to make Marcade's entrance in the last scene of *Love's Labour's Lost* dramatically effective. He is dressed in black and probably moves slowly as a bearer of ill-tidings; this is in such contrast to the comic bustle already filling the stage that his entry draws immediate attention and will give to his first, simple-seeming words, 'God save you, madam!', the widest possible relevance; for a moment, before the announcement of the death of the Princess's father, the characters confront a general, intuitive fear.

'*Exeunt*' is also an important moment for business. When the tribunes stay behind after crowded scenes in *Coriolanus*, their action in drawing together in secrecy, which is emphasized by repetition, speaks visually for their mutual dependence, a motivation which in time of triumph they do not utter and may not recognize. So Shakespeare has given a sense of personal danger to the early proceedings of the tribunes and prepared the audience for their sudden collapse. In *Julius Caesar*, after the assassination in III.1, all except the conspirators flee from stage — with the further exception of Publius. Brutus directs the audience's attention to this aged and hitherto insignificant senator: suddenly he will be noticed, standing silent amid the uproar, 'quite confounded with this mutiny'. Brutus tries to reassure him and Cassius urges him to leave, but there is no verbal reply: Shakespeare has used the helpless horror-struck presence of Publius, accentuated by his absolute silence, to give a sharp contrast to the general noise and movement. Before he leaves the stage he has shown the fear in the storm, the paralysis of mind and body that the conspirators have brought about and which they will in part share at the end of the drama.

Silence is often used by Shakespeare to accentuate a reaction that can only be expressed physically. When Macduff hears that Macbeth has had his wife and children murdered, there is dialogue to support and identify the central dramatic fact of his silent gesture; it is Malcolm who speaks:

> What, man! Ne'er pull your hat upon your brows;
> Give sorrow words. The grief that does not speak
> Whispers the o'erfraught heart and bids it break.
>
> IV.3.208-10

Joy also is expressed by an inarticulate response, identified in the comments of bystanders, as Leontes and Hermione are reunited at the end of *The Winter's Tale*: 'She embraces him.... She hangs about his neck' (V.3.112-13). Again the central fact is the silent and, on this occasion, mutual gesture. Sometimes no verbal description is provided: what, for example, should be the bearing of Volumnia, after Rome has been saved by the sacrifice of her son and she enters, with Valeria and Virginia, to be welcomed by the united cheers of senators and plebeians? She is acclaimed as the 'patroness, the life of Rome!' but she does not speak a single word in her passage across the large stage (V.5). Certainly all eyes will be fixed upon her, and the performer of the role has a large opportunity to express anger, suffering, helplessness, stoic pride — whatever seems appropriate after the earlier events.

*

Shakespeare's reliance on silent physical reaction in this context is one measure of the trust he placed in gesture and stage-business. It also shows how much he left to the actor, for the passion given predominance here can sway the balance and meaning of the whole tragedy. And, on reflection such responsible choices are everywhere facing actors and directors in his plays: as gesture and business are important, so they crucially affect the total impression of a play.

For an example, how should Prince Hal answer in the charade episode of *I Henry IV*, when he is pretending to be his father and Falstaff has been speaking in Hal's person in defense of himself?

> No, my good Lord: banish Peto, banish Bardolph, banish Poins; but, for sweet Jack Falstaff, kind Jack Falstaff, true Jack Falstaff, valiant Jack Falstaff — and therefore more valiant, being, as he is, old Jack Falstaff — banish not him thy Harry's company, banish not him thy Harry's company. Banish plump Jack, and banish all the world.
>
> II.4.457-63

How should the answer be given: 'I do, I will?' In the 1964 Stratford-upon-Avon production, the second half of the short speech came after a moment's silence which was a 'gesture' of deliberation. The same year in a production by Joan Littlewood at the Edinburgh Festival, all four monosyllables were spoken rapidly, as Hal hastily dismounted from his improvised throne because of the knocking at the door; here, in the mounting urgency before the Sheriff enters, it was Hal's later words that gained by deliberation: 'thou art a natural coward' to Falstaff, and of himself, 'Now, my masters, for a true face and good conscience.' Which of these pieces of stage business was correct? Should Hal dismount quickly or slowly? It has been remarked that the knocking on the door *following* 'I do, I will' (as at Stratford but not at Edinburgh) is intended to break the perplexed silence caused by Hal's speech; but the knocking was first marked in the text by the editor, Capell; neither the Quarto printed from foul papers, nor the edited Folio version has any sign of it. As far as the original texts go Bardolph might enter without warning and interrupt Hal in the middle of a sentence. Or another completely opposite interpretation is possible: perhaps 'I do' should be said firmly and deliberately, *after* the 'gesture' of a direct look at Falstaff — that is, 'at this moment I most certainly do' — and then lightly, with quick movement and laughter, 'I will' — that is 'no; not yet'. (Hal certainly seems in high spirits when he next speaks: 'Heigh, heigh! the devil rides upon a fiddle-stick'.)

The main points here are that this text needs interpretation — these four monosyllables do not sufficiently control performance — that some kind of stage-business is demanded by the interruption of the charade whenever it should come, and that the stage-business and verbal interpretation together significantly alter the dramatic fact. And so in earlier examples: how much pain should be indicated when the asp bites Cleopatra, and how violently should she die? How long should Macbeth continue the fight, and how easily should he be vanquished?

There is no escape from this dilemma. Some scholars have argued that Shakespeare's plays should be performed with the minimum of business; but the text often invites unspecified gestures and movement, and we know that in Shakespeare's own day these were important elements of performance. He had inherited a visually expressive theatre and his actors were famed for their 'action'. It was reported that when a company travelled in Germany, the people not 'understanding a word they said, both men and women, flocked wonderfully to see their gesture and action'.[3] When *Othello* was performed at Oxford in 1610, a member of the audience noted that:

> Desdemona, killed by her husband, in her death moved us especially, when, as she lay in her bed, her face only implored the pity of the audience.[4]

In the text Shakespeare seems to acknowledge the power of this purely visual spectacle:

> *Look* on the tragic loading of this bed.
> This is thy work. — The *object* poisons sight....
>
> V.2.366-7

Acknowledging Shakespeare's occasional demand for silent physical presentation and the momentary power of gesture and business to extend or modify the verbally sustained performance, we must ask how much depends on all this. I have chosen numerous examples from *Coriolanus* to suggest a continued influence in a single play, and chapters 6 and 7, by following single roles throughout their plays, will show its influence on character presentation. Here I shall try to show, from

Hamlet, that physical confrontations, a silent exeunt and a few simple gestures can work with a more verbal drama to illuminate the interplay of character and, perhaps, the presentation of story and theme.

The Closet Scene (III.4), in which Gertrude acknowledges that Hamlet has 'cleft my heart in twain' and he gains new impetus that will alter his behavior to the King and take him to England and back again, is generally acknowledged to be central in the tragedy. It is the most sustained and intense scene, and is an immediate contrast with the spectacle and movement of the Play Scene and Hamlet's abortive resolution to kill the King. The Ghost appears for the last time just before its climax and subsequently Hamlet appears for only three short scenes before being absent for more than five hundred lines. Its events lead directly to the catastrophe, for Claudius now takes more open measures against Hamlet and the death of Polonius provides him with a fit instrument in Laertes. But if so much is generally agreed, its consequences may be puzzling if judged by words alone. In the next two Acts Hamlet hardly speaks to his mother, the only direct duologue being in the last scene in which he says simply:

> Good madam!...
> I dare not drink yet, madam; by and by....
> How does the Queen?...
> Wretched queen, adieu!

The passions of the Closet Scene, its central position and sustained and intimate excitement appear to have little consequence in the presentation of Hamlet's character, and no resolution fittingly held back for the conclusion of the play.

But this is to judge by the spoken words alone. In performance, the tragedy often seems eloquently shaped: where words would have been impracticable or inadequate Shakespeare has used a physical language, and the form and pressure of his tragedy depend upon it.

Hamlet and Gertrude meet again at Ophelia's grave. He is calm and dignified — 'This is I, Hamlet the Dane' — but soon he is grappling, hand-to-hand, with Laertes. A stage direction in the Folio text (which records some prompt-book additions) says that Hamlet leaps into the grave; certainly Laertes cries 'The devil take thy soul', and Hamlet's response seems to grow in emotion and strength. Attempts are made to part them and, significantly, Horatio's words suggest that Hamlet is quite as incensed as Laertes:

KING: Pluck them asunder.
QUEEN: Hamlet! Hamlet!
ALL: Gentlemen!
HORATIO: Good my lord, be quiet.

As they are forcibly restrained, Hamlet reaches a crest of verbal excitement, at least:

Why, I will fight with him upon this theme
Until my eyelids will no longer wag.

Then Gertrude speaks: 'O my son, what theme?' Her words are simple, but momentarily they transform Hamlet so that he speaks with equal simplicity: 'I lov'd Ophelia'. The transition of mood and tone is astonishing and the audible cause of it is his mother's bare question. It could easily be unconvincing in performance, but we should also notice that Gertrude's verse-line remains incomplete, involving a break of metrical pattern and almost certainly a pause before or after: surely Hamlet must have faced his mother and in the silence responded to her physical presence. By even a slight hesitation in the course of his violent activity the audience will be encouraged to look closer and become aware of a mutual 'gesture' between the two characters, and by that means recognize an unspoken and perhaps unconscious communication.

Turning to Laertes, the apparent cause of his passion, Hamlet again speaks wildly, and the Queen, as if she does not realize the source of her earlier power, ineffectually orders the attendants to 'forbear him'. He drives the scene forward to its verbal climax:

And, if thou prate of mountains, let them throw
Millions of acres on us, till our ground,
Singeing his pate against the burning zone,
Make Ossa like a wart! Nay, and thou'lt mouth,
I'll rant as well as thou.

Then Gertrude again stills the storm and, partly by the bare-faced but effective device of repetition, the audience is drawn again to recognize the power of her physical presence over Hamlet. She speaks first to others:

This is mere madness;

> And thus awhile the fit will work on him....

So she fulfills Hamlet's last request in the Closet Scene by affirming that he is 'essentially in madness', not 'mad in craft', and by this act of loyalty she gains attention and holds it. Gentle words now control Hamlet so that he probably turns towards her — at least he must be still in order to listen; and by choosing a female image Gertrude seems to tell him that she herself is now true as the dove:

> Anon, as patient as the female dove
> When that her golden couplets are disclos'd,
> His silence will sit drooping.

The text requires a quiet, low pitch and lengthened, softer rhythms, and these will best be contrived if mother and son have again confronted each other, communicating on the deepest level of their natures. Hamlet says nothing to Gertrude, but as he turns back to face Laertes he is transformed in utterance and, therefore, bearing:

> Hear you, sir:
> What is the reason that you use me thus?
> I loved you ever....

Gertrude has nothing more to say; Hamlet has answered by his attention to her words and can speak now without passion.

The fuller issues of the situation are not forgotten, but mastered: he reasserts his full responsibility by the ironic and perhaps feignedly distracted:

> But it is no matter.
> Let Hercules himself do what he may,
> The cat will mew, and dog will have his day.

He leaves the stage at once and in six brisk lines the King concludes the scene; the crowded stage empties silently, although Horatio, Laertes and Gertrude are each individually addressed. The mute *exeunt*, like a wave receding after breaking on the shore, gives an impression of power expended and of danger postponed by some force that has not been acknowledged verbally. Gertrude's exit, in tempo and bearing, should be contrasted with the movement of others for they have not borne the emotional center of the scene: and here again the audience is prompted to observe the expression of feelings which are out of reach of words — of them not even Hamlet has spoken.

In the tragedy's last scene Gertrude's presence and actions are again more eloquent than her words: what she says merely directs and underlines her gestures. She crosses from her throne by the side of Claudius towards her son, gives her napkin to him and drinks to his fortune. With 'Come let me wipe thy face' she finds an intimate gesture by which she can treat him tenderly as if he were still a child, and she wholly his mother. After the narrow excitement of the duel (itself a gesture of new resolve and, later, of passion), Hamlet's first words show concern for Gertrude, and hers are an indictment of Claudius' treachery. Their verbal exchange is very brief but it must involve another confrontation, and it is from this deeply realized moment that the widest issues of the tragedy spring to life: Hamlet assumes authority and then, in passion and haste, he kills the King and ends his own part in a kind of peace.

In *Hamlet* words are spoken almost incessantly and they suggest worlds of interest. But they are not all the play; at least one strand of the story depends for its most deeply charged moments upon physical action and silent, or almost silent, confrontations.

FOUR

Subtext

ALREADY, in the presentation of Hamlet, Gertrude, Coriolanus, Volumnia, Cleopatra and Prince Hal, we have seen that Shakespeare could give dramatic expression to reactions, conscious and subconscious, that lie beneath the words that are spoken, that qualify what the text explicitly says. Despite the rhetoric, music and excitement of his words, this subtextual communication is an almost constant element of his stagecraft and one that imaginative actors delight to exploit.

So far the subtext has been observed through Shakespeare's use of gesture, stage-business and silent physical confrontations; to these means must be added the text itself: sudden shifts in subject or in tone and tempo, broken syntax or metre, the introduction of unusual words or disproportionate reactions, all need to be sustained by the actor's expression of the unspoken reactions that cause them. If the text is to sound like an 'imitation of life' it needs a subtext. Here is Brutus deliberating in *Julius Caesar*:

> It must be by his death;... and for my part,
> I know no personal cause to spurn at him,
> But for the general:... He would be crown'd...
> How that might change his nature, there's the question....
> It is the bright day that brings forth the adder,
> And that craves wary walking. Crown him... that!...
> And then, I grant, we put a sting in him.
>
> II.1.10-16

Read this aloud, conscious only of the meaning of each syntactical unit, and the consecutive meaning and development of the whole passage will hardly be communicated. At each juncture marked with three dots in the text printed above there is a transition of thought and feeling for which the words represent only the beginning and the end, the change of verbal reaction but not the process that is its cause. Why after 'It must be by his death' does Brutus continue 'and for my part'? The text does not say — but an actor can show that the idea of Caesar's death awakens in Brutus a need to justify himself. Then, from considering political problems, Brutus simply names the crux of Caesar's ambition, 'He would be crown'd', as if he were more concerned with the person than the policy. But then from considering Caesar's 'nature', Brutus moves away again to generalities, as if too close a knowledge of the man must be avoided. If the abrupt 'that', after the precise 'Crown him', were not spoken with some strong and precise feeling, it would be a slight hesitation, out of key with the pressures of the soliloquy; it must be able to carry the transition through the reasonable qualification of 'And then, I grant' and the more evasive plural pronoun 'we', to the sharp image of 'put a sting in him'. Textually, the soliloquy is a series of disjointed statements in which lofty and political considerations are uppermost; its continuous dramatic life depends on subtextual impressions of suspicion, guilt, pride and emulation, that can be expressed physically and by variations of stress, pitch, texture, phrasing, rhythm, volume, tempo.

Shakespearian dialogue is like a stone that reveals its deep veins and rich color only when it is carefully and appropriately polished; or like a personal letter that makes sense only to those who know the writer and can 'hear' his or her voice in its words; or like a map that must be read by someone already familiar with the terrain. Always it demands exploration until every peculiarity of its textual surface can be sustained in dramatic reality, until the hints it contains of subtextual impulses are used to enliven and give substance to a performance and to reveal conscious and unconscious motivation.

When Juliet waits for Romeo, syntax, rhythm and imagery are clues to an impression of sexual excitement and virginal fear that should underlie the words:

> Come, night; — *and this quickly suggests the more direct idea* — come, Romeo; — *then the two ideas come together making a sharper perception* — come, thou day in night; —
>
> *and now an explanation holds this moment of awareness more leisurely but persistently, and shows its fuller implications* — For thou wilt lie upon the wings of night — *Romeo's coming is associated with 'lying', as on a bed, and with flight, as sexual excitement is often represented in dreams* —
>
> Whiter than new snow on a raven's back — *the idea of cold virginity, has been doubly asserted in 'white' and 'new snow'*[1] *and the vague threat of 'wings of night' defined with the* 'raven' *of death.*
>
> *Then Juliet, afraid of the twin implications of sexual encounter and death, reverts quickly to the original, simpler eagerness; but now this is amplified* —
>
> Come, gentle night, — 'gentle' *because night and death are now her*

rivals to be placated — come, loving black-brow'd night — 'loving' *and the more physical* 'black-brow'd' *associate* 'night' *with sexual concerns* —
Give me my Romeo; — *but having is now associated with loss* — and when he shall die
Take him and cut him out in little stars, — *she tries to reduce her fears by assuming the scale of nursery games, by taking refuge in childish fantasy and rivalry* —
And he will make the face of heaven so fine
That all the world will be in love with night,
And pay no worship to the garish sun. — *this thought is more extended because it is only entertained as play; but the deeper reality of her sexual involvement then takes over in an inarticulate exclamation and she utters her longing in two close-packed metaphors, both images common in sexual fantasy and dream* —
O, I have bought the mansion of a love,
But not possess'd it; and though I am sold,
Not yet enjoy'd.

III.2.17-28

For Juliet's soliloquy, subtextual thoughts and feelings provide an impulse towards speech that supports and extends textual meanings; for Brutus' soliloquy, the subtextual impression, besides making his words seem necessary, suggests that those very words disguise the true nature of his concern with the conspiracy against Caesar. These are two, out of the many, ways in which Shakespeare used the actor's ability to give dramatic life to thoughts and feelings 'under' his dialogue.

*

Of course, the word 'subtext' was unknown to Shakespeare. It is not listed in *The New English Dictionary* or its *Supplement* of 1939. It comes from Stanislavski's writings about the actor and is still particularly associated with the 'method' of acting that was first developed while Chekhov was writing for the Moscow Art Theatre. Subtext was then defined as:

> the manifest, the inwardly felt expression of a human being in a part, which flows uninterruptedly beneath the words of the text, giving them life and a basis for existing,... a web of innumerable, varied inner patterns inside a play and a part,... all sorts of figments of the imagination, inner movements, objects of attention, smaller and greater truths and a belief in them,

> adaptations, adjustments and other similar elements. It is the subtext that makes us say the words we do in a play.[2]

The new word and its definition were so quickly adopted because they provided a more precise way of discussing the manner in which spoken stage dialogue can reveal, as ordinary speech seldom can, the innermost processes of thought and feeling, and how that dialogue is related to physical and emotional performance. Stanislavski's concept is particularly appropriate for Shakespeare's plays which for centuries have held audiences' attention by truth of utterance, and by reality and depth of characterization.

At the end of the nineteenth century Henry Irving quoted Macready, the actor he most admired, to explain the importance in performance of 'the thoughts that are *hidden under words*':

> What is the art of acting?... It is the art of embodying the poet's creations, of giving them flesh and blood, of making the figures which appeal to your mind's eye in the printed drama live before you on the stage. 'To fathom the depths of character, to trace its latent motives, to feel its finest quiverings of emotion, *to comprehend the thoughts that are hidden under words*, and thus possess one's self of the actual mind of the individual man' — such was Macready's definition of the player's art.

In the same lecture he translated this into his own words:

> the actor who has no real grip of the character, but simply recites the speeches with a certain grace and intelligence, will be untrue. The more intent he is upon the words, and the less on the ideas that dictated them, the more likely he is to lay himself open to the charge of mechanical interpretation. It is perfectly possible to express to an audience all the involutions of thought, the speculation, doubt, wavering, which reveal the meditative but irresolute mind.... In short, as we understand the people around us much better by personal intercourse than by all the revelations of written words — for *words*, as Tennyson says, '*half reveal and half conceal the soul within*' — so the drama has, on the whole, infinitely more suggestions when it is well acted than when it is interpreted by the unaided judgement of the student.[3]

In an earlier age recitation of 'the speeches with a certain grace' and order and balance of deportment were more highly regarded than in Irving's or Macready's but, nevertheless, the best actors of those days were also remarkable for the impression of feeling that sustained their words and sometimes modified them. So, in 1748, it was said of

Betterton's Brutus in *Julius Caesar*, that when he:

> was provok'd, in his Dispute with Cassius, his Spirit flew only to his Eye; his steady look alone supply'd that Terror, which he disdain'd an Intemperance in his Voice should rise to.[4]

Richard Steele described in *The Tatler* the 'wonderful agony' when Betterton's Othello:

> examined the circumstance of the handkerchief...; the mixture of love that intruded upon his mind upon the innocent answers Desdemona makes, betrayed in his gesture such a variety and vicissitude of passions, as would admonish a man to be afraid of his own heart,... Whoever reads in his closet this admirable scene, will find that he cannot, except he has as warm an imagination as Shakespeare himself, find any but dry, incoherent, and broken sentences; but a reader that has seen Betterton act it, observes there could not be a word added....[5]

Changes of taste have modified what actually happens on the stage, but the actor's pursuit of an 'imitation of life', display of 'passion', and 'natural' elocution (to use Shakespeare's phrases) and, indeed, the continuing necessity to make some 'incoherent and broken' passages, like those of Brutus or Othello, comprehensible to an audience, have led always to the discovery and expression of 'subtext'. Despite the comparative novelty of this word, 'that which makes an actor say his words in a play' has, for centuries, been sought out and expressed through gesture, bearing and elocution, in order to give a 'personal and exact life'[6] to Shakespeare's dialogue.

*

Sometimes we can observe Shakespeare's conscious experiment with these dramatic techniques, most clearly in his presentation of his characters as actors.

At the end of *Love's Labour's Lost* various country-folk speak as Worthies in a pageant. Sir Nathaniel with brave words attempts to declare 'I am Alisander': but he is mocked for his pains — 'Your nose says, no, you are not' — so that the 'conqueror is dismay'd' and runs away. He is 'o'erparted', for he cannot provide the emotional or physical performance required by his words; he fails to express an adequate subtext. Moth has no words as the infant Hercules and so his performance is not open to challenge in the same way. Holofernes describes what the boy presents quite fluently, but when he ceases to be the schoolmaster-chorus and speaks as Judas Maccabaeus he cannot find the spirit to complete more than one line of his part — despite the fact that he probably wrote it himself. Armado as Hector, however, does not speak so much as a line before criticism begins: his leg is thought 'too big for Hector's' and his 'faces' are not acceptable. Costard, as Pompey, is the only one to speak out his part, but he probably did not attempt too 'great' a verbal performance; he had earlier explained:

> It pleased them to think me worthy of Pompey the Great; for mine own part, I know not the degree of the Worthy; but I am to stand for him.
>
> V.2.504-6

In this display Shakespeare has obviously used varying discrepancies between text and subtext, between attempted and achieved performance, for comic effect: as the Princess says, 'Their form confounded makes most form in mirth'.

At the end of *A Midsummer Night's Dream*, in the play of *Pyramus and Thisbe*, the device is repeated in a more elaborate way, and, in preparation, Theseus explains that he values subtext above text, tongue-tied 'modesty of fearful duty' above 'saucy and audacious eloquence':

> Where I have come, great clerks have purposed
> To greet me with premeditated welcomes;
> Where I have seen them shiver and look pale,
> Make periods in the midst of sentences,
> Throttle their practis'd accent in their fears,
> And, in conclusion, dumbly have broke off,
> Not paying me a welcome. Trust me sweet,
> Out of this silence yet I pick'd a welcome;
> And in the modesty of fearful duty
> I read as much as from the rattling tongue
> Of saucy and audacious eloquence.
> Love, therefore, and tongue-tied simplicity
> In least speak most to my capacity.
>
> V.1.93-105

Clearly, Shakespeare was aware of more than comic implications of a failure to sustain a part by an appropriate impression of emotional and physical truth. Some of his earliest major characters are portrayed as actors of varying achievement. Richard of Gloucester is confident of a successful performance:

> Why, I can smile, and murder whiles I smile,
> And cry 'Content!' to that which grieves my heart.
>
> *III Henry VI*, III.2.182-3

But in contrast, when Richard II has seen his own face in a glass, he knows that his words have been less powerful than his silent feelings:

> My grief lies all within;
> And these external manner[s] of lamen[t]
> Are merely shadows to the unseen grief
> That swells with silence in the tortur'd soul.
> There lies the substance.
>
> *Richard II*, IV.1.295-9

Later, in solitary confinement, he recognizes that he has 'play[ed] in one person many people, and none contented' (V.4.31-2). In *Julius Caesar*, Brutus counsels the conspirators to hide their true feelings:

> Let not our looks put on our purposes,
> But bear it as our Roman actors do,
> With untir'd spirits and formal constancy
>
> II.1.225-7

and Casca is said to put on a 'tardy form' of speech in order to disguise the 'quick mettle' of his wit which might be dangerous if spoken openly (I.2.294-301). In these instances Shakespeare requires, specifically, that an actor in his play should represent a man whose subtextual reality is different from what his words imply: more murderous, more cunning, or more pained.

Hamlet's first long speech to his mother is perhaps the most comprehensive account of this, but here the imperfect performance is mostly in action and appearance:

> 'Tis not alone my inky cloak, good mother,
> Nor customary suits of solemn black,
> Nor windy suspiration of forc'd breath,
> No, nor the fruitful river in the eye,

Nor the dejected haviour of the visage,
Together with all forms, moods, shapes of grief,
That can denote me truly. These, indeed, seem;
For they are actions that a man might play;
But I have that within which passes show —
These but the trappings and the suits of woe.

I.2.77-86

The actor of Hamlet must represent a man who says his behavior is like an imperfect actor's performance, that what he does is not fully true to his inward and hidden nature; yet he, himself, does not know, at this stage in the play what actions could 'denote him truly'. By such theatrical metaphors, and by the failure of 'overparted' actors in the pageant of the Worthies and *Pyramus and Thisbe*, we know that Shakespeare distinguished verbal, or outward, performances from true, or 'inward', performances, and that he sometimes required his actors to sustain a subtextual reality beneath a false or imperfect textual performance.

By the use of conscious disguise Shakespeare also devised situations in which inward emotion or thought is opposed to the words spoken, denying the meaning of speech or extending its reference. This is clearest in comedies like *Twelfth Night* or *As You Like It*. When Orsino asks his page, Cesario, 'How dost thou like this tune?' the reply is

It gives a very echo to the seat
Where Love is thron'd.

Twelfth Night, II.4.19-21

Through these stilted words Viola's subtextual affection for Orsino is expressed, so that the seeming boy is said to speak 'masterly'. Later in the same scene, when Orsino talks about his love for Olivia and Cesario — or rather the disguised Viola — interrupts with, 'Ay, but I know...', the Duke suddenly stops his own line of thought to ask 'What dost thou know?' (ll.102-3). This is an incomplete verse-line, probably indicating a pause while Viola remembers that she is Cesario; she then continues in a vein a little more like the boy's: 'Too well what love women to men may owe'. But as her hidden concern was not wholly disguised by her words, so she is not capable of keeping it silent; she proceeds:

My father had a daughter lov'd a man,
As it might be perhaps, were I a woman,

I should your lordship.

These are not remarkable words, but their subtextual feeling completely holds Orsino's attention so that he forgets his own concerns to listen to this supposed fiction and insists on knowing her 'history'. When Viola, gaining confidence in verbal expression of her love, has told how:

> She pin'd in thought;
> And with a green and yellow melancholy
> She sat like Patience on a monument,
> Smiling at grief....

she reassumes her role of Cesario and it is again Orsino who presses the question, 'But died thy sister of her love, my boy?'. At last Viola can use Cesario to extricate herself from the too-revealing pathos and intimacy, and asks briskly, 'Sir, shall I to this lady?'; and only now does Orsino remember his own 'theme'. At least twice in this scene Cesario gains far more attention than his words could ever claim without a sustaining and overwhelming emotional performance; only the power of subtext could so draw Orsino's attention away from his obsession with Olivia. If the pause and sudden changes of rhythm, language and subject-matter are to be enacted in 'imitation of life', the characters' inward feelings must be expressed in contradiction to the verbal and costume disguise.

Rosalind posing as Ganymede often gets Orlando to betray his deepest feelings in supposedly fictitious words, and expresses her own love while speaking against love. But when she recovers from her swoon on seeing Orlando's bloody handkerchief and tries to act the man, she cannot convince Oliver:

> This was not counterfeit; there is too great testimony in your complexion that it was a passion of earnest.
>
> IV.3.167-8

In this instance, her inward feelings lag behind the bravery of her verbal performance so that she, in effect, denies her words even as she speaks them.

There are many disguises in Shakespeare's plays which do not use costume at all. So, in *Much Ado*, the unconscious attraction of Benedick and Beatrice to each other is concealed by their words and expressed at first only by the way in which they draw together on each entry and awaken unusually forceful antagonism. When two invented conversations are staged for their benefit, they accept the fictions as true — despite the inefficiency of Leonato who 'dries' in his role and the fantastic elaboration of both sets of performers — because their hidden feelings prompt them to believe, against almost everything they have said, that they love each other. Verbal disguise of this sort is found in every play — sometimes consciously assumed, as by Richard III or Casca; sometimes unconsciously, as by Richard II or Brutus; sometimes half-intentionally, as by Hamlet.

Here, as in the two plays-within-plays, Shakespeare has forced the actors to distinguish text from subtext; and sometimes subtext becomes uppermost so that the words which conceal also reveal, directly by quibbles or allusiveness, or indirectly by the marks of subtextual tension that must be sustained in physical performance — sudden changes of subject matter, tone or tempo, broken syntax or metre, apparently disproportionate or surprising reactions.

*

When he was defining subtext, Stanislavski said that it 'flows uninterruptedly beneath the words of the text', and this continuity (as contrasted with intermittence of verbal performance) is an important source of its effectiveness. Often Shakespeare's strategy is to start impressing the inner nature of a character by merest hints in the text, or other outward activity, and to reveal only one part of the subtextual basis at a time until a complex interplay of conscious and unconscious motivation has been built up through a continuous series of impressions. When the ground has been prepared, subtextual reality is at last expressed directly in the text as well. Benedick and Beatrice are obvious examples, declaring their mutual love in words only at the end of the very last scene; by that time, what was earlier said to be impossible has become inevitable and is acknowledged fully in the text.

Claudius, in the first Acts of *Hamlet*, is an example of a character whose deep sense of guilt is progressively revealed and also a contrary, and conscious, subtextual effort to suppress it. In Act III, Scene i, some moralizing from Polonius releases a long aside that gives textual definition to the insecurity of his disguise as a confident and powerful king up to that moment:

O, 'tis too true!
How smart a lash that speech doth give my conscience!

> The harlot's cheek, beautied with plast'ring art,
> Is not more ugly to the thing that helps it
> Than is my deed to my most painted word.
> O heavy burden!
>
> III.1.49-54

In a reading of the play this aside may seem like a brash intrusion of obsolete stagecraft that falls too pat after Hamlet's talk of the 'conscience of the King' in the last line of the previous scene. But in performance it seems necessary because it gives textual expression to an inner consciousness which has already been suggested in a sequence of subtextual revelations.

Claudius does not enter until immediately after the Ghost has provoked curiosity and concern, so the audience will attend closely and perhaps sense a purposeful evasion when his public speech begins by showing most art where its matter is most strange: discretion 'fighting' with nature, 'mirth in funeral', 'our sometime sister, now our queen', and so forth. Power, ease and astuteness are dominating textual impressions, but his reliance on embellishing art — or 'most painted word' — can serve the actor as occasion for expressing a need to 'cover up'. Contrasted with his talk of haste and immediate business, Claudius' words of dismissal:

> Take thy fair hour, Laertes; time be thine,
> And thy best graces spend it at thy will!
>
> I.2.62-3

can go beyond their obvious meaning and sound like a regret for his own strict concerns, especially if the syntactical separation and metrical strength of 'time be thine' are given full value. Answering Hamlet's scorn with continuing urbanity, Claudius can turn talk of love and gentleness into a show of force. When he twice breaks in between Hamlet and his mother, his speech, movement and bearing can seem motivated by fear of some unnamed consequence. All this is before the Ghost has told his story; after that the audience will be more ready to notice a cloaked forcefulness in Claudius' smooth words and to observe his uneasy movements. Shakespeare now uses other characters to emphasize what Claudius does not say: the uncertainty of Rosencrantz in reply to entreaties where he had expected 'commands', or the way in which Polonius is allowed to run on in expounding Hamlet's love for Ophelia so that Claudius seems lost in thoughts he will not, or cannot, express. The King's silence here also contrasts with Gertrude's impatience; his replies are short and infrequent, and (when state affairs have just established him as prompt and careful in detailed planning) he leaves practical suggestions to Polonius. Judged over three Acts and in relation to other characters, the inner tensions of Claudius are not expressed in one sudden and blunt aside, but are manifested progressively on his every appearance.

It is often necessary to look backwards over a role in order to appreciate the opportunities for subtextual expression. At the beginning of *The Winter's Tale*, Leontes' silence as he holds center-stage and the terseness of his speech can be seen as expressions of his insecure and self-regarding nature, once we have read on and come to his jealous outbursts. Similarly Henry IV's early appearances must be revalued after studying his death-bed scene in Part II: guilt, loneliness and weariness had been his deepest reactions while he gave commands and appeared as the crowned King of England among his nobles. Henry V's prayer before Agincourt:

> More will I do;
> Though all that I can do is nothing worth,
> Since that my penitence comes after all,
> Imploring pardon.
>
> IV.3.298-300

leads an actor to reassess the King's anger at the French Ambassador, his demands for absolute proof of his right in France, his response to the traitors as to 'Another fall of man' (II.2.142), his ruthlessness before Harfleur, and so on. Beneath his verbal assurance there is a fear, that can be expressed subtextually until Henry acknowledges it textually, just before the crucial battle.

In *Macbeth* the hero's non-textual response is obvious and large from the very beginning, but still Shakespeare has made the audience wait until the close of the first scene before beginning to identify it textually: so Macbeth's instinctive responses seem more deep-seated and his power to conceal more impressive. Here again the other characters on stage have important parts to play in marking silent reactions. When he enters, marching to a drum, his first words seem unmotivated — 'So foul and fair a day I have not seen' (I.3.38) — unless we suppose that he instinctively senses the Witches' presence before be sees or hears them; such an unwilled response is implied by the fact that he echoes the Witches' words from the play's first scene (l.10). Certainly Banquo's reply — 'How far is't call'd to Forres?' — because no true response to what was said, can suggest that his companion is unable to enter Macbeth's thoughts. When the Witches become visible, Macbeth says nothing although their interest is centered on him: now some subtextual response holds him silent; Banquo interrogates, until Macbeth asks curtly, 'Speak, if you can. What are you?' So Banquo has again helped to present Macbeth, for his speculation suggests by contrast that his leader accepts the strange creatures in his silence, and expects a message. When Macbeth has been greeted three times with three hopeful prophecies, he is again silent and Banquo describes his reaction: and it is a surprising reaction, neither incredulity, nor hope, nor pleasure, but 'fear':

> Good sir, why do you start, and seem to fear
> Things that do sound so fair?

In whatever style the actor performs Macbeth, he must show a total response through gesture, bearing, and movement, through his physical performance; it must be a response large enough to include thought and conscious reaction and yet be stronger than all these because uncontrolled by them — the valiant Macbeth would not intend to reveal fear. Held by his secret feelings, he does not respond to Banquo's question. From his later words we know that he listens, but he takes no part in the continuing interrogation. Then as the Witches 'Hail' him together with Banquo, he speaks directly to them ignoring his partner; his questions are now concerned with himself, and are clear, precise and astute. This transition restores the earlier impression of decisiveness; his powers have been increased, not diminished, by the chiefly inward excitement of the encounter. To deliver this kind of dialogue and to hold the center of the complicated scene, the actor must make silence as real, complex and forceful as words, and show, in a continuous and integrated performance, how an instinctive reaction over-masters, and then is controlled by, conscious intention.

When the Witches vanish, it is again Banquo who speaks first, but Macbeth now responds and his contrasting speech, by accounting for the disappearance of the Witches as a matter of fact, reveals how much further they have taken hold of his imagination than of the still speculative Banquo's. Then he adds 'Would they had stay'd'; there is little logical progression of thought here, so the words will seem motivated subtextually by thoughts and feelings drawing his mind away from Banquo's. It must be spoken in a manner that prevents reply, for

Banquo continues to wonder about the nature of the Witches. The next time Macbeth speaks he ignores Banquo's direct question to elicit a response about the prophecies themselves: 'Your children shall be kings!' Since it is made clear later, in soliloquy, that he has been considering his own 'imperial theme', the actor must again give an impression of words disguising thoughts. This time Banquo seems to catch the subtextual implications:

> MACBETH: Your children shall be kings.
> BANQUO: You shall be King.
> MACBETH: And Thane of Cawdor too; went it not so?

Banquo's straight reply contrasts and therefore underlines the indirection of Macbeth: why had he spoken of Banquo rather than himself? and why does he then pass by the immediate challenge of his own royal hope to speak of secondary matters? He is both disguising his inner thoughts and seeking confirmation of them; he wants to be sure of the prophecies and he wants to hide their true effect on himself. He is so engaged in what pretends to be casual talk that only Banquo hears approaching footsteps. And it is when Ross and Angus have hailed him as Thane of Cawdor that Macbeth is at last given an aside to make his unspoken consciousness more explicit. Shakespeare resorts to this device only when the instinctive, emotional and physical reactions have already been established, and the conscious attempt to conceal them. Yet still there are reserves, to show that Macbeth cannot name 'that suggestion Whose horrid image doth unfix my hair', even to himself; for nowhere does he name the man his thought would murder. Besides the astonishing fear, that could come only from immediate and guilty thoughts of murder, there is also a half-spoken sensitivity to guilt or to the suffering of others. At the end of the scene he speaks aside to Banquo, with disguising easiness and assurance, of a 'free heart'. Since he is later to suffer for the loss of 'troops of friends' (V.3.25), it might be appropriate for the actor to suggest a desire, stronger than his words, for a life of trust and affection — even when considering murder. He rejoins the others with a brief 'Come friends', which is certainly a verbal disguise of his fears and intentions, but perhaps, also, a yearning for what he is about to destroy.

*

Of course, subtext is not 'read' so easily as the text. The first task is to discover where it must be expressed by some means in order to make sense of the words, and where gestures, stage-business or emotional performance necessarily take over from words. But then its precise nature and strength, at any moment, must be defined in relation to the text of the complete play.

In practice, the subtextual implications of any one role in performance will depend considerably on what the individual actor can do, on his temperament and physical being which are the medium for its enactment. Each actor is like a unique colored filter, that emphasizes certain aspects of a part and is incapable of transmitting others.

The last words of Malvolio in *Twelfth Night* show what freedom an actor has in interpretation — or, to put this another way, how much depends on his gifts and decisions. The words 'I'll be reveng'd on the whole pack of you' (V.1.364) *read* like a quick conclusion to a practical joke with allusions to revenge which are unusual in a comedy. But in performance Malvolio speaks the line after a long silence in which he has heard how the trick was played on him and has refused to respond either to a plea to be reasonable, or to sympathy. The management of the scene focuses attention on his silence, so that his reactions to all he sees and hears will be noticed. When at last he speaks, his total performance will seem to express previously hidden thoughts. The audience will be made to realize that Malvolio is isolated and incapable of being helped; but the actor can choose what emotion or thought is the cause of this: humorless self-concern, pride, stoicism, contempt, bewilderment, suffering, fantastic daydreaming. When an actor tries to portray any of these motivations, he is not attempting to express 'more than is set down for him', but he is giving a substance and clarity to the brief words , which have been rendered obligatory by the long silence. Shakespeare has also given him an exit with which to enforce his response with protracted physical movement (there were long distances to be crossed on Elizabethan stages), and he has marked a hiatus following his departure by Olivia's 'He hath been most notoriously abus'd' and Orsino's 'Pursue him, and entreat him to a peace'. Moreover this expression of inward feeling is placed at the latest point in the play, a position of great importance after the affairs of Viola, Orsino, Olivia, Sebastian, Sir Toby and others have been concluded; there follows only a concluding speech by Orsino that has no narrative or character development, and then the riddling song of Feste.

Even when there is a great deal of text for the actor to speak — the choice of subtext can be difficult and bold decisions must be taken, preferably after experimentation in rehearsal. For example, it might be argued that Hamlet's 'To be, or not to be — that is the question...' should be acted so that the subtext implies 'To be, or not to be — that is not the question....' (I know that this has proved practicable for some actors of the role.) The textual argument of the soliloquy draws together in:

> Thus conscience does make cowards of us all...
> And enterprises of great pitch and moment,
> With this regard, their currents turn awry
> And lose the name of action.

The spoken words throughout are concerned, as the famous first line says, with the task of making up one's mind to act. But then Hamlet sees Ophelia, and there is a surprising verbal transition:

> Soft you now!
> The fair Ophelia. — Nymph, in thy orisons
> Be all my sins rememb'red.

After the conscious deliberation of the soliloquy there is an unexpected call on Hamlet's emotions, but his reaction to this disturbance is not disturbed; his words are not ill-formed or obviously unprepared. The tempo changes, and mood, tone and phrasing: and smoothly so. From his tough, practical considerations he can move easily to peace, softness, woman and guilt ('all *my* sins'), as if these thoughts had lain, ready for expression, under the earlier soliloquy. Noticing this transition, we should revalue the earlier text: the incidental color of its images and the changes in direction of its argument may seem more important than they did at first. What the words had only hinted at may have been Hamlet's deepest concerns, and capable of subtextual expression: the pain in *slings and arrows*, *heartache*, *natural shocks*, *rub*, *whips and scorns*, *spurns*; and the desire for a natural peace in *sleep*, *consummation*, *devoutly*, *quietus*, *bourn*. 'To be or not to be' is quite certainly not the only question; under the concern expressed in these words must be another, at first merely suggested but then wholly expressed to Ophelia; and it must prove, finally, to be the stronger. This is not the Hamlet of indecision who attempts to resolve his turbulent thoughts in 'enterprises of great pitch and moment', but the Hamlet who at the end of the play will allow his mother to wipe his brow, the Hamlet who looks for felicity beyond death and accepts silence.

Shakespeare wrote poetic drama of great verbal power; but the words are not all. Always the text is accompanied by continuous physical performance which can transform the effect of spoken words. An unspoken reaction is sometimes necessary for mere intelligibility of its words. Silence and gesture are also important. And the text often lies.

FIVE

Shakespearian Actors

> Behind the dialogue of Greek drama we are always conscious of a concrete visual actuality, and behind that of a specific emotional actuality. Behind the drama of words is the drama of action, the timbre of voice and voice, the uplifted hand or tense muscle, and the particular emotion. The spoken play, the words which we read, are symbols, a shorthand, and often, as in the best of Shakespeare, a very abbreviated shorthand indeed, for the acted and felt play, which is always the real thing. The phrase, beautiful as it may be, stands for a greater beauty still.

THESE words by T. S. Eliot, in an essay on *Seneca in Elizabethan Translation* (1927), sharply delineate the central difficulty in understanding plays in theatrical terms. For Shakespeare, as they suggest, the literary text is a particularly abbreviated account because of the scope for physical and emotional performance that his dialogue gives to actors. Granville-Barker judged that a play of any quality is 'like the iceberg, floating one-ninth above water and eight-ninths submerged';[1] the 'literary record' is the one-ninth we can see.

Granville-Barker went on to say that 'Ideally, everything should be implicit in the record...: set the play in motion and all the hidden things *should* come to light and life.' It follows that, first of all, we must learn to set the play in motion for ourselves, in the theatre of our mind. We can learn to hear the words as we read, to recreate changes of tempo and rhythm, deduce the places where gesture and stage-business are important and look for opportunities for subtextual impressions and for the progressive clarification of that physical and emotional reality which lies beneath the observed text.

The main difficulty is that the theatre of the mind is intangible. When we only *imagine* that a play is in performance, the actual physical facts can slip out of mind, and we can find our attention engrossed by one interesting detail. We can forget, too, the temporal control and sequence of performance, and that sense of scale which comes by witnessing a whole play without a break. Our imaginary enactment is too indulgent of our own interests, and of course it is severely limited by our own particular talents and experience.

The other recourse is to actual performances. These are tangible, and in them almost the whole play can be heard and seen, and studied. Moreover the text has been studied before performance by the persons for whom Shakespeare wrote, individual actors. They are not

Elizabethan actors, of course, but in many of their instincts and skills are more like Elizabethan actors than most readers and students of Shakespeare. Moreover an actor's interpretation must be one that is convincing to himself as a performer, and it must make consistent sense — physically, emotionally and, in some degree, intellectually — to his audiences. The evidence of performance is of crucial importance.

But actual performances are also of limited use for learning about Shakespeare's plays. Productions are created under difficulties of casting and organization; there's too little time and too little money to provide satisfactory conditions, to take sufficient risks, develop imaginative acting, learn enough about the demands of the text or appropriate ways of staging. They are limited, too, by the talents of the performers, and obscured by the additions and alterations which no creative artist seems able to resist making to Shakespeare's text. And we as spectators are also unsatisfactory, especially limited in our response to effects which are new to our experience.

Both the theatre of the mind and actual performances need to be supplemented by reading accounts of earlier productions. Here we shall find approaches to the text that are now out of fashion but of proved validity for audiences, and the effects appropriate to different theatres and styles of performance some of which may be closer to Elizabethan conditions than any known today. Moreover only the greatly gifted actors have left sufficient evidence behind to be usefully studied and so through theatre history we can share imaginative and appropriately ambitious readings of the texts. We do not respond here to actual performances, but we can study the wide range of descriptions, sympathetic and hostile, that these earlier interpretations have provoked; sometimes the records illustrate the development of a performance during ten or twenty years of repertory playing.[2]

Present and past productions are, then, essential stimulants and guides in our pursuit of a theatrical understanding of Shakespeare's plays. History proves that, among the great quantity of dross in theatre productions, the riches of Shakespeare's dramatic invention are constantly rediscovered. Each age, each decade, has its own way of performing and producing, and every one reveals some new elements that have been hidden in the text until the moment when an actor, with a particular style and experience, has been able to effect the surprise. On the first performance, a famous Shylock was praised in rapid doggerel:

hnnnnnnnnnnnnb

and every year reviews speak of 'revelation', 'originality' and

Shakespeare's play being 'given' new value or coherence.

For example, a detailed report from *The Examiner* of 5 June 1814 shows how Edmund Kean sought a deep consistency and unusual psychological truth in his roles, and so developed the contrasts implicit in situations. It concerns his Iago:

> The actors of this part in general... stab Roderigo, and then walk away with perfect ease and satisfaction. Mr Kean... gives and repeats the atrocious thrust, till it may be supposed no life remains; but he feels this to be a matter too important to be left in doubt. He therefore, though he at the same time converses coolly with those about him, throws his eye perpetually towards the prostrate body...: sometimes he walked by it carelessly, and surveyed it with a glance too rapid to be observed; sometimes he deliberately approached it, and looked at it with his candle...: and thus he continued to hover over and watch it till he leaves the stage.

If the tension created by this business seems like an intrusion upon the text, we should remember that the usual playing of this incident on the modern stage often evokes laughter from the audience at Iago's and, possibly, the play's expense. Perhaps Kean discovered the secret of how to play this dispersed, short-phrased and oddly cloak-and-dagger scene. Certainly, few Iagos have been so admired.

When a study of performances goes intimately with a renewed study of the theatrical detail of the texts, it will lead us closer to the acted and felt play that lies hidden behind the printed words. If we find more possible interpretations than certain ones, that may be a sign that we begin to respond to the full wealth and demands of Shakespeare's imagination. We should always be willing to test the value of an actor's discovery by reference to the text, to the character as a whole and the play as a whole. We should, as it were, keep the plays in constant rehearsal in the theatre of our mind.

Michel Saint-Denis has a description of an actor's approach to a part that suggests an appropriate encounter with Shakespeare, always remembering that we have to consider the wider dramatic effects as well as individual roles. It is a stern and exciting direction:

> In a classical play [and, specifically, he includes Shakespeare's in this class] the actor must not hurry or jump upon the character. You must not enslave the text by premature conception or feeling of the character. You should not hurry to get on the stage and try to act, physically and emotionally, too soon. Psychological and emotional understanding of a character should come through familiarity with the text, not from outside it. You must know how to wait, how to refuse, so as to remain free. You must be like a glove,

open and flexible, but flat, and remaining flat at the beginning. Then by degrees the text, the imagination, the associations roused by the text penetrate you and bring you to life. Ways are prepared for the character to creep in slowly and animate the glove, the glove which is you, with your blood, with your nerves, with your breathing system, your voice, with the light of your own lucid control switching on and off. The whole complex machinery is at work; it has been put into action by the text...[3]

SIX

Creating a Role: Shylock

EVER since 14 February 1741, when Charles Macklin persuaded the management of Drury Lane to restore Shakespeare's text in place of George Granville's adaptation and to allow him to play Shylock, *The Merchant of Venice* has nearly always been revived for the same purpose — to give some actor the chance of playing the lead. For that is what Shylock is: although he appears in but five of its twenty scenes and not at all in the last Act, he can dominate every other impression and display the powers of many kinds of actor. He often takes the final curtain-call, without Portia or Bassanio, without Antonio, the merchant of Venice. This tradition is so strong that it is easy to forget how strange it is: how odd that a villain — the one who threatens the happiness of the others — should so run away with a play that is a comedy by other signs, and that makes only a passing, unconcerned allusion to him at its conclusion. But the records are unequivocal.[1] In the theatre it is his play. Fortunately the records are also unusually detailed, so that we are able to reconstruct the different ways in which Shylock has been given life and observe the qualities in Shakespeare's text which make this a star part. And from this inquiry, other questions arise: have ambitious actors misrepresented Shakespeare's play? is one interpretation, one reading of the actor's opportunities, more faithful than another? is a fully realized Shylock incompatible with a well proportioned *Merchant of Venice*, one that is satisfactorily concluded?

*

At first the part seemed to have been written especially for Macklin, as Boaden's *Memoirs of J. P. Kemble* (1825) affirm:

> His acting was essentially manly — there was nothing of trick about it. His delivery was more level than modern speaking, but certainly more weighty, direct and emphatic. His features were rigid, his eye cold and colourless; yet the earnestness of his manner, and the sterling sense of address, produced an effect in Shylock, that has remained to the present hour unrivalled.
>
> i.440

It was thought that Shakespeare had drawn Shylock 'all shade, not a gleam of light; subtle, selfish, fawning, irascible, and tyrannic', and that Macklin's voice was:

> most happily suited to that sententious gloominess of expression the author intended; which, with a sullen solemnity of deportment, marks the character strongly; in his malevolence, there is a forcible and terrifying ferocity.
>
> Gentleman, i.291

He cast his performance between two extremes, sullen and malevolent; and the two were linked by weight and power in his deportment and his eyes:

> There was, beside his judgment which went to the study of every line of it, such an iron-visaged look, such a relentless, savage cast of manners, that the audience seemed to shrink from the character.
>
> *Memoirs*, pp.405-6

His performance began sullenly:

> when Shylock and Bassanio entered... there was an awful, a solemn silence.... He approached with Bassanio.... Still not a whisper could be heard in the house. Upon the entrance of Anthonio, the Jew makes the audience acquainted with his motives of antipathy against the Merchant. Mr Macklin had no sooner delivered this speech, than the audience suddenly burst out into a thunder of applause, and in proportion as he afterwards proceeded to exhibit and mark the malevolence, the villainy, and the diabolical atrocity of the character, so in proportion did the admiring and delighted audience testify their approbation....
>
> Kirkman, i.258-9

Macklin himself spoke of the first scenes as 'rather tame and level,' but:

> I knew where I should have the pull, which was in the third act, and reserved myself accordingly. At this period I threw out all my fire;... the contrasted passions of joy for the Merchant's losses, and grief for the elopement of Jessica, open a fine field for an actor's powers,...
>
> *Memoirs*, p.93

For this scene with Salerio and Solanio, and then with Tubal, he 'broke the tones of utterance' and ensured that his 'transitions were strictly natural' (Kirkman, i.264). But for the trial he reverted to what he called 'a silent yet forcible impression' (*Memoirs*, p. 93):

> Macklin...'stood like a TOWER,' as Milton has it. He was 'not bound to *please*' any body by his pleading; he claimed a right, grounded upon LAW,

Figure I. Macklin as Shylock, IV.1: 'Most learned judge! a sentence; come prepare' (from Bell's *Shakespeare*)

> and thought himself as firm as the Rialto.[2]

The kind of detail that impressed an audience can be judged from this account in a letter by a German visitor, Georg Lichtenberg, who saw Macklin in 1775:

> Shylock is not one of those mean, plausible cheats who could expatiate for an hour on the virtues of a gold watch-chain of pinchbeck; he is heavy, and silent in his unfathomable cunning, and, when the law is on his side, just to the point of malice. Imagine a rather stout man with a coarse yellow face and a nose generously fashioned in all three dimensions, a long double chin, and a mouth so carved by nature that the knife appears to have slit him right up to the ears, on one side at least, I thought. He wears a long black gown, long wide trousers, and a red tricorne, after the fashion of Italian Jews, I suppose. The first words he utters, when he comes on to the stage, are slowly and impressively spoken: 'Three thousand ducats.' The double 'th', which Macklin lisps as lickerishly as if he were savoring the ducats and all that they would buy, make so deep an impression in the man's favour that nothing can destroy it. Three such words uttered thus at the outset give the keynote of his whole character. In the scene where he first misses his daughter, he comes on hatless, with disordered hair, some locks a finger long standing on end, as if raised by a breath of wind from the gallows, so distracted was his demeanour. Both his hands are clenched, and his movements abrupt and convulsive. To see a deceiver, who is usually calm and resolute, in such a state of agitation, is terrible.[3]

Macklin's imitators cheapened this portrait, presenting a Shylock 'bent with age and ugly with mental deformity... sullen, morose, gloomy, inflexible, brooding over one idea, that of his hatred, and fixed on one unalterable purpose, that of his revenge.'[4] If this mood was relieved it was by laughter at Shylock's expense, especially in the Tubal scene which often excited 'a mixture of mirth and indignation'.[5] But then, on 26 January 1814, Edmund Kean played the Jew at Drury Lane with 'terrible energy'; like Macklin he established a reputation overnight and founded a new tradition.

His Shylock was not so easy to imitate, for it depended on most unusual gifts. His voice had a range 'from F below the line to F above it', its natural key being that of B flat. His hard guttural tone upon G was said to be 'as piercing as the third string of a violoncello', and his mezzo and pianissimo expressions as 'soft as from the voice of woman'. This instrument he learned to control so that it gave sudden and thrilling effects: he could give 'the yell and choaked utterance of a savage':

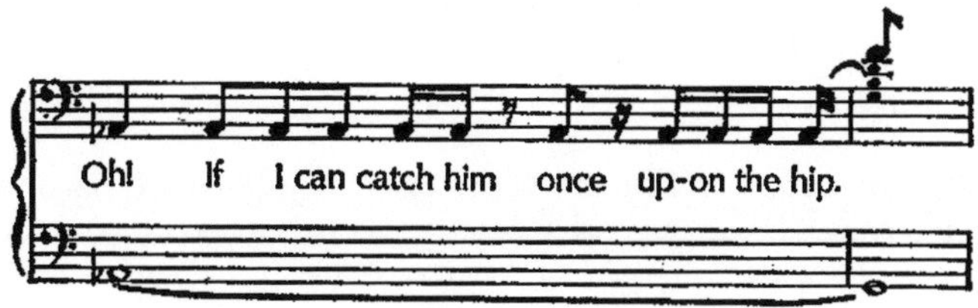

At times he gave 'a torrent of words in a breath', yet with 'all the advantages of deliberation'. His pauses could give a 'grandeur', speaking 'more than the words themselves':[6]

Kean was fond of 'abrupt transitions... mingling strong lights and shadows with Caravaggio force of unreality'. He gave an irregular performance, always seeking 'points' for passion and power. This might have degenerated into trickery, but he 'vigilantly and patiently rehearsed every detail' until his artistic sense was satisfied; and he acted with his whole being, watching the after-effects of passion as well as its sudden expression:

> a strong emotion, after discharging itself in one massive current, continues for a time expressing itself in feebler currents.... In watching Kean's quivering muscles and altered tones you felt the subsidence of passion. The voice might be calm, but there was a tremor in it; the face might be quiet, but there were vanishing traces of recent agitation.
>
> Lewes, pp. 2-8

His arms, hands and large eyes were, with his voice, eloquent of intelligence, spirit and power.

Kean's first scene as Shylock started, as Macklin's did, slowly, but added dignity and a crushing, sardonic humour:

> From the first moment that he appeared and leant upon his stick to listen

> gravely while moneys are requested of him, he impressed the audience,...'like a chapter of Genesis'. [Then followed] the overpowering remonstrant sarcasm of his address to Antonio, and the sardonic mirth of his proposition about the 'merry bond'...
>
> Lewes, p. 11

As he spoke of Laban and his flock (I.3.72-91), he seemed 'borne back to the olden time':

> Shylock is in Venice with his money-bags, his daughter, and his injuries; but his thoughts take wing to the east; his voice swells and deepens at the mention of his sacred tribe and ancient law,...

But he can change rapidly:

> The audience is then stirred to enthusiasm by the epigrammatic point and distinctness with which he gives the lines:
>
> Hath a *dog* money? Is it possible
> A *cur* can lend three thousand ducats?
>
> Hawkins, i. 129

In Shylock's second scene, taking leave of Jessica, Kean revealed yet another facet of his powers, for in his calling 'Why, Jessica! I say' there was a 'charm, as of music' (Doran, pp. 429-30). But his chief triumph was, like Macklin's, in III.1. This became the crucial test for all succeeding Shylocks; Squire Bancroft, discussing one particular failure at the end of the century, noted that:

> The fact of rushing on the stage in a white-heat frenzy, with nothing to lead up to its passion, I take it, is the main difficulty.

He had seen only Kean's son, Charles, assay it satisfactorily, and he closely reproduced his father:

> Apropos of which, Mr Wilton often spoke to me; he having once, when quite a young actor, played Tubal to the Shylock of Edmund Kean. The great actor did not appear at rehearsal, but sent word that 'he should like to see the gentleman who was to be the Tubal at his hotel'. Mr Wilton obeyed the summons, and spoke always of the kindness with which Kean instructed him, after saying, 'We'll run through the scene, Mr Wilton, because I'm told that if you don't know what I'm going to do I might frighten you!' Mr Wilton described the performance as *stupendous*! and said that, although

> prepared beforehand, at night Kean really frightened him.'

For this scene Kean could use his flashing transitions; he showed, in a manner long remembered, the alternate passions:

> Shylock's anguish at his daughter's flight; his wrath at the two Christians who make sport of his anguish; his hatred of all Christians, generally, and of Antonio in particular; and then his alternations of rage, grief, and ecstasy, as Tubal relates the losses incurred.
>
> Doran, p. 430

In the speech beginning 'He hath disgraced me, and hindered me half a million....'

> He hurried you on through the catalogue of Antonio's atrocities and unprovoked injuries to him, enforcing them with a strong accentuation and a high pitch of voice; and when he had reached the *climax*, he came down by a sudden transition to a gentle, suffering tone of simple representation of his oppressor's manifest un-reason and injustice, on the words
>
> 'I am a *Jew*![8]

In the trial scene was noted:

> His calm demeanour at first; his confident appeal to justice; his deafness, when appeal is made to him for mercy; his steady joyousness, when the young lawyer recognizes the validity of the bond; his burst of exultation, when his right is confessed; his fiendish eagerness, when whetting the knife; — and then, the sudden collapse of disappointment and terror, with the words, — 'Is *that* — the LAW?'...
>
> Then, his trembling anxiety to recover what he had before refused: his sordid abjectness, as he finds himself foiled, at every turn; his subdued fury; and, at the last, (and it was always the crowning glory of his acting in this play), the withering sneer, hardly concealing the crushed heart, with which he replied to the jibes of Gratiano, as he left the court.
>
> Doran, pp. 430-1

To this account must be added the return of his sardonic humour, in lines like:

> An oath, an oath! I have an oath in heaven.
> Shall I lay perjury upon my soul?
>
> IV.1.223-4

or in, 'I cannot find it; 'tis not in the bond' (l. 245), which, according to *The Examiner*, was accompanied with a 'transported chuckle'. There was in Kean's performance, as the same journal noted, a 'union of great powers with a fine sensibility': for Macklin's malevolence he had given sardonic intellect and fiery spirit; for his sullen strength, he had emphasized family love and racial pride, both being subjected to suffering and pain. Everything had been expressed with a series of instantaneous, forceful effects. So he reversed a tradition, and, for Hazlitt, Kean's Jew was:

> more than half a Christian. Certainly, our sympathies are much oftener with him than with his enemies. He is honest in his vices; they are hypocrites in their virtues.[9]

Irving's Shylock at the Lyceum on 1 November 1879 was the next to be generally accepted as an original reading. He accentuated earlier suggestions of dignity, and was venerable, lonely, grieved, austere: he moved with pride and grace; his humour was coldly cynical, rather than sardonic; his thought was meditative, not sullen, and his anger was white and tense; in defeat he called forth pity and awe. When he first played the role he bent all his effort toward gaining sympathy, but later he allowed his Shylock to become more 'hard, merciless, inexorable, terrible' (Winter, pp. 175 and 178). Irving's elevated tone was established in that early, 'tame and level' scene: his first lines were spoken half-turned away from Bassanio, in a subdued monotone, and the whole was played more deliberately than was customary, even in the sneers and expressions of anger. In III.1, to Salerio and Solanio, he spoke wildly at first, but then with the 'calm tone of desperate resolve' (Irving, p. 341). He eliminated the 'almost incessant movement [and] explosive vociferation' that was customary, but gave a 'lightning flash' at 'To bait fish withal' (l.45); and, after a pause of suspense, 'there ensued the torrid invective... uttered at first in an almost suffocated voice,... but presently in the fluent tones of completely liberated passion' (Winter, pp. 187-9). With Tubal be played for pathos; there was a break-down after 'would she were hearsed at my foot....' (ll.77-84), and the speech finished ('no tears but o' my shedding') with sobs; on 'I will have the heart of him, if he forfeit', he tore open his robe, repeatedly striking his breast.

But unlike other Shylocks, Irving made his strongest effects in the beginning of the Trial Scene. Here his dignity had full scope: he entered in dead calm, as 'a priest going to the altar', or as 'a figure of

Fate — pitiless, majestic, implacable'.[10] Yet he was also a 'lethal monster, sure of his prey, because bulwarked behind the pretense of religion and law' (Winter, p.196); there was a:

> momentary flashing out of a passionate delight, where Portia's words to Antonio, 'You must prepare your bosom for his knife,' seem to put within his grasp the object of his hate.

And both these impressions contrasted finely and surprisingly with:

> the total collapse of mind and body, when at a glance the full significance of the words - 'This bond doth give thee here no jot of blood' (l.301) — burst upon his keen intellect. In these words, and what follows, he seems to receive his death-blow.... We feel the prop is in effect gone 'that doth sustain his life'. But he keeps a firm front to the last, and has a fine curl of withering scorn upon his lip for Gratiano, as he walks away to die in silence and alone.[11]

Yet this was not all: he moved away slowly and with difficulty, as if opposing a fatal weakness by an act of will; at the door he nearly fell, to recover and 'with a long, heavy sigh' to disappear (Winter, p.195).

After Macklin, Kean and Irving, no one has so completely captured the public's imagination with an original Shylock. Most actors have moved somewhere within the earlier limits while frankly comic interpretations, or a woman in the role, have been short-lived eccentricities; occasionally there have been clear failures. Lewis Casson, Ernest Milton and John Gielgud were at first among the most assured and independent. Casson, performing with the Old Vic Company in 1927, stripped Shylock of romance, dignity and moral stature; this gave a 'new comic quality, in his lighter scenes', and in the trial held attention without relying on purely 'theatrical effects'.[12] St John Ervine in the *Observer* complained that this Shylock lacked the 'magnificence of baffled rage and the courageous abandon of a man whose life is filled with despair'. But to this Casson replied that he could find neither of these qualities in Shakespeare's text: instead of dying for his religion and his oath or remaining scornful to the end, Shylock replies, 'I am content,' and to Casson that was 'contemptible' conduct.[13] He acted within an everyday and even petty idiom: his first scene was the 'ordinary bluff of commerce, common to all tired businessmen'; he dined ,with Antonio, against his religious scruples, to satisfy mere 'spite'. Casson believed that what is mean, malicious, cunning, cruel and cowardly — traits found in almost every man — draws Shylock on to his 'abominable acts', and this process he tried to portray. The performance was continuously interesting (especially to experienced playgoers), but not compelling; and it did not establish a tradition.

Ernest Milton, five years later, likewise avoided easy theatricality; he played the opening scenes lightly, but with a studied Jewishness, and then, on discovering that Jessica has fled, 'the lamp he is carrying falls from his hand and fate suddenly and savagely transforms him'.[14] From this point he showed more power, but without spectacular strokes, and the final prolonged moment before he leaves the court, as he looks round and 'shows his teeth in a snarl of impotent but silent hatred'[15], was one that could be successfully attempted only by an actor who had played with consistent and minute truth, and with progressive tension.

John Gielgud came to the role in 1938, influenced by a highly acclaimed Chekhov season. He thus saw his problem as that of acting 'in style', appropriate to Shakespeare's language and period, while still acting 'in character'; and as he rehearsed he came to believe that Shakespeare himself had 'obviously calculated' on this attempt, and given full scope for it.[16] As with Casson's, some critics complained that his Shylock fell 'rather from the pavement to the gutter, than from the mountain to the abyss',[17] but Gielgud had added intensity, throughout. He provoked the *New Statesman* to give a detailed account:

> Mr Gielgud is riveting as the Jew,... most careful not to sentimentalize the part.... When he is on the stage you can feel the whole house motionless under the painful weight of his realism. In the trial scene he obliged us to suspend disbelief in the impossible story, and when he stropped his knife upon his shoe, we were appalled, not by fear for Antonio, but by the sight of hatred turned to madness. His appearance throughout was extraordinary — gummy, blinking eyes, that suggested some nasty creature of the dark, and loquacious hands with as many inflections as his voice. 'But stop my house's ears,' 'I had it of Leah when I was a bachelor,' 'I am not well' — the intensity with which he delivered such phrases lingers in the memory.

Shylock could sustain Chekhovian attention to subtext, and could evoke pathos without sentimentality, intensity without theatricality.

*

After World War II, Peter O'Toole at Stratford-Upon-Avon, in 1960, was the first Shylock to achieve comparable authority. At twenty-eight years old, he was "arresting and flamboyant..., an actor who knows how to hold the audience and possess the stage, as if by some innate and royal prerogative."[18] The text became new-minted:

> This was less through the longer speeches than in short phrases, snatches or bites at single words: 'I *hate* him... If I can *catch* him... Even on *me*... I have an oath in *heaven*... Is *that* the law?'

This was not a pathetic alien:

> 'No tears but of my shedding' was not said for sympathy, but with ritualistic beating on his breast. He expressed pain here, and at the memory of Leah, by showing his effort to bear it himself, with clenched control.... As Portia drew the trial towards an issue, the shorter phrases — a shouted 'I stand for judgement...' stilled the angry court — and the intense sharpening of the knife had full power. After the collapse of his 'rights', Shylock regained some of his strength with his dignity; he laughed at the sparing of his life and prided himself still on his sense of right — 'send the deed after me, And I *will* sign it.'
>
> ... Neither director nor actor stressed the 'inhumanity' of Shylock: his rapaciousness was not evident, for he was dressed too well for a miser; he walked too upright to suggest cunning or unbridled hatred.... Moreover, this 'magnificent Shylock', as one review called him, was opposed by a gushing, nervous, trivial band of Christians.[19]

Laurence Olivier's Shylock, for the National Theatre in 1970, was in a production by Jonathan Miller who set the play in the late nineteenth century, a status-seeking, mercantile world:

> Olivier jettisons altogether the rabbinically bearded tribal figure (on his lips the very word 'tribe' approaches a sneer). He is not a Jew of the Renaissance ghetto, but one who has come into his own in a mercantile age and can almost pass for a Christian merchant; in his morning suit, gold spectacles, and top hat, he is indistinguishable from Antonio.
>
> Within, however, he has been incurably maimed by the process of assimilation. His delivery is a ghastly compound of speech tricks picked up from the Christian rich:... 'I am debatin' of my present state', he spits out, fingering a silver-topped cane; and then spoils the gesture by dissolving into paroxysms of silent, slack-jawed laughter.

His performance was not "sympathetic", but showed "the kind of monster into which Christian societies transform their aliens."[20] His care for appearance served both to make his murderous intention seem less outrageous and to mark the deeper involvement and pain that finally possessed him. With considerable ingenuity Olivier softened the effect of sharpening the knife which is to kill Antonio. In the trial scene, he:

> ...was accompanied by a servant, to whom Bassanio's line: 'Why dost thou whet thy knife so earnestly?' was addressed, and on whose behalf Shylock replied: 'To cut the forfeiture from that bankrupt there!'[21]

Seventeen years later, at Stratford-upon-Avon, Anthony Sher explored the more horrendous aspects of the role, and of the play, with unmistakable passion:

> Kicked, beaten, abused and spat upon by his Christian tormentors, Anthony Sher's grotesquely bearded Shylock seethes like some possessed dervish, hyped-up beyond the reach of reason in his rage for revenge.

So reported the press, when the production by Bill Alexander reached London in 1988. This uncompromising reading of the text:

> haunted by the memory of the holocaust, and, in the appalling racism of Antonio and his cronies, gives a sharp reminder of how often anti-semitism and racism lurk beneath an apparently civilized veneer. In the circumstances, Shylock's behavior becomes, if not justified, almost entirely understandable.[22]

'The villainy you teach me I will execute' (III.1.62-3) became the key-line in the performance, and the trial scene demonstrated its consequences:

> Brandishing a dagger, ranging the scales and blood-splattered towel in front of the pinioned Antonio, chanting in a ritual of revenge, Sher is mesmerised like some predatory animal poised for the kill.[23]

But the interpretation was not without complexities:

> Sher's heavily accented Shylock... wobbles vertiginously between tactical fawning and an insolent parody of fawning, roaring wrath and momentary subsidences into helpless nerves...
> When daughter Jessica deserts the family home, carting off a pile of money and jewels, most Shylocks invite a superior sneer as they comically mix up ducats and daughters and so betray their distorted priorities. But Mr Sher's almost Lear-like anguish at daughterly ingratitude powerfully suggests that it is in his heart and not, despite all he might shout, in his cash-box that she has wounded him, and that his subsequent furious actions have less to do

with money than with the devious settling of an emotional score.[24]

Each actor must find his own way through the challenges and opportunities of the text. Only a year later, in 1989 at the Phoenix Theatre in London, Dustin Hoffman brought a wholly different technique and sensibility to the role, in a production by Sir Peter Hall. The key to this performance, according to the Jewish Chronicle, was when:

> after his daughter has run away, he tells Tubal: 'The curse never fell upon our nation until now.' Tubal looks at him as if to ask: 'What kind of world have you been living in?' and Shylock quickly responds: 'I,' he stresses, 'never felt it until now.'... And like any ordinary man who has been warped by a lifetime's humiliation, when revenge comes hobbling over the horizon he greets him like a long-lost brother and spits as he has been spat on and burns with eagerness to turn the knife as it has been turned on him....
>
> By contrast with the revellers who steal his daughter and his ducats, Hoffman, small and neat in a long buttoned-down-to-the-middle gown, his beard grizzled, two slim ringlets flanking his cheeks, a short pigtail hanging beneath a black velvet yarmulke, is an austere, though intellectually slight, figure.[25]

Quietly, his Shylock drew attention, as he seemed to rethink his whole life:

> It is only when armed with his courtroom knife... that Hoffman manages to acquire anything like the mesmeric theatricality that we have come to expect from the role as played by the likes of Olivier, O'Toole and Redgrave.[26]

When Shylock is defeated by the lawyer-Portia:

> there is not even a spasmodic blaze of anger at his forced conversion, and he goes to his fate unprotestingly, hustled out of the court by the gentry and clearly destined for a beating; an ordinary little man who thought he could take on the Venetian establishment.[27]

*

Literary critics might complain that these various Shylocks tell more about the 'pitiful ambition' of the actors who invented them than about Shakespeare's play. They could cite, in evidence, the 'No, no, no!' which Kean added after his '...would she were hearsed at my foot, and the ducats in her coffin!', or Irving's interpolated scene of Shylock's return at night after Jessica's escape, to knock at his closed door and wait as the curtain fell.[28] Or they might recall the "long, withdrawing and hardly human wail" with which Laurence Olivier concluded his performance after Shylock had left the stage in the Trial Scene,[29] or the crowd of young louts who pelted Anthony Sher's Shylock with stones at the beginning of III.1, and who chanted their hatred with 'Jew! Jew!' as he fled from them. But as surely as such additions alter Shakespeare's play, so surely did the interpretations they serve arise from that play: all these Shylocks, despite their contradictions, exist only in and through *The Merchant of Venice;* nothing else could inspire them. The text itself shows how they exploit opportunities given to the actor by Shakespeare.

Shylock's entry is delayed until I.3, when the audience has already seen Antonio, Bassanio and Portia. The heroine leaves the stage with tripping rhyme:

> Come Nerissa. Sirrah, go before.
> Whiles we shut the gate upon one wooer, another knocks at the door.

and Shylock enters with Bassanio or, rather, Bassanio with Shylock, for the Jew but echoes him:

> SHYLOCK : Three thousand ducats — well.
> BASSANIO: Ay, sir, for three months.
> SHYLOCK: For three months — well.
> BASSANIO: For the which, as I told you, Antonio shall be bound.
> SHYLOCK: Antonio shall become bound — well.
> BASSANIO: May you stead me? Will you pleasure me? Shall I know your answer?
> SHYLOCK: Three thousand ducats for three months, and Antonio bound.
> BASSANIO: Your answer to that.

Shylock's words are pedestrian on the printed page, but they are not so when acted. Of course, repetition without variation would deflate the 'strongest' scene; but no actor would be guilty of that in this situation. Shylock's slow movement and speech at first contrasts with the gay departure of Portia and Nerissa; thus a distinct impression is made at once and the very flatness of the words arouses curiosity. Then as Bassanio becomes more impatient — 'Ay, sir...' and 'as I told you' —

Edmund Kean as Shylock
(H. Meyer, after W.H. Watts; 1814)

Henry Irving as Shylock

Antony Sher as Shylock
(Photo: Joe Cocks Studio)

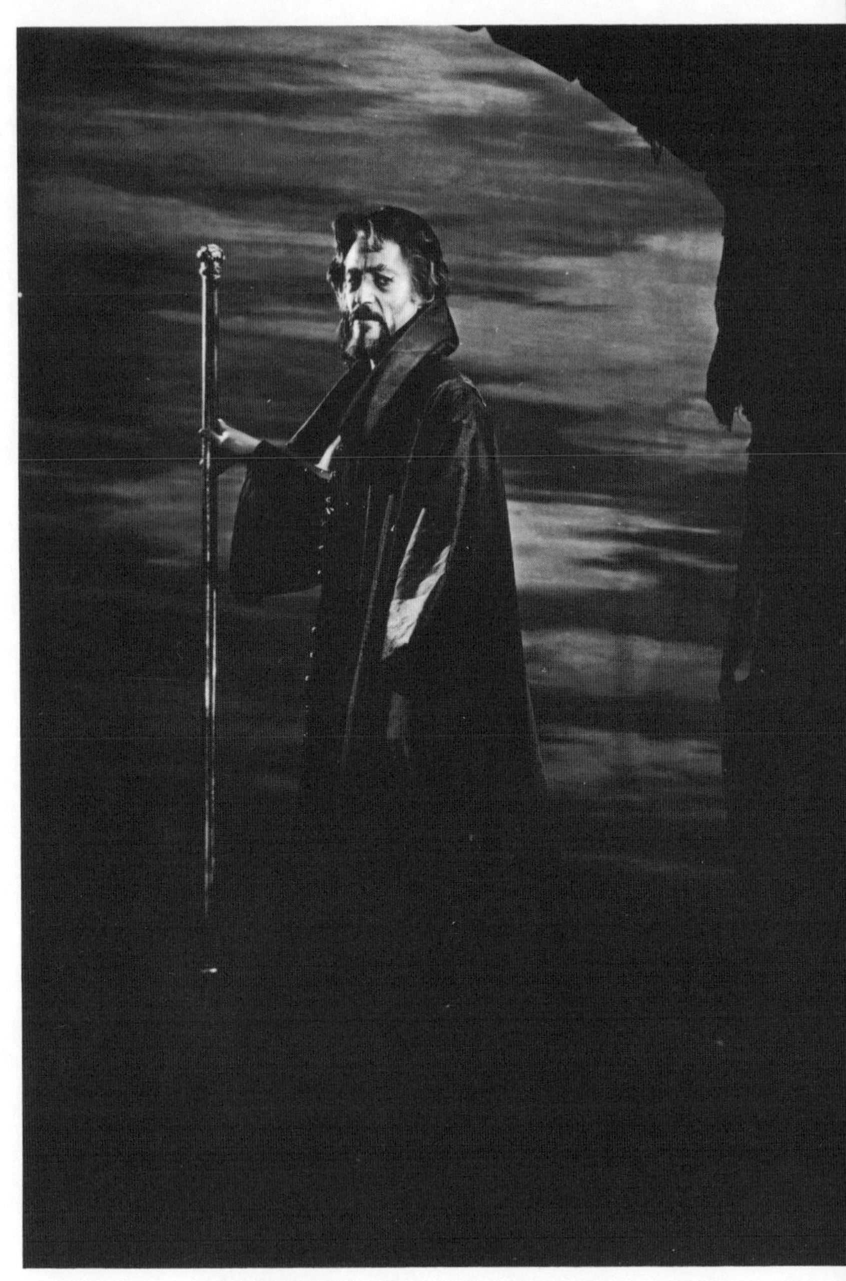

Peter O'Toole as Shylock
(Photo: Angus McBean)

ILLUSTRATIONS FROM GORDON CRAIG'S CRANACH PRESS *HAMLET*:

Hamlet Alone

First Court Scene

Ophelia, Laertes & Polonious

Frighted by False Fire

John Conklin's Candlelit Setting for the Masque in *The Tempest*
(Photo: Lanny Nagler)

Prospero and Ariel in Julie Taymor's production of *The Tempest*, designed by G. W. Mercier
(Photo G.W. Mercier)

G.W. Mercier's Setting for the Masque in *The Tempest*
(Photo: G.W. Mercier)

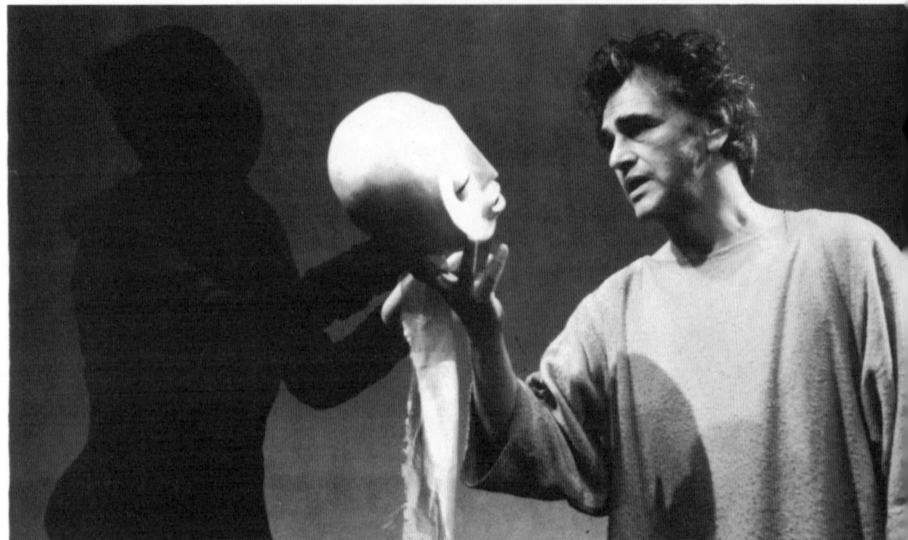

Prospero, Ariel and the Actor of Ariel in Julie Taymor's *The Tempest*
(Photo: G.W. Mercier)

Shylock's repetitions, in his own tempo and intonation, assure the audience that this man has his own time and his own thoughts; he neglects the three urgent questions to repeat earlier points yet again. And in distinguishing his delivery from Bassanio's, the actor can find many suggestions from the text. As Lewis Casson played him, he is a canny business man, by flat repetitions drawing his client out to show how much he needs the money. For Macklin, the echoing would be sullen and heavy, a slow savoring of 'it now appears you need my help' (l.109). With Kean the repetitions would show a sharper satisfaction with the twice repeated 'Antonio bound', supported by 'I will feed fat the ancient grudge I bear him' (l.42), and:

> Fast bind, fast find —
> A proverb never stale in thrifty mind.
>
> II.5.53-4

The repetitions need a subtext, or 'under-meaning', in order to sustain the introduction of the new character. Probably the stronger they are, the closer they will be to Shakespeare's intention. The ambiguous 'well's (variously printed as exclamations or questions by editors) can allow two under-meanings to each speech: Shylock's repetition of Bassanio's words can thus be so private with hatred that the 'well' is a necessary declension towards conversation; or the repetition could be falsely bland and the 'well' spoken aside, voicing a private satisfaction. In any case the effect of thus introducing Shylock with thoughts and feelings not directly expressed in the words themselves is to awaken a precise curiosity, induce an intense focus, as the audience watches for explicit statement.

If so far only the privacy of Shylock's thoughts has been fully established, the duologue at once proceeds to further complication:

> SHYLOCK: Antonio is a good man.
> BASSANIO: Have you beard any imputation to the contrary?
> SHYLOCK: Ho, no, no, no, no:...

The emphatic reply suggests that the Jew is surprised at being misunderstood, or pretends to be, and it can be used to add to the impression of guile which may already be implicit in the way in which he made Bassanio talk. At once he explains patiently:

> ...no, no; my meaning in saying he is a good man is to have

> you understand me that he is sufficient....

Shylock's intellectual superiority is nicely established by this elaboration, and by the ironic tone of 'good' and 'sufficient'. And the impression is strengthened by the ease with which he proceeds to make the rich merchant seem a bad security, by his precise and humorous enumeration of risks, his parenthetic explanation of 'water-rats', and his final show of modesty — 'I think I may take his bond'. Bassanio's short-phrased and, perhaps, short-tempered reply — 'Be assur'd you may' — enhances Shylock's control by contrast; and the repetitive rejoinder — 'I will be assur'd I may' — gives opportunity for re-impressing the ominous subtext of the opening.

So far the dramatic issues have been most strongly expressed through contrasts and a controlled manner of speaking, but then Shylock is stung by a chance word of Bassanio's:

> SHYLOCK: ... May I speak with Antonio?
> BASSANIO: If it please you to dine with us.

Possibly, the invitation is diffident, for it implies a show of familiarity with someone the speaker despises; but, however it is spoken, Shylock's reply has contrast enough in its forceful vocabulary and phrasing, and in the sudden particular scorn of 'Yes, to smell pork, to eat....' The projected bargain is forgotten, apparently by a stronger impulse:

> ... to eat of the habitation which your prophet, the Nazarite, conjured the devil into! I will buy with you, sell with you, talk with you, walk with you, and so following; but I will not eat with you, drink with you, nor pray with you. What news on the Rialto?

The sharp, piled-up phrases culminate in his first allusion to religious observances in 'pray with you'; then, as if by an enforced recall to immediate concerns, there is the sudden anti-climax of 'What news on the Rialto?' and, quickly, the feigned ignorance of 'Who is he comes here?' The *power* of Shylock is first shown in this sudden gust of utterance so firmly subdued for some subtextual reason; and its cause is not money or personal animosity, but race and religion. As Bassanio briefly identifies Antonio and joins him, Shylock is left alone for a soliloquy which, at last, expresses directly what has hitherto been suggested under the lines, by 'sheer acting'; and Shakespeare has prepared for this moment the audience's curiosity and expectation.

Yet as Shylock speaks now, with the greater control of verse, all is not made plain. His hatred, avarice and cunning become unequivocal, but there is confusion about the relative importance of two grounds of hatred. The first statement is quick, as if unstudied:

> I hate him for he is a Christian.

But the second, while claiming to be more important, has a show of reason which makes it sound considered rather than passionate:

> But more for that in low simplicity
> He lends out money gratis, and brings down
> The rate of usance here with us in Venice.

His next phrase, 'If I can catch him once upon the hip', is both an everyday idiom and a possible allusion to Jacob's wrestling with the angel (Gen.xxxii); certainly it is no casual thought, for it awakens, in 'I will feed fat the ancient grudge I bear him', the physical idea of devouring as a beast, linked with the solemn connotations of 'ancient'. Then racial consciousness is uppermost again with 'He hates our sacred nation'; and, as this new intensity echoes in tempo and words the first rush of feeling, so it also is followed more reasonably, with explanation and enumeration:

> ... and he rails
> Even there where merchants most do congregate,
> On me, my bargains and my well-won thrift,
> Which he calls interest.

The soliloquy concludes sharply:

> Cursed be my tribe,
> If I forgive him!

The actors were all, in their partial interpretations, responding to the opportunities of the text: the Shylock who confronts Antonio has had opportunities for inviting an intense and precise scrutiny, for suggesting cunning, avarice, deliberation, power and control—and a hatred that is private and considered, and then irrational and uncontrolled. And in all this he towers — in force, intellectual finesse and quick sensation —

over Bassanio, the romantic hero.

With Antonio present Shylock still dominates the scene and calls the tune. As Bassanio recalls him from soliloquy he makes a sudden transition to blandly assumed simplicity and forgetfulness. He taunts Antonio by reminding him that he breaks his principles in asking for money on interest. He tests the importance of the loan by making Antonio listen to a detailed story of Laban and Jacob, his ancestors, and at the same time shows his isolation by being himself absorbed in it. When Antonio turns aside to talk to Bassanio, he can draw him back, simply by mentioning 'Three thousand ducats'. Moreover he shows that he has a keener awareness of the situation than Antonio: the Christian's assumed and brief courtesy —'shall we be beholding to you?' — is answered with sharp parody and a scornful reminder that he has been kicked and spat upon; he even imitates the fawning reply which Antonio seems, somewhat naively, to expect. The Christian deals shortly with Shylock to good purpose, because he hates his avarice and cruelty and because he is thinking of his friend, but little is said or done to draw the audience's attention to this; the handling of the scene makes the audience follow Shylock, for he most fully, consecutively and immediately responds to the situation.

Antonio now drops his pretence to Shylock and, dilating on truly generous friendship as his love for Bassanio allows him to do, asks for the loan 'as to thine enemy'. The two men are irreconcilable, but, whereas Antonio sounds annoyed, Shylock is self-possessed and knows that, in 'a merry sport', he can now propose his bond for the forfeit of a pound of flesh if the debt is not repaid in three months. He seems to have arranged the impasse purposely: the audience will have been reminded by his mockery that he seeks to catch Antonio 'on the hip' and will now intently watch his hypocritical finesse and relish:

Why, look you, how you storm!
I would be friends with you and have your love.

The ploy works and, after more mockery, he leaves the stage, ostentatiously busy with mundane considerations. He has given a new direction and uncertainty to the action, and the brief comments that follow his subtextually triumphant exit only accentuate the danger by suggesting that Antonio and Bassanio underestimate the inflexible hatred and the cunning management of this man.

Shylock is allowed to grow in the audience's knowledge independently of the other major characters, for while he is often spoken of during the next two Acts, he is seen only with minor characters until just before the trial. With Launcelot and Jessica he appears in a new setting, his own household. He easily dominates this scene (II.5), still isolated ('Who bids thee call?'), sarcastic at Antonio's expense (expecting his 'reproach'), concerned with his race ('By Jacob's staff, I swear'); and, in short time, much is added to his realization on the stage — chiefly his concern and affection for his daughter. Characteristically there are no long speeches of explicit feeling, but the lines require subtextual feeling to support them. Hatred of the Christian is expressed by his willingness to 'eat pork' to further it and by an allusion to fabulous tales of Jews eating Christian flesh:

> I am not bid for love; they flatter me:
> But yet I'll go in hate, to feed upon
> The prodigal Christian.

From this build-up of hatred there is a sudden transition:

> Jessica, my girl,
> Look to my house.

Its rapid contrast, the simplicity of 'my girl' at the line-ending, the suspicion implied in 'Look to my house', show Shylock exposed, touched, in need, for the first time. This must be the right reading, for now he can express fear:

> I am right loath to go:
> There is some ill a-brewing towards my rest,
> For I did dream of money-bags tonight.

The 'money-bags' turns the subject to one in which the audience may laugh at Shylock as a mere miser, but only after the sudden transition to tenderness and fear has brought them closer to him than before. Macklin's solemnity, the musical 'charm' of Kean's voice and Irving's dignity, all found scope here. The scene proceeds to show Shylock concerned that Jessica shall not hear the music of the masque nor 'gaze at Christian fools with varnish'd faces', and watchful for his 'sober house'. During this the audience is made aware at least twice that his daughter is about to rob him and escape from the home she calls a 'hell', and so discovers that Shylock is limited in knowledge, ignorant about the affection for which he has shown his need. After this disclosure, challenging and therefore reawaking earlier ones, the plot interest quickens and Shylock leaves intent on 'Fast bind, fast find'. No other character in the play holds comparable interest for the audience in his own development, as distinct from that of the action and interplay of characters; Shylock alone has such surprising and developing responses.

The opportunities for the actor in the scene (III.1) with Salerio and Solanio, and then Tubal, are well displayed in accounts of performances, but the points of emphasis need to be distinguished. Shylock's first entry, in grief and anger, is an overwhelming visual contrast to his early control. His immediate and direct reproach to the gossiping young men and their freedom to quip and jest at his expense represent loss of cunning and command. His outright self-exposure:

> My own flesh and blood to rebel!... I say my daughter is my flesh and my blood...

shows him impervious to mockery and shame. However much he later laments his loss of money and jewels, all these unguarded, unpremeditated moments show the center of his grief: his family, home, authority, race. And thus his heart is alarmingly exposed. The two young men turn the talk to Antonio and this provokes the first of the great 'transitions' of the scene, used to such powerful effect by Macklin and Kean; the change is to vivid and personal scorn of Antonio, but this develops to a hope of revenge, and his scorn then returns. Now he openly lists Antonio's deeds which he counts injuries, and this halts only for the second, and greater, transition:

> ... cooled my friends, heated mine enemies. And what's his reason? I am a Jew.

Then through the rest of the speech — remarkable for its range of sensation, from laughter to tears and thoughts of death, for its sarcasm and its pleas for acceptance as a human being (his reasoning in this respect is much like Henry V before Agincourt[30]) — he draws away from this fact to a still more sustained threat of villainy and revenge. The mere release of energy, of crowded and baffling impressions, makes this unanswerable; the young men go without replying, quickly responding to a message from Antonio. Shylock stands now silent, alone, unapproachable; the actor can, and must hold the whole theatre silent.

Tubal, a fellow Jew, enters and with him Shylock, still unexhausted, has a series of transitions between grief (for the loss of his daughter and his ducats) and pleasure (in the 'good news' of Antonio's losses). He concludes it after Tubal's account of Jessica's exchange of a ring for a monkey. This must be the climax of the scene, not only by its position but also because here alone Shylock remembers a freer past ('I had it of Leah when I was a bachelor') and sees the difference between himself and his daughter: 'I would not have given it for a wilderness of monkeys'. The last phrase may be a wry or helpless jest; certainly 'wilderness' seems to release from his unspoken thoughts a sense of desolation.[31] The overwhelming effect of these feelings upon him is shown in his reaction to Tubal's next piece of news about Antonio: this time, instead of exulting, he makes deliberate and practical plans to 'have the heart of him'. Shylock is now so alone, intemperate, inhuman and assured, that the scene, if acted slackly, would be ludicrous and muddled. With absurd, painful, powerful earnestness, he twice appoints Tubal to meet him 'at our synagogue'–again words which touch his deepest feelings — and he does not wait for an answer. For this central manifestation — a moment of clarity and powerful utterance, an opportunity for Irving's pathos and Kean's terror –Shakespeare has contrived the impression that Shylock is driven by feelings too deep to be resisted or fully uttered. The Jew at once dominates the play and makes it appear unable to contain him; the emotions which drive and threaten him cannot be made fully articulate in sustained speech.

Before the trial, a short scene (III.3) shows that the manacled Antonio confronting Shylock is resigned to death, if only Bassanio will return. However, this is already known from his letter, and a more important development is the return of Shylock's sardonic humour in this scene, and the emphasis it gives to his inflexible intention to 'have his bond'.

By this means, when Shylock enters the Trial Scene (IV.1), silent and alone, to listen to the Duke's last plea, and when he makes his politely and solemnly phrased reply, the audience can at once recognize the deadly inhumanity underneath his 'performance'. So his long taunting speeches and sharp rejoinders alike show confidence and composure without concealing his savage, fixed intent. Shylock's stature is maintained to the last possible moment (here Irving's dignity had strong effect) and, in contrast, Bassanio's most generous sentiment is lightly mocked by Portia and considered a trifle by Shylock. Antonio is not belittled, but this is through lofty resignation, the acceptance of himself as the 'tainted wether of the flock, Meetest for death'; he seems to live outside the issues of the court-room. In her disguise, of course,

Portia withstands Shylock, and her plea for mercy — more solemn and sustained than any of his speeches — brings before him the antithesis of his hatred: but he is unmoved and, once more, demands the forfeit. His defeat, therefore, comes very suddenly, by a verbal quibble, as he is about to kill the silent Antonio; the surprise is instantaneous and as thrillingly dramatic as Claudius' 'Give me some light', or Hal's 'I know thee not'. Portia and Shylock are opposed and, as it were, spot-lit.

It may at first seem strange that Shylock should be denied any words with which to express his immediate reaction to the reversal in full measure; yet this is the very means by which Shakespeare has, once more, drawn almost all of the audience's interest to him. He collapses physically as Portia elaborates the case against him and then, after Gratiano has had time to taunt him, there is probably a moment of total silence (the break of the verse-line suggests this) before he speaks, incredulously: 'Is that the law?' On the other side they now speak in turn, but he alone faces them and they must wait for his answers; there are more pauses, in some of which Gratiano mocks him or Portia questions. Except for the garrulous Gratiano, his opponents do not speak of their joy in victory, and so Shylock holds the dramatic focus until he leaves the stage. As the audience waits on his words to satisfy their interest, they will watch closely and see that he is struggling inwardly to understand and come to terms: rapidly he tries two bolt-holes and then a plea for death. But there is no escape and he must listen to his full sentence and the 'utmost' mercy of his enemies, which is a life of poverty and the outward acceptance of his daughter's husband and his enemies' religion. The verbal conclusion of his role is:

> I am content

and

> I pray you, give me leave to go from hence;
> I am not well; send the deed after me
> And I will sign it.

The speeches are brief and must be sustained by subtextual feelings; so they can express renewed control — a dignity (especially in the assurance of fulfilling his word), or a new, hidden purpose (as of suicide or revenge), or an accepted hopelessness. And there is yet the silence in which Shylock leaves, hearing the Duke's curt command and Gratiano's jibe: this cannot fail to impress the audience, at least with his physical weakness as he moves slowly and with difficulty, and probably with his restraint and isolation in saying nothing more; and if he turns towards

Gratiano for a moment only, there will be an impression of rekindled scorn for such Christians, or of now-impotent hatred. The slow, silent exit is an unmistakable invitation for the actor to reinforce at the conclusion the salient traits of his characterization; and it was surely meant to be powerfully affecting, for Shakespeare immediately changed the subject, providing a contrast in relieved inquiries about dinner-engagements.[32]

By many devices Shakespeare has ensured that in performance Shylock is the dominating character of the play; none other has such emotional range, such continual development, such stature, force, subtlety, vitality, variety; above all, none other has his intensity, isolation, and apparent depth of motivation. The various interpretations that have become famous are responses to an unmistakable (and unavoidable) invitation to make a strong, adventurous and individual impression in the role.

SEVEN

Playing for Laughs: the Last Plays

SHAKESPEARE'S company, in common with earlier Elizabethan acting groups, would have been quick to find how to get laughs from his plays. Each company had good comics — enough to play Malvolio, Sir Toby, and Sir Andrew as well as Feste, or to bring Jonson's *Bartholomew Fair* to its abundant life — and the chief clown[1] was often its most important member. Richard Tarlton of Queen Elizabeth's Men, who died in 1588, was the first of a line of comedians who could claim to be the funniest men in England. The succession passed to the Chamberlain's Men and then to the King's in the clowns William Kempe and Robert Armin. In notoriety these men surpassed the heroic and romantic actors like Alleyn, Burbage, and Perkins. Professor Nungezer, who has collected eye-witness accounts in his *Dictionary of Actors... in England before 1642*, found that:

> No other Elizabethan actor has been the object of so many notices in contemporary and later writing as Tarlton, or has been remembered with such various and practical tokens of esteem.
>
> p.355

His face was instantly recognizable and inns were named after him; as Joseph Hall satirically announced:

> O honour, far beyond a brazen shrine,
> To sit with Tarlton on an ale-post's sign!
>
> *Satires* (1599), vi; l.204

The great clowns were star actors, capable of thriving on their own verbal wit or their own projected personalities. Tarlton was famous for solo 'jigs' (or song-and-dance routines) and for extemporizing verses on themes proposed by members of his audience. Kempe left the Chamberlain's Men about 1599 to exploit his individual talents, as by dancing from London to Norwich and writing a book about it. Armin, who was known as a writer before succeeding Kempe, wrote a play, *The Two Maids of More-Clack* (1609), in which he could act himself — taking three distinct parts, not counting the occasion when in his second role he pretended to be in his first. These clowns were prepared to succeed without much help from the literary art of others. If we merely read the roles they accepted we shall get a dull and unvaried impression: as in low comedy at all times, falls, blows, knavery, mimicry, stupidity, and surprise provided constantly recurring jokes. There was, indeed, good reason for clowns to say and do more than was set down for them; they needed new ways of sustaining old routines; they had to be individual and original to succeed. In a crazy, exaggerated, and energetic art, Tarlton, Kempe, and Armin established themselves — themselves rather than their authors or their roles.

Certainly the individual art of the chief clowns helped to sustain the ubiquitous comedy in the plays of the time; and Shakespeare was well aware of the talents of his company's clowns. In four of the plays originally printed from his autograph manuscript, or a good copy of it, the names of actors found their way into the speech-prefixes or stage-directions, usurping the characters they were meant to sustain. Twice it was the thin man of the company, John Sincklo, who in *II Henry IV* played the Beadle described as an 'anatomy' or skeleton, and could not have been replaced easily; but twice the actors named were clowns. In *Much Ado About Nothing*, Kempe appears in IV.2, instead of '*Dogberry*' or '*Constable*', and Cowley for '*Verges*', '*Headborough*' or '*Con. 2*'. In *Romeo and Juliet*, IV.5, the direction '*Enter Will Kemp*' appears instead of '*Enter Peter*'. In each case the actor seems to have been more formative in Shakespeare's creating mind than the character he had invented; none of the names of the straight actors of the company ever crept into stage directions in the same way.

Shakespeare, whose Hamlet could reprove clowns for speaking more than was set down for them, used clowns for important roles in almost all his plays; his respect for the single judicious auditor did not banish fools, fights, and merry bawdy incidents from his plays. Between the slapstick incidents of *The Comedy of Errors* and *The Taming of the Shrew* and the subtle and elaborate foolery in *Twelfth Night*, or between the crazed and cruel humour of *Titus Andronicus* and *Henry VI* and the intensities of the crazed Lear and his Fool, there is an obvious refinement and deepening of comedy; but this should not be allowed to obscure the prat-falls and absurdities of his neatest comedies — Maria promises that Sir Toby shall 'laugh himself into stitches' — or the tripping-up and abuse of Oswald by Kent in *King Lear*. If *Henry VIII* is wholly by Shakespeare he there introduced two comic porters with a pushing crowd in despite of the play's prologue that scorned both 'fool and fight': here are blows enough, and the usual bawdy jokes about 'the Indian with the great tool', about women, honor, and cuckoldom — and all this by way of preparation for a great prophetic concluding scene.

If we wish to understand Shakespeare's plays in performance, we must learn to notice the cues he has provided for these clowns to get their laughs. First there are opportunities for impressing a dominant personality. Often a role will begin with a solo entry, without much reference to the existing dramatic situation and often without reference to any other character. This is varied by immediately providing the chief comedian with an obvious foil or 'feed'. Often the textual provision is most detailed at this point, as if Shakespeare felt the need to insist on the clown taking some color from his author's conception on the all-important first impression. Verbally the comic parts tend to peter out when a sufficient head of dramatic energy has been established; at the end of a successful low comedy performance the actor's hold over an audience ensures that a very little material will go a sufficiently long way.

Whatever the demands of plot or theme the clown had to be able to use his traditional business, and Shakespeare must have known that his words would stand more chance of being respected if they invited this usual cooperation. Any reference to an ugly face, for example (or, ironically, its opposite good looks) would be taken up at once, for clowns, then as now, exploited out-of-the-ordinary features. Henry Peacham used the effect of this as an almost mythological simile:

> As Tarlton when his head was only seen,
> The tirehouse door and tapestry between,
> Set all the multitude in such a laughter
> They could not hold for scarce an hour after...
>
> *Thalia's Banquet* (1620)

Other clowns used a 'scurvy face' as a circus clown uses exaggerated make-up. Grimaces were invented and grotesque gestures. Thomas Gaffe wrote in the Praeludium to his *Careless Shepherdess* (1618-29):

> I've laughed
> Until I cried again to see what faces
> The rogue will make. O it does me good
> To see him hold out's chin, hang down his hands,
> And twirl his bauble. There is ne'er a part
> About him but breaks jest...

Silent by-play was often accompanied by trite words. In the 'bad'

Quarto of *Hamlet*, the prince takes his complaint of clowns a step further than in the authoritative text:

> And then you have some again, that keep one suit
> Of jests, as a man is known by one suit of
> Apparel, and gentlemen quote his jests down
> In their tables before they come to the play, as thus:
> 'Cannot you stay till I eat my porridge?' and 'You owe me
> A quarter's wages', and 'My coat wants a cullison',
> And 'Your beer is sour'; and blabbering with his lips
> And thus keeping in the cinquepace of jests,
> When, God knows, the warm clown cannot make a jest
> Unless by chance, as the blind man catcheth a hare.
>
> Sig. F2f.

Many authors, including Shakespeare, provided running gags of this sort for their clowns, as popular television programs today have their "trade marks" in a presenter's words of greeting or farewell, or in odd clothes, or constantly repeated gestures or grimaces.

The clowns also had more normal skills and these had to be provided for. They could play on tabor and pipe. They were active and nimble, Tarlton being a fencing master and Kempe a notorious dancer. They were skilled, too, in mimicry, becoming sad or gay on demand, and were often given speeches which allowed them to imitate different kinds of behavior within a short compass, as in Touchstone's party-piece on the various degrees of quarreling. In this way they could show their imitative skill and project shrewd and compendious social comment. When the Clown enters in Thomas Heywood's *Rape of Lucrece* (1609) and is asked for news, he offers court-news, camp-news, city-news, country-news, and news-at-home, and is asked for them all (C2v-3). The Porter in *Macbeth* was probably meant to mimic the walk and talk of the farmer, equivocator, and tailor whom he imagined at the castle gate; so played the scene is still continuously funny today.

One of the greatest strengths of the clowns was their ability to call forth abnormal responses, to make pathos, villainy, wisdom, or cowardice both funny and acceptable. As Launcelot Gobbo is given opportunity to mock his blind and mistaken father in *The Merchant of Venice*, so the servant-clown in *The Miseries of Enforced Marriage* (1607) mocks his mistress's misery:

> From London am I come, though not with pipe and drum,

> Yet I bring matter, in this poor paper,
> Will make my young mistress, delighting in kisses,
> Do as all maidens will hearing of such an ill,
> As to have lost the thing they wish'd most —
> A husband, a husband, a pretty sweet husband —
> Cry: 'Oh, oh, oh,' and 'Alas!' and at last 'Ho, ho, ho!'
> as I do. Sig.C3

Thieving is a common occasion for enjoying the clown's skill: Mouse, the clown in the long-popular romance *Mucedorus*, steals a pot of ale and a stage-direction follows to describe his subsequent engagement with the ale-wife:

She searcheth him, and he drinketh over her head, and casts down the pot. She stumbleth at it, then they fall together by the ears; she takes her pot and goes out.

Often these escapades were mixed with an element of cowardice, as when Cuckedemoy in Marston's *Dutch Courtezan* (1603-4) picks the pocket of Malheureux as he is going to execution. Sometimes two divergent responses were called forth together, notably bawdy enjoyment with some piece of social criticism or a mocking imitation of some unamorous activity; the school lessons in *The Taming of the Shrew*, are opportunities for this, and the clown's tilt at pedantry in his disavowal of any intention to flirt with Lucrece's maid in Heywood's play:

> If ever I knew what belongs to these cases, or yet know what they mean; if ever I used any plain dealing or were ever worth such a jewel, would I might die like a beggar; if ever I were so far read in my grammar as to know what an interjection is, or a conjunction copulative... why do you think, madam, I have no more care of myself, being but a stripling, than to go to it at these years; flesh and blood cannot endure it. I shall even spoil one of the best faces in Rome with crying at your unkindness
> D4f.

Here too is the obvious lie, superlative overstatement, mock weeping, and ugly face. And here is the clown's deliberate and two-faced concern with sexual virility: so, in *As You Like It*, Touchstone complains that Corin brought the 'ewes and rams together' and betrayed a 'she-lamb of a twelve-month to a crooked-pated, old, cuckoldly ram', and then justifies his attachment to Audrey in that as 'horns are odious, they are necessary'. Launcelot Gobbo is allowed to complain that Lorenzo 'raised the price of hogs' by making more Christians and then boast of the dishonesty of the Moor whom he, himself, has got 'with child' (III.4.16-37).

The strangeness and license that the clowns' humour sometimes required is well illustrated by their animal disguises. *Ram Alley* (1607-8) by Lording Barry has a clown who dresses as an ape to do lewd dances; Fletcher's *Mad Lover* has a dog-barking episode by a clown who had been in a masque of beasts. A tract called *This World's Folly: or a Warning-Piece discharged upon the Wickedness thereof* written by I. H. and published in 1615 has much to say about 'obscene and light jigs, stuff'd with loathsome and unheard-of ribaldry, suckt from the poisonous dugs of sin-swell'd theatres'. This critic singled out Greene of the Queen's Men for his 'stentor-throated bellowings, flash-choaking squibbles of absurd vanities' and his speciality of dancing as a baboon, 'metamorphosing human shape into bestial form'.

*

Performances of the clowns and fools of Elizabethan theatres are well documented compared with those of their fellow actors, but even so our knowledge is fragmentary. But, as fooling is timeless, we can learn more from later-day comics who have left detailed memoirs. Three extracts, in place of many, can show the unchanging form of clowning and suggest something of the actors' art behind the brief facts that have survived from Shakespeare's time.

The clown's 'scurvy' face and comic dress has always been sufficient cause of laughter. *The Life of the Late Famous Comedian, Jo Haynes* (1701) tells how:

> There happen'd to be one night a play acted call'd *Catiline's Conspiracy*, wherein there was wanting a great number of senators. Now Mr Hart, being chief of the House, wou'd oblige Jo to dress for one of these senators, altho' Jo's salary, being then 50s. per week, freed him from any such obligation. But Mr Hart, as I said before, being sole Governor of the Playhouse and at a small variance with Jo, commands it and the other must obey. Jo, being vex'd at the slight Mr Hart had put on him, found out this method of being reveng'd on him: he gets a Scaramouch dress, a large full ruff, makes himself whiskers, from ear to ear, puts on his head a long Merry Andrew's cap, a short pipe in his mouth, a little three legg'd stool in his hand, and in this manner follows Mr Hart on the stage, sits himself down

> behind him, and begins to smoke his pipe, to laugh and point at him.
>
> p. 23

A century later *Oxberry's Dramatic Biography* (new series, i; 14 April 1827) gave a compendious picture of Grimaldi that illustrates how a clown can center attention on his assumed character no matter what is happening elsewhere on the stage and can make the audience laugh at actions that would usually evoke an anxious concern:

> The hopelessness of one who knows not what to do next, he hits to a nicety — he always appeared to us to represent a grown child waking to perception but wondering at every object he beholds. Then, his exuberance of animal spirits was really miraculous; what a rich ringing laugh! — the very voice of merriment! Then, the self-approving chuckle, and the contemptuous look, half pity, half derision, that he gave to the dupe of his artifice; his incessant annoyance to *Pantaloon* and his feigned condolence for the very misfortunes of which he was the author; his amazement and awe of *Harlequin*, his amorous glances at *Columbine*, and his winks at the imbecility of the doting and the dandyism of the young lover; his braggadocia blustering, his cautious escapes from detection and his ludicrous agony during fustigation, an operation duly performed on *Clown* by all the personages of the motley drama — were all his, and HIS ALONE. He was the very *beau ideal* of thieves: robbery became a science in his hands; you forgave the larceny, for the humour with which it was perpetrated. He abstracted a leg of mutton from a butcher's tray, with such a delightful assumption of *nonchalance* (he threw such plump stupidity into his countenance, whilst the slyness of observation lurked in his half-closed eyes). He extracted a watch, or a handkerchief, with such a bewitching eagerness — with such a devotion to the task — and yet kept his wary eye upon the victim of his trickery. He seemed so imbued with the spirit of peculation, that you saw it in him, merely as a portion of his nature, and for the which he was neither blamable or accountable. His pantomimic colloquies with the other sex, too, were inimitable — his mincing affectation, when addressing a dandizette; his broad bold style, when making love to a fisherwoman — were all true to Nature.

A clown's struggles to be funny have been disclosed in some memoirs. In *Grock, King of Clowns* (tr. 1957) the great twentieth-century circus artist has contrasted himself with a straight actor:

> Unlike an actor who has his set part to play, a clown can vary and embroider his part every night if he chooses. The chief thing is that what he does makes a hit.
>
> p.83

He is free to improvise for each new audience but he is also imprisoned by the absolute need to raise a laugh. Grock tells the story of how he invented his 'piano-lid trick'. At each routine joke with the piano, his feed, Antonet, had been saying 'Do you think that was funny?... Do you really think that was funny?' and so had killed his effects. Grock became truly enraged and took off the piano lid to strike Antonet:

> My costume and make-up must have made my genuine rage incredibly funny. The public shrieked with laughter. I came to my senses and pursued Antonet no further.

Grock returned to the piano to put the lid on, but failed to do so:

> Something had to be done to amuse them now that I was alone in the ring. But what on earth was I to do? I rested the lid against the lefthand side of the piano, sloping to the ground from the end of the keyboard. At the sight of it, the idea came to me to let my hat slide down it. No sooner thought than done. My hat tobogganed merrily to the ground. I was just going to pick it up and put it on when the great inspiration came! Why not toboggan down after my hat? I climbed up on to the piano, slid down the slope straight to my hat, which I put on and then walked proudly off. The effect was stupendous!
>
> pp. 85-6

Anger and a ludicrous face; obvious child-like pleasure; unexpected and disproportionate behavior; the simple action of putting on a hat; these can raise stupendous laughter and applause, given a clown's agility, resilience, and sense of scale and timing.

*

Read with the eyes of a clown Shakespeare's plays offer abundant cues for business and improvisation. *The Winter's Tale*, which E. M. W. Tillyard has called a presentation of 'the whole tragic pattern from prosperity to destruction, regeneration, and still fairer prosperity',[2] can be taken as an example.

For clowns Autolycus is the star part. He enters with a solo song, with no immediate dramatic task beyond the establishment of his assumed *persona*. The words Shakespeare has given him invite mimicry and business on the four times repeated 'With heigh', and on the 'tirra-lirra' for lark-song and the contrasting references to thrush and jay. A brief, prose speech serves to connect the character with 'Prince Florizel' and so, vaguely, to the plot, but at the same time, makes pointed reference to his comical rags, being 'out of service' like himself, and also provides an excuse for imitating a superior person dressed in 'three-pile' velvet. At once he has another song, contrasting in mood with the first:

> But shall I go mourn for that, my dear?
> The pale moon shines by night;...

The imitation of the forlorn lover is quickly revalued as a prelude to mischief when a second stanza presents Autolycus again as an adventurer, this time with a reference to punishment in the 'stocks'. Even here there is an inversion of ordinary moral judgement of a kind customary in clowns' dialogue, for he will 'avouch' his account in the stocks as if formally claiming right while being punished for wrong. With his prose speech that immediately follows Autolycus is established by name and by his thieving; and as something of a coward and an indolent innocent:

> beating and hanging are terrors to me; for the life to come, I sleep out the thought of it.
>
> ll.29-30

With the entry of the shepherd's son, he lets the audience share his hope of successful trickery and at once goes into a new imitative routine: this time he is a poor robbed and beaten man crying out for death. Tears will bring laughter here; and so will his dexterity in picking the young shepherd's pocket while talking of a 'charitable office'. The comic business has its surprises, for his victim offers to give him money and so threatens to discover the robbery, and Autolycus himself nearly spoils everything by talking in his assumed role about his real one and so nearly giving himself away by calling his vices virtues. Before he successfully shakes off the shepherd's son, the joke of imitation is taken a step further as he has to pretend to be a bigger coward than the coward he really is. Alone again, he raises expectation for his next appearance at the sheep-shearing — and makes the obvious word-play in hoping that the 'shearers prove sheep'. With a further glance at 'virtue' he leaves the stage with a third song —which again invites imitative gestures and picks up the pace of the performance:

> Jog on, jog on, the footpath way,
> And merrily hent [jump] the stile-a...

It also justifies his villainy by the merriment it brings, and gives a further opportunity for mimed action:

> A merry heart goes all the day,
> Your sad tires in a mile-a.

A master-clown would use this introductory scene to show off many of his tricks and gain the connivance of the audience.

His next entry is a further transformation. Now a pedlar he enters with yet another song, this time giving opportunity for by-play with his audience on the stage and a run of sexual innuendoes. After telling tall stories to the credulous rustics he 'bears' his part in a song for three voices: — 'you must know 'tis my occupation' he says, with a clown's extra-dramatic statement about his own interests and a glancing jest at the expense of puritans whose accustomed phrase this was. He leaves the stage to follow his dupes with a brief aside to keep the audience aware of his intentions ('And you shall pay well for 'em') and with another song asking questions of 'My dainty duck, my dear-a' and, finally, telling even his victims that 'Money's a meddler'.

His second appearance in IV.4 begins with another soliloquy, as Camillo, Perdita, and Florizel talk aside. Autolycus is in full triumph after his 'sheep-shearing', but when he thinks he is overheard he has only one thought: 'hanging'. Camillo supplies a spoken stage-direction in case the actor does not see the cue for yet another transformation:

> How, now, good fellow! Why shak'st thou so? Fear not, man; here's no harm intended to thee.

He is asked to exchange his poor clothes for Florizel's and when his benefactors leave him outwardly transformed to a gentleman with a 'Farewell, my friend', he is ready for his new role in 'Adieu, sir:' comically he is only *just* ready, for he is still wearing his pedlar's false beard (cf. l. 702)

In soliloquy he congratulates himself on coping with business somewhat out of his usual line of pickpocketing. He is allowed a glance, too, at the traditional art of the clown: 'Sure, the gods do this year connive at us, and we *may do anything extempore*'; he, the clown as well as Autolycus, proclaims himself 'constant to my profession'. Then more 'matter for a hot brain' enters with the shepherd and his son; more 'work' for a 'careful man' he claims, indulging a clown's customary transference of values.

A few preparatory asides and the business of taking off a false beard and he is then ready to encounter the rustics as a full-fledged courtier. Here the clown can satirize the familiar distinctions between town and country, and would give himself away to anybody but fellow clowns by picking his teeth and wearing his clothes 'not handsomely' (ll.738 and 742). The necessary plot-development being complete, the episode ends with Autolycus terrifying the shepherd's son with a description of tortures and at the same time assuming the role of outraged and self-secure morality. The others leave Autolycus behind for a soliloquy in which he expostulates about his embarrassment of riches:

> If I had a mind to be honest, I see Fortune would not suffer me; she drops booties in my mouth.

The last scene in which Autolycus appears (V.2) would seem an anti-climax to any actor but a clown. He is now in Sicilia and at first he is but one of an audience for the news of Perdita's reunion with her father. But his presence from the start of the scene ensures that he can react to the new situation and allows him a soliloquy immediately before the shepherd and his son enter dressed in new finery. He is dejected:

> Now, had I not the dash of my former life in me, would preferment drop on my head...

His 'merry' philosophy has let him down and he is even envious:

> Here come those I have done good to against my will, and already appearing in the blossoms of their fortune.

But dejection for a clown is a new ploy, even if it appears unassumed. The actor will take advantage of the silence with which he answers the first overtures of the now irrepressible shepherds, and will give a dawning irony to his belated response: 'I know you are now, sir, a gentleman born' (l.130). After hearing further chat he is ready to make a cumbersomely humble approach. His last words promising to 'prove' a tall fellow, is no large conclusion for Autolycus, but that is provided by the last words of the shepherd's son: 'Come, follow us; we'll be thy good masters.' The crucial point is that Autolycus makes his exit after them: for a clown, this is an invitation to provide his own idiosyncratic business. He can take his choice: simple mimicry, or a renewed picking of pockets (this became a stage tradition, with words added from David Garrick's version of the play) or, more comprehensively using grimace and gesture, a rehabilitation of the clown's hopefulness, his nose catching the smell of new trickery, a dawning satisfaction at the prospect of his old comfortable discomfort, his old virtuous vices. With a good clown as Autolycus — and the part calls for one — the mere call to *follow* the others off-stage ensures that he has the last laugh. As Grock would say: 'The chief thing is that what he does makes a hit'.

Autolycus does not attract much attention from readers of *The Winter's Tale* and most literary critics pay only passing recognition. Even in performance he can fall flat. *Punch* of 1 February 1933 said of an Old Vic production:

> There was little in this dark gymnastic gipsy of Mr Geoffrey Wincott to suggest that here was one of the great Shakespearean characters. It is not a part which plays itself....

Comment in other papers agreed with this, and with the *Manchester Guardian*'s judgement of 7 July 1948, that a Stratford-upon-Avon production had a 'rather too zealously grotesque Autolycus'. The part comes to life only when a clown contributes his own art and personality, and takes up most of the cues that Shakespeare has given him.

In the great age of English pantomime, Garrick's *Florizel and Perdita* held the stage instead of Shakespeare's play. Besides curtailing the action of the play this version gave considerable prominence to Autolycus and the shepherds. But a prompt-book for Kean's revival of Shakespeare's play at the Princess's Theatre in 1856 (now in the Folger Library) shows another way with Autolycus — to cut him down in the interest of stage spectacle and narrative clarity: here, for example, he makes no appearance in Act V. In the theatre Autolycus must be a clown's star performance, or nothing.

A very well-documented production is one sponsored by a famous clown at his own theatre and for his own Autolycus. A published Collection of the *Critical Opinions... of 'The Winter's Tale' at Burton's Theatre, New York* gives some idea how Simon Forman, a Jacobean playgoer, came to note in his diary after seeing a performance: 'Beware of trusting feigned beggars or fawning fellows'. The New York *Sunday Times* said of William Burton:

> He seems to have entered completely into the spirit of the thing; he is so jovial a vagabond, so amusing a specimen of rascality, and commits petit larcenies and small swindling transactions in such a funny, jolly sort of way, that one cannot help enjoying the entertainment he creates as a set off against his natural and unconquerable depravity. The rags are worn with such a jaunty swaggering air, and he is altogether a most magnificent specimen of the 'bummer' of antiquity. One can hardly help admiring the lazy nonchalance and consistent independence of the honest labor with which he gains a questionable livelihood.... In an age of large financial speculation, he would have been a great capitalist, and we admire and respect him accordingly.

The *Albion* also saw contemporary point in Burton's Autolycus — successful clowning is timeless and therefore free to mirror the concerns of any particular age:

> He is the embodiment of the vulgar idea of success and the sharpest satire on the worship of the almighty dollar. His 'revenue is the silly cheat'. O, Wall Street, behold thy King! 'Hanging and beating are terrors to him; for the life to come, he sleeps out the thought of it!' Comfortable nodder, in the deep wall pew, behold thy ancestor!

The *Sunday Dispatch* described the effect of this Autolycus on the play as a whole:

> Our only regret is that Master William Shakespeare does not send that rogue Autolycus upon the stage before the fourth act, when, in reality, that life which alone can give general popularity to the play only begins. Burton is grand, rich, unctuous, racy, roguish, and funny all at one and the same time in the part....

Burton had much the same creative qualifications for the role as an Elizabethan clown. Like Tarlton and Armin, he had published his *Waggeries and Vagaries*; and he wrote several farces. 'Mirth', it was said, 'came from him in exhalations', and 'the resources of by-play, grimace, and mimetic effect, were his at command' (W. Keese, *Actors and Actresses*, iii (1886), p. 224).

> The secret of Burton's power did not lie in any single gift; it was not only his mirth-provoking face, his ability to infuse character and comicality together into his countenance, though doubtless this was the most peculiar of his talents; he had others.... Burton had a creative faculty. He did more for many of the characters he played than the author of the piece. His *Toodle* and *Sleek* were absolute creations, and indicated an ability quite akin to that

> of a great dramatist.... He could play with success scenes of great pathos, and would often have brought tears to the eyes of his auditors were it not for their recollections of his more familiar comic scenes.
>
> *Sunday Times*, New York, 12 Feb. 1860

A full clown's performance in *The Winter's Tale* importantly affects the theatrical life of the play. In a story that moves from prosperity through destruction to regeneration, from separation to reconciliation, the clown presents a character who is both a failure and a success. In an intensely felt narrative he evokes from the audience laughter, connivance and appreciation, relaxation and admiration. In a drama about the influences of time, he provides a timeless artistry, and remains unchanged at the conclusion. He brings topicality to a fantastic tale, an escape from the consequences of knavery to a moral confrontation, and a grotesque embodiment of irresponsible fears and aggressions, of vigorous and sexual activity, to a shapely and often refined romance.

The relevance of his role can be gauged partly through particular verbal contact with the rest of the play: Florizel calls Perdita a goddess, as Autolycus sings his wares 'as they were gods and goddesses'; Polixenes calls her a 'knack', the word he used for Autolycus' pedlar's wares; Perdita's 'blood looks out' at Florizel's whisperings, after Autolycus had hailed 'red blood' that reigns in 'winter's pale'; and Florizel had disappeared from court, as Autolycus' ballad promises:

> Get you hence, for I must go
> Where it fits not you to know.

So the clown's disguise, trickery, thieving and easy excitement of 'summer songs.... While we lie tumbling in the hay' are shown to be relevant to the affairs of the main plot. Later the very clothes for disguising Florizel are taken from Autolycus' disguise, and the fearful trembling of this clown is a reminder of the dangers the King's son is risking.

But Autolycus' contribution to the play is greatest at its most general. His heightening of the 'mirth of the feast' — the license of instinctive and irresponsible enjoyment — enables Shakespeare to present Florizel and Perdita without stiffness and yet with contrasting carefulness; it also enables the dance of the wild 'men of hair' to make its contrast with the earlier decorous dance with immediate acceptance as another divertissement. The last exit for Autolycus in Act V, with its climactic and possibly silent humour, is an important device to relax the critical attention of the audience immediately before Hermione is revealed as a painted statue. Grock used to play Verdi on a diminutive concertina at the end of his act, and it always seemed powerfully seductive to the audience; and so here, the audience's contentment at the invincible humour and roguery of Autolycus disposes it to accept the strange, severe and sweetened (cf.l.76) theatricality of the concluding scene. Laughter and dreams alike release our fantasies from the restrictive control of our censoring minds; so, having joined everyman's laughter at the undeserved and unfounded resilience of Autolycus, the audience will more readily accept the dreamlike conditions of the final scene, the living statue that

> Excels whatever yet you look'd upon
> Or hand of man hath done.
>
> ll.16-17

Laughter has contrived the relaxed and uncritical condition suitable for the acceptance of a further and solemn fantasy.

'Dreams are toys' argues Antigonus in III.3, and at the end of *A Midsummer Night's Dream* Puck asks that the whole comedy should be accepted as an idle dream. So much Shakespeare certainly knew about the connections between fantasy and humour, and his contemporaries accepted it too. The total solemnity of much criticism of the last plays that is current today would strike Elizabethans and Jacobeans as pompous and restrictive. Romance, for them, spelt wonder, delight, *and* mirth. The prologue to the romantic comedy *Mucedorus* expresses this directly:

> Mirth drown your bosom, fair Delight your mind,
> And may our pastime your contentment find.

And *The Winter's Tale* has more 'pastime' than Autolycus. The two shepherds are traditional rustic comics, with muddled meetings and muddled speeches; they mix comedy and pathos in discovering the disastrous end of Antigonus; they mistake meanings, labor slowly in witticisms, attempt mimicry, and, like Autolycus, leave the play with more troubles obviously to come. There is comedy, too, in the earlier scenes of the main plot, especially in the contrasts between the forthright Paulina and the timid jailer and courtiers, and the two husbands, Antigonus and Leontes. All the comedy contributes to the final effect of the play, by its fantasy and freedom, obviously; but also by the individuality, topicality and robust vitality that are required to perform the more comic roles.

*

Shakespeare understood the acting talents of clowns and gave them scope — but always appropriately to his main design. The other romances use clowns' performances in various ways, according to their narratives and themes. *Pericles*, which is probably not wholly by Shakespeare, has least comedy. In the last three Acts, where the authorship is less disputed, humour is concentrated in the brothel scenes, allowing a kind of ease or 'delight' to incidents out of tone with the thrusting and evocative narrative of the rest of those Acts. The whole incident takes some color from Boult, notably in a short scene (IV.5) with the memorably exaggerated line, 'Come, I am for no more bawdy-houses. Shall's go hear the vestals sing?', with which an anonymous gentleman suggests a zany impracticability in sudden conversion. Boult remains unchanged when he leaves the play, but subdued to Marina's purposes and having voiced, in unusually solemn tones, the clown's usual defense of his misdeeds — that is, that the fault lies in the world, or with 'others':

> What would you have me do? Go to the wars, would you, where a man may serve seven years for the loss of a leg, and have not money enough in the end to buy him a wooden one?
>
> IV.6.168-70

In *Cymbeline*, Shakespeare uses a tighter rein. The jailer is the only outright clown's part, but his clown's defense, 'I would we were all of one mind, and one mind good' (V.4.200), is an important verbal preparation for the Soothsayer's final:

> The fingers of the pow'rs above do tune
> The harmony of this peace.
>
> V.5.464-5

Cloten looks at first to be a loutish clown, amusingly and coarsely interrupting the courtly scenes and then becoming the foolish wild man of the woods who ineffectually tries to ravish Imogen and kill Posthumus. But in his two soliloquies, 'I love and hate her' and 'Meet thee at Milford Haven!' (III.5.70-81 and 131-46), he is presented with too strong an impression of pent-up and self conflicting feelings to remain either a clown or a comic villain. His end is funny, like a typical braggart's combat, but Belarius reminds the audience of the risks he has so far taken:

> not frenzy, not
> Absolute madness could so far have rav'd
> To bring him here alone.
>
> IV.2.135-7

and he differs from other braggarts in actually taking the initiative in the last engagement — 'Yield, rustic mountaineer' — and actually, though off-stage, dying.

In *Cymbeline* humour is dispersed throughout the action; but the relaxed enjoyment of comedy is seldom unalloyed: the Queen, Posthumus, Iachimo, Pisanio, Belarius, Guiderius, Arviragus, Cymbeline himself perhaps, and certainly Imogen, all raise laughter at times, as does the contrivance of the plot, and yet all these characters, at times, command the audience's closest and directest sympathy. When Imogen mistakes Cloten's headless body as Posthumus', laughter and tears are brought together most sharply. For Imogen the experience is specifically like a 'dream'. The apparent reality as expressed here—

> Pisanio might have kill'd thee at the heart,
> And left his head on.

—is so absurd that very few actresses have dared to use all the words provided. Bernard Shaw recognized that Shakespeare had successfully created the 'dim, half-asleep funny state of consciousness' but he nevertheless advised Ellen Terry to cut 'A headless man' from her performance:

> This is what I cannot understand; and I believe it is an overlooked relic of some earlier arrangement of the business.[3]

The whole soliloquy so mixes abrupt comedy with deepest feeling that, temporarily, the comedy is entirely subdued, becoming part of the terror of Imogen's nightmare-dream. Only out of dramatic context, without the passion and uncertainty of the 'felt' situation, are the lines at all funny; trust the mixture of absurdity and fantasy, and the scene becomes wholly affecting.

In the last scene the persistent mingling of comedy and affecting dramatic narrative is smoothly resolved. The characters file off-stage together, no one drawing all sentiment to himself but all moving at the bidding and with the reassurance of the Soothsayer, Philarmonus. All are 'o'erjoy'd' (l.401): 'joy'd' that others are what they are, and prepared to 'laud... the gods' and wonder at the new 'peace' (ll. 424 and 474-83). It would be wrong to cut from this last scene its hints of comedy, the laughter that can so readily be raised by Posthumus' 'Shall's have a play of this?', Cymbeline's 'Does the world go round?', the Doctor's 'I left out one thing, Belarius' 'My boys, There was our error' and 'Not too hot ...I am too blunt and saucy', and the sudden reappearance of the Doctor for the ludicrously neat 'By the Queen's dram she swallow'd'. At these and other points the contrivance of the play's conclusion can appear hilariously complicated; and the laughter that will undoubtedly come during rehearsals must be prized and its occasions carefully retained and possibly augmented in order to help present the delight and fantasy of the happy ending. This romantic play uses clowns and comic dialogue as an entry and support for fantasy, and so gains moments of feeling that are all the sharper for contrast; and it arrives at a conclusion that in performance can seem sublime because it is not always perfectly serious and so not always obviously impossible.

The conclusion of *The Tempest* is the most grave and considered of all. But in this play, too, the importance of the clowns' roles can be under-estimated. The last arrivals when Prospero stands revealed as the rightful Duke of Milan are a drunken jester and butler, and a 'thing of darkness': such emphatic placing alone requires respect. Obviously Trinculo and Stephano seeking shelter or profit from Caliban is a normal clown's trick, like the disguises and trickery of Autolycus. The songs 'Freedom' and 'Scout 'em and flout 'em', and the falling-out about the finery Prospero sets as a trap, invite comic team-work, and embellishment. Caliban himself as a strange 'monster' is partly a clown's role; even his attempted rape of Miranda and attack on Prospero, together with his care for the island's beauties, are in the comic tradition. Bremo, the wild man in *Mucedorus*, tries to woo Amadine by offering, like Caliban to Stephano:

> If thou wilt love me thou shalt be my queen;
> I'll crown thee with a chaplet made of ivory,
> And make the rose and lily wait on thee.
> I'll rend the burly branches from the oak,

> To shadow thee from burning sun,
> The trees shall spread themselves where thou dost go,
> And as they spread, I'll trace along with thee...
>
> IV.3

and much more. The clown, William Burton, played Caliban in his own theatre, along with Autolycus, Bottom, Belch, Falstaff, and a host of his farcical creations:

> The most superb performance of Burton's which I remember was his *Caliban.* A wild creature on all fours sprang upon the stage, with claws on his hands, and some weird animal arrangement about the head partly like a snail. It was an immense conception. Not the great God Pan himself was more the link between the man and beast than this thing. It was a creature of the woods, one of nature's spawns; it breathed of nuts and herbs, and rubbed itself against the back of trees.
>
> *New York Times*, 20 June 1875

To give Caliban to a clown does not mean underplaying the obvious pathos and power of feeling in the role:

> His Caliban we have tried to forget rather than remember; [wrote W. L. Keese in his memoir of Burton] it terrified us and made us dream bad dreams; but for all that, we know that it was a surprising impersonation.
>
> p. 175

There are, in fact, changes in Shakespeare's use of his comics: from the beginning of this play their characters carry a more than usual burden of immediate and inescapable feeling. They are closer to Cloten than to Autolycus or the shepherds. Trinculo and Stephano are afraid of the storm, the monster, the island and strange noises, but are denied the compensating resilience of other clowns; they are saved by mutual recognition (II.2.92-3) and later by Caliban's 'Be not afeard. The isle is full of noises...' (III.2.130-8). The coward revealed under Trinculo's jesting and the bully under Stephano's good cheer are displayed at last without the usual chance of laughing away the consequences. The last appearance of the trio raises an obvious laugh from the callow Sebastian, but their ludicrous débâcle produces a muddled exhortation that is more surprising than the jailer's or Boult's last resort, less obviously hypocritical than that of Autolycus:

> Every man shift for all the rest, and let no man take care for

himself; for all is but fortune.

V.1.256-7

In the confrontation that follows, the severe moral tone of Prospero's judgement quenches the irresponsibility of fooling:

> TRINCULO: I have been in such a pickle since I saw you last that, I fear me, will never out of my bones. I shall not fear fly-blowing.
> SEBASTIAN: Why, how now, Stephano!
> STEPHANO: 0 touch me not; I am not Stephano, but a cramp.
> PROSPERO: You'd be king o' the isle, sirrah ?
> STEPHANO: I should have been a sore one, then.
> ALONSO [pointing to Caliban]: This is as strange a thing as e'er I look'd on.
> PROSPERO: He is as disproportioned in his manners
> As in his shape. Go, sirrah, to my cell;
> Take with you your companions; as you look
> To have my pardon, trim it handsomely.
> CALIBAN: Ay, that I will; and I'll be wise hereafter,
> And seek for grace. What a thrice-double ass
> Was I to take this drunkard for a god,
> And worship this dull fool!

Each of the trio makes a forced jest at his own expense; but not as a comic escape route. The despatching words do not suggest a funny *exeunt*:

> PROSPERO: Go to; away!
> ALONSO: Hence, and bestow your luggage where you found it.
> SEBASTIAN: Or stole it, rather.

They do not have the usual chance to encourage sympathy. Laughter has been aroused by the earlier meetings and conspiracy, but, remembering them, Prospero had been so disturbed that his daughter had never seen him 'touch'd with anger so distemper'd' (IV.1.144-5).

Shakespeare has tightly reined all other laughter in this deliberately judicial play. Miranda's first encounters with Ferdinand cause her to 'prattle something too wildly', to ask outright 'Do you love me?', to announce unbidden 'I am your wife'. Prospero's comment when he finds them together suggests the incipient comedy — 'Poor worm, thou art infected! This visitation shows it' — but within forty lines he is caught by a very different response:

> Fair encounter
> Of two most rare affections! Heavens rain grace
> On that which breeds between 'em!
>
> III.1.32-76

In the last scene too, Miranda's 'Sweet lord, you play me false' and

> How beauteous mankind is! O brave new world
> That has such people in't!
>
> V.1.172-84

may well bring laughter for their ironical innocence; but, even more quickly than at the end of *Cymbeline*, this comedy is lost in wonder and in the joy of reconciliation.

So Antonio and Sebastian's jests with Gonzalo turn awry as 'Widow Dido' is introduced and Alonso is forced to think anew of his lost son and daughter. When the lords mock, the idealism of Gonzalo's utopian discourse, the jesting gives place to a conspiracy to kill Alonso.

Ariel has some flashes of irresponsible, Puck-like humour, as in:

> The King's son have I landed by himself,
> Whom I left cooling of the air with sighs
> In an odd angle of the isle, and sitting,
> His arms in this sad knot —
>
> I.2.221-4

He imitates the grief-stricken prince, to raise laughter as any clown might do, and he seems to relish joining the clownish quarrels of Trinculo and Stephano. But Ariel is also, from the first, a 'moody spirit', and one who is busy in order to win freedom from contact with everyone in the play. Once he does sing '... merrily. Merrily, merrily....', but that is only when his own freedom is in sight. He does not answer Prospero's 'I shall miss thee' (V.1.95) and he is almost silent on his last errands. Dismissed in the very last speech of the play he has no words of farewell to Prospero — perhaps he should laugh 'merrily' after he has left the stage, 'delighted' and free.

Shakespeare depended on comic performances, giving laughter to all his romances, mixing mirth with delight and dreaming. But the clowns must observe the implied limits; in the play which ends with a solitary man wanting:

> Spirits to enforce, art to enchant;
> And my ending is despair
> Unless I be reliev'd by prayer....

he banished laughter before its conclusion; it is lost in punishment, in wonder and joy, in conspiracy and treachery, and in the escape of Ariel.

EIGHT

Interplay

THE presence of Salerio, Solanio and Tubal in *The Merchant of Venice* allowed Shakespeare to give a somewhat broader view of how Christians and Jews behave in the Venice of this comedy. But as individual characters they hold little interest, not one of them having a moment when he gathers all attention to himself. Their chief function is to provide interplay with other characters, notably with Shylock in Act III scene i, when the dramatic focus on the central character has to be both intense and sustained. Here their dialogue, action, and very presence on the stage open up new responses from Shylock, displaying the inner movements of his consciousness in a way that his own deliberations could not, and perhaps revealing more of himself than he himself could know.

Shakespeare was the master of such interplay. In the trial scene of *The Merchant* (IV.1) the main characters are closely and inescapably involved with each other, and as its drama develops they are revealed more and more deeply. After judgement has been pronounced, Shylock's concluding silence and Portia's mischievous pleasure in her own power are reactions which go beyond conscious choice but display reactions which alter the audience's perception of both characters. These effects are by-products of the main action, the result of interactions between the characters present, but they are nonetheless essential to Shakespeare's purposes, the very structure of his play depending on them.

Such interplay is one of the most characteristic qualities of Shakespeare's plays in performance. From it derives that sense of spontaneity which makes their action seem lifelike and their characters believable. So far in this book, for the sake of clarity, attention has been paid mostly to individual characters, but from time to time, where it is essential to dramatic development, a wider view has also been recognized. While Hamlet the prince dominates the action of *The Tragedy of Hamlet*, and his individual viewpoint is established in a series of soliloquies and asides, we have also seen how different impressions of his character are revealed, often against his conscious will, in scenes with his mother, Ophelia and Laertes. Claudius addresses his court decisively as king and has soliloquies with which to express his more private thoughts, but Shakespeare also used the presence of Polonius, Laertes and Gertrude, and even of such a minor character as

Rosencrantz, to show how Claudius is drawn away from the role he has set himself to play by feelings which are not entirely under his control. At the beginning of *Macbeth*, we have seen how Banquo's response to the Witches is in purposeful contrast to Macbeth's; it is part of that bewildering experience which unsettles the mind and being of the victorious general, rendering him almost unable to take charge of himself or the situation:

> function is smother'd in surmise,
> And nothing is but what is not.
>
> I.3.141-2

Interplay between characters is more than an occasional element in these plays and should be studied as an essential part of Shakespeare's dramaturgy. His *dramatis personae* do not encounter each other like fixed and separate participants in a game — various pieces on a chess board — but they engage with each other at levels of consciousness deep within themselves, and they are changed in the process. Instead of simple oppositions leading to unequivocal victories or defeats, the resources of these characters are revealed progressively to each other, to themselves and to their audiences.

*

From the earliest plays onwards, an impression of interplay grows stronger and more necessary to an understanding of character and action . In *The Two Gentlemen of Verona* Proteus has only to see Sylvia to fall in love with her; they exchange very few words on first meeting and the audience must wait until Proteus is next alone to understand what has happened:

> Even as one heat another heat expels
> Or as one nail by strength drives out another,
> So the remembrance of my former love
> Is by a newer object quite forgotten.
>
> II.5.188-91

Self-consciously he voices his own sense of the encounter which the audience has just witnessed. In *Romeo and Juliet*, however, after one ardent speech by Romeo which springs out of his silent observation of Juliet in the dance, the two come together and their intertwined thoughts, their irresistible attraction towards each other, and their sense of awe and hesitation, are expressed in the words of a regular sonnet, shared between them. They give words and ideas to each other:

ROMEO: If I profane with my unworthiest hand
 This holy shrine, the gentle fine is this:
 My lips, two blushing pilgrims, ready stand
 To smooth that rough touch with a tender kiss.
JULIET: Good pilgrim, you do wrong your hand too much,
 Which mannerly devotion shows in this;
 For saints have hands that pilgrims' hands do touch,
 And palm to palm is holy palmers' kiss.
ROMEO: Have not saints lips, and holy palmers too?
JULIET: Ay, pilgrim, lips that they must use in pray'r.
ROMEO: O, then, dear saint, let lips do what hands do!
 They pray; grant thou, lest faith turn to despair.
JULIET: Saints do not move, though grant for prayers' sake.
ROMEO: Then move not while my prayer's effect I take.

I.5.91-104

At first this is almost too controlled to be believable, but a more instinctive impression is given as the third quatrain is split between the speakers. Besides, after the kiss at the close of the sonnet, their thoughts overflow the formal bounds; the dialogue continues with rhymes shared evenly and shorter questions, and sharper and, from Juliet, more colloquial responses; and almost certainly there is shared laughter. A new sense of some unspecified 'sin', as if they sense that something is wrong, is recognized in jest:

ROMEO: Thus from my lips by thine my sin is purg'd.
JULIET: Then have my lips the sin that they have took.
ROMEO: Sin from my lips? O trespass sweetly urg'ed!
 Give me my sin again.
JULIET: You kiss by th' book.

As they kiss a second time, the Nurse's 'Madam, your mother craves a word with you' breaks their intimacy, and Juliet leaves silently. Neither she nor Romeo needs a soliloquy here to make their feelings evident; reactions to each other have overtaken such means of expression. By later standards, the thoughts of these two characters are very explicit in their verbal interplay, but the audience can sense an unspoken complicity expressed through the shaping, timing and pitch of the sonnet, as it is spoken, and in the more playful rhymes that follow.

In *Much Ado About Nothing*, written three or four years later, Shakespeare showed from the beginning that his two principal characters were drawn to each other despite what they said, even while engaged in self-protective or aggressive dialogue. These lovers start under a heavy verbal disguise, wooing each other, but too wise or too wary to 'woo peaceably'; or, to put it another way, too fearful to acknowledge how much is at risk. A good deal of obvious comedy derives from this game of hide and seek, not least in the response of others to their difficulties. In performance much will depend on how the two lovers are cast; their interplay can be almost painfully vigorous or foolishly light-headed, or even dull and predictable. But in more ambitious ways of playing the parts, their words are a disguise which traps them by setting their imaginations racing, so that they are led into responses which surprise and delight themselves and, when honesty and profound feelings make huge demands, frighten them too.

From almost the first moment, Benedick says that he is aware of the distinction between 'simple true judgement' and the words of a 'professed tyrant' to the opposite sex (I.1.142-5); but he learns during the play how nearly impossible are the words or deeds which have to answer the promptings of another person's 'soul.' Although he could not kill Claudio, his friend — 'not for the wide world' (IV.1.288) — yet he must if he is to trust Beatrice:

> BENEDICK: Think you in your soul the Count Claudio hath wrong'd Hero?
> BEATRICE: Yea, as sure as I have a thought or a soul.
> BENEDICK: Enough, I am engag'd; I will challenge him...
>
> IV.1.325ff.

Slowly, with surprising delicacy as well as with abrupt and obvious humour, Benedick and Beatrice become truly alive together before the eyes of the audience, without either character being fully aware of any change until it has happened; and then they hardly know how to speak of it, except in a way that is ridiculous and draws even their own laughter. At the end, Shakespeare dismisses them with a dramatic trick which allows everyone to laugh: surreptitiously they have written clumsy love poems to each other and these written proofs of their mutual involvement are made public simultaneously. They want to hear and see no more, and so Benedick cries for a truce and a retreat: 'Peace; I will stop your mouth' (V.4.97) he announces, as he kisses her. Beatrice remains less at the mercy of events, for she is able to choose how she 'yields' — if, indeed, she does.

In most productions, when the first war of words becomes part of a more complex interplay and the two actors are fully engaged, it becomes clear that Beatrice is the stronger, more ready to commit herself to new experience and more able to hold her own counsel. But this is a matter for individual actors to discover for themselves, once they have explored and made their own every detail of the text. Perhaps neither is the stronger, or the more foolish, or the more enlightened by the subtle process. The prime fact that anyone staging the play has to grasp is that these two characters can be realized only through interplay that is adventurous and honest. Each has soliloquies and scenes with other people in which to make their feelings for the other person more or less clear, but the fun and the heart of the matter is in the actors' own hands during the comparatively brief scenes when they meet face to face and must make what they can of their encounter.

Their exchange of eleven short speeches in the first scene would not score highly out of context in any contest for repartee. But Beatrice has already had opportunity to show her interest in Benedick when she asked a Messenger for news of him and gave a riddling account of earlier engagements:

> He set up his bills here in Messina, and challeng'd Cupid at the flight; and my uncle's fool, reading the challenge, subscrib'd for Cupid, and challeng'd him at the bird-bolt. I pray you, how many hath he kill'd and eaten in these wars? But how many hath he kill'd? For, indeed, I promised to eat all of his killing.
>
> I.1.32-7

This message is mixed, for 'bird-bolt' was an easy, harmless trial of accuracy which used blunt-headed arrows; and the eating of dead men is so grotesque an image that it will not register with any seriousness — unless Beatrice is determined that it should. Perhaps she should, for the Messenger is rendered speechless and Leonato intercedes with 'Faith, niece, you tax Signior Benedick too much; but he'll be meet with you, I doubt it not'. Surely he intends no pun with 'meet', as the Messenger does not when he replies 'He hath done good service, lady, in these wars', but Beatrice's imagination is still harping on food and feeding:

> You had musty victual, and he hath holp to eat it; he is a very

valiant trencherman; he hath an excellent stomach.

Out of this preliminary interplay with other characters, Beatrice has gained a head-start on Benedick in the audience's understanding. Perhaps this is sufficient to turn her first words to him into a joke: 'I wonder that you will still be talking, Signior Benedick: nobody marks you' (ll.99-100). But if it registers as a joke, it will be partly at her own expense, for she had agreed with the Messenger's 'I see, lady, the gentleman is not in your books' (l.64). Perhaps Benedick has been aware of her presence and for that reason has been making intrusive comments (by way of boorish jokes) in a conversation which is of no direct concern to him personally. Perhaps he has been angling for her attention: many actors will play the scene in this way so that his response — 'What, my dear Lady Disdain! Are you yet living?' — does not mark an abrupt surprise, but issues a challenge in return for a challenge. On the other hand, this response could be said with pleasure, quickly covering any small wound that Beatrice might have made. Timed neatly, phrased with assurance, and played with mutual understanding, even this first exchange, which verbally seems to offer little, can be a delight and create a sense of expectation in a theatre. How much do they care for each other or for the words they use to sustain contact? Each pairing of actors will suggest different ways of bringing life to the short episode and so, without striving to do so, they will also establish themselves in the audience's favor.

This introductory talk is like a preliminary rally at tennis, between two players who know each other very well and enjoy their long shots and hard-driving returns. Almost no exposition is achieved, no motivation established unambiguously, no plot-line set up, no points scored in earnest. But they flirt with many issues, as a list of the nouns and verbs they use will quickly discover. The principal verbs are to wonder, live, mark, die, feed, convert, come, love (three times), find, trouble, thank, hear, bark, swear, keep (twice), escape, scratch, make, wish, do, end, know; almost all are active, strong, and compact; the exceptions are concerned with desire and hope. Among the nouns they use are the traditional ones of lovers' talk: disdain, courtesy, heart, ladies, ladyship, gentleman, happiness, suitor, blood, God, face. But these are mixed with less civilized nouns, and these come eventually to predominate: dog, crow, parrot-teacher, bird, beast, horse, continuer, jade, trick. Halfway through the encounter, their words show that they become more aware of each other's physical presence, as if for a moment they realize the effect of being close together. Beatrice first speaks of Benedick coming into Courtesy's 'presence'; and then after Benedick's talk of his 'heart', she speaks of her blood, her dog, 'a man'; then follows Benedick's ladyship, mind, and face — the last of which Beatrice picks up, aggressively and promptly. Then follows talk of birds and beasts. Have they come close to each other, and then veered away?

If the opening encounter is read with an eye for how thoughts change, how each other's words and presence awaken their imaginations in different and in similar ways, the interplay is no longer composed of contrived and self-conscious verbal repartee of moderate skill and considerable obscurity. It becomes the means of showing two persons instinctively alight with desire, and with fear and hope; for one brief moment, moving towards a common response. Almost certainly neither character should recognize how far they are committed to each other at this early point in the play, but it can help the actors if they sense and use the underlying excitement:

> BEATRICE: I wonder that you will still be talking, Signior Benedick; nobody marks you.
>
> BENEDICK: What, my dear Lady Disdain! Are you yet living?
>
> BEATRICE: Is it possible disdain should die while she hath such meet food to feed it as Signior Benedick? Courtesy itself must convert to disdain if you come in her presence.
>
> BENEDICK: Then is courtesy a turncoat. But it is certain I am loved of all ladies, only you excepted; and I would I could find in my heart that I had not a hard heart, for, truly, I love none.
>
> BEATRICE: A dear happiness to women! They would else have been troubled with a pernicious suitor. I thank God, and my cold blood, I am of your humour for that: I had rather hear my dog bark at a crow than a man swear he loves me.
>
> BENEDICK: God keep your ladyship still in that mind! So some gentleman or other shall 'scape a predestinate scratch'd face.
>
> BEATRICE: Scratching could not make it worse, an 'twere such a face as yours were.
>
> BENEDICK: Well, you are a rare parrot-teacher.
>
> BEATRICE: A bird of my tongue is better than a beast of yours.
>
> BENEDICK: I would my horse had the speed of your tongue, and so good a continuer. But keep your way a God's name, I have done.
>
> BEATRICE: You always end with a jade's trick; I know you of old.

Much of the pleasure of *Much Ado About Nothing* in performance derives from the interplay of Benedick and Beatrice. But a certain mystery is retained in the progress of their wooing. The next meeting is in masks, for the dance at the 'great supper'(II.1), and therefore their talk is severely limited, though wild and also tight-lipped. When Beatrice returns to meet Benedick face to face, he refuses the encounter, declaring to everyone that he would prefer almost any other duty than 'three words' conference with this harpy' (II.1.241-2). Then their next meeting is at crossed purposes, so that each retains a different impression from the interview: Benedick has been tricked into believing that Beatrice pines for him, but is provided here with the very minimum of encouragement. *She* does not understand what he means; *he* turns everything she says into a covert protestation of love:

> Ha! 'Against my will I am sent to bid you come in to dinner' — there's a double meaning in that. 'I took no more pains for those thanks than you took pains to thank me' — that's as much as to say 'Any pains that I take for you is as easy as thanks'.
>
> II.3.234-7

Beatrice had left the stage quickly, seeing no advantage in staying, but Benedick stays long enough to 'take pity of her'. Finding himself alone, he resolves to 'go get her picture' (239) so that he may enjoy the shadow, if not the substance, of her presence.

Their only sustained encounter is reserved for a much deeper and more equal encounter. The scene is in church (IV.1), after Claudio has denounced Hero, his bride, as a common whore. Both Benedick and Beatrice are exposed to contrary and seemingly irreconcilable demands, and when the rest of the congregation has left, he goes over towards 'Lady Beatrice' who is still weeping for her wronged cousin. As he tries to express his concern, instinctively they begin to play with words again, as if their minds are excited and restless in ways that cannot be contained by simple expressions of grief or sympathy. They seem to need each other and need conflict; so they take each other's words and turn them to advantage or to challenge. Soon both are speaking of their love:

> BENEDICK: I do love nothing in the world so well as you. Is not that strange?

BEATRICE: As strange as the thing I know not. It were as possible for me to say I lov'd nothing so well as you;...
ll. 266ff.

But Beatrice becomes aware that her words may be taken to mean more than she intended, or that she had momentarily intended more than she could say 'freely'. Allowing no reply, she goes on, either stumbling or speaking with sudden rapidity:

> but believe me not,and yet I lie not; I confess nothing, nor I deny nothing.I am sorry for my cousin.

Thoughtlessly asserting a male prerogative or, more purposefully, heightening the pressure of his words, Benedick cannot stop speaking of their love: 'By my sword, Beatrice, thou lovest me'(l.272). So he tries to confirm her love, or to ask or plead for a return of his own.

The interplay can now go several ways, according to their involvement up to this moment. Beatrice may seek refuge from too much exposure by speaking of his sword, not of her own love; or, seeing in a flash how she might test his love, she may begin to work towards a further confrontation. Either way she is soon able to be more open about her own love for Benedick. With clashing and ricocheting wordplay, in short exchanges that are so weighted that they seem to tremble with tension, much of her speech can be quiet and very serious; or shockingly brutal; or it can be quickened with laughter at herself, as well as at her suitor:

BENEDICK: By my sword, Beatrice, thou lovest me.
BEATRICE: Do not swear, and eat it.
BENEDICK: I will swear by it that you love me; and I will make him eat it that says I love not you.
BEATRICE: Will you not eat your word?
BENEDICK: With no sauce that can be devised to it; I protest I love thee.
BEATRICE: Why, then, God forgive me!
BENEDICK: What offence, sweet Beatrice?
BEATRICE: You have stayed me in a happy hour; I was about to protest that I loved you.
BENEDICK: And do it with all thy heart.
BEATRICE: I love you with so much of my heart that none is left to protest.

> BENEDICK: Come, bid me do anything for thee.
> BEATRICE: Kill Claudio.

Just before the close of this interplay, Beatrice is more gentle and whole-hearted than she has ever been to Benedick; and he may be less aggressive or self-assured than before. The actors must listen carefully to each other and respond to each other's pitch, tempo, phrasing, emphasis, so that the speeches intertwine in meaning and measure of conviction. But then the command 'Kill Claudio' is abrupt, harsh and devastatingly practical, even if Beatrice knows that it is so outrageous that it can seem impossible, absurd, or laughable. Then all wordplay stops: Benedick's answer is uncompromising; and following one more riposte, her reply is final:

> Ha! not for the wide world.
> You kill me to deny it. Farewell.

Interplay has become impasse, shocking in its suddenness and seemingly complete.

Dramatic interest is here dependent entirely on what has gone before, sustaining the words but not fully expressed by them. Some Beatrices break away to leave Benedick and the place where they have met, so that he has to cry out 'Tarry, sweet Beatrice', and hurry to hold her back. But there are many ways of playing this moment. Beatrice may have been overcome by thoughts of love as soon as she spoke of them, and all that followed was a struggle to return to other concerns; so she might now find it impossible to leave Benedick and as she says 'Farewell' she does not move. Or she may have seized the opportunity to persuade Benedick to kill Claudio as a way of testing his worth, so that she spoke with conviction and energy and now adds to the pressure by leaving without sign of reluctance or indecision. Or the two may have been drawn together from the very start of this dialogue, while Beatrice was still weeping, and now hold each other in their arms; the whole exchange would then be very quiet, and Beatrice may now be telling herself to leave, but without any effect until she begins to regain her wits with: 'I am gone though I am here; there is no love in you; nay, I pray you, let me go.'

In any way of playing the scene, Beatrice denounces all the men she has ever known with an unequivocal force which nearly silences Benedick, and outstrips the righteous indignation with which Claudio had previously declared that Hero was a whore. She sees herself as more capable and more wholehearted than any man:

> O that I were a man! What! Bear her in hand until they come to take hands, and then with public accusation, uncover'd slander, unmitigated rancour — O God, that I were a man! I would eat his heart in the market-place....

This demands such total committal that each actress will act the moment differently as she draws upon her fullest resources. Benedick cannot withstand her anger, unless she weakens a little before she turns away; then, immediately, Benedick could cry out 'Tarry, good Beatrice'. But probably her energy is not yet spent and her conclusion has no hint of pathos as she begins to leave the stage; a shared silence would then follow before Benedick can speak.

> ...manhood is melted into curtsies, valour into compliment, and men are only turn'd into tongue, and trim ones too. He is now as valiant as Hercules that only tells a lie and swears it. I cannot be a man with wishing, therefore I will die a woman with grieving.

Either way, Benedick's response is surprisingly gentle, and yet strong enough to regain her attention:

> BENEDICK: Tarry, sweet Beatrice. By this hand, I love thee.
> BEATRICE: Use it for my love some other way than swearing by it.

Again both actors will discover how they meet here but, after Beatrice's less prescriptive challenge to use his hand for her love, the scene is ready to close. Soon she has no more to say, and Benedick has the last words.

So far as the plot goes, much remains in the balance, but after all the changeable, witty, passionate, puzzling, simple, and absurd speeches in this scene, the interplay between the two characters must have established some kind of trust which is almost independent of their words. On a deep level of consciousness, a mutual understanding has been forged which stands, in the play, as mutual love. But the comedy is not yet concluded: they have to learn to live with their love and to acknowledge it publicly and formally, and this needs two more scenes as lively and unpredictable as any that have gone before, and equally touched with both trusting idealism and disbelieving candor. Only when Benedick claims 'A miracle!'(V.4.91) do they find a way to end the play by joining in a dance of celebration for their own happiness and for other unions and conquests which are rather less amazing.

*

'Kill Claudio.' — 'Ah! not for the wide world' in *Much Ado* is a short exchange which is open to different interpretations and liable to change, so that it is slightly different each time it is played. But this crux is placed at so critical a time in the development of the drama that its instability seems to be a calculated effect, as if Shakespeare delighted to lay upon his actors this responsibility and this spur to adventurous playing. Open and critically placed moments of this kind are found throughout the plays: in *Henry IV*, *Part I*, 'Banish plump Jack, and banish all the world.' — 'I do, I will' (II.4.463-9), or in *Hamlet* 'I did love you once.' — 'Indeed, my lord, you made me believe so' (III.1.115-6), and several more in the same scene between the prince and Ophelia.

These open moments using the simplest dialogue are perhaps more frequent in the tragedies than elsewhere. They are the means of establishing the deep involvement of the characters and of encouraging the audience to become aware of that level of reaction. In *King Lear* several are placed in the very first scene. 'Nothing, my lord.'— 'Nothing!' — 'Nothing' (ll.86-8) is notoriously capable of being played in many ways, all of them drawing intense scrutiny to the public confrontation of father and daughter; and the main action of the play seems to spring from the disturbance experienced here. Kent's first interjection to Lear, Cordelia's silent responses to the King of France, and some terse phrases in the exchange between Goneril and Regan provide other moments in the first scene which call for finely tuned interplay and expose deep-seated conflicts and attachments. The earlier dialogue between Edmund and his father, and between his father and the Earl of Kent, provides several replies in which a few words suggest a silent resentment, ambition, or idealism. Edmund, standing at some distance from his father while he is being talked about in the third person as if he were not present, can make a strong impression by his very presence and maintain this in the following interchange.

One of the most remarkable achievements of *King Lear* is another form of interplay. Nearly all its leading characters seem at the last to be overcome by the 'weight', or pressures, of its performance:

> The weight of this sad time we must obey;
> Speak what we feel, not what we ought to say.
>
> V.3.323-4

Actors must open themselves to all that has happened between the characters and carry a sense of that to supply a basis for the words they speak now, and to ensure the authenticity of the entire experience. The text itself is often a mere indication of silent reactions that have become inevitable and intensely personal: all that has happened, says Albany, 'makes us tremble' (V.3.230); a messenger has to be urged twice to 'speak' (ll.222 and 225). Lear himself is in his own mental world, where his loving daughter, his fool, the 'slave that was a-hanging' Cordelia, and a memory of Kent all play their parts. But those who watch may well believe:

> He knows not what he says; and vain is it
> That we present us to him.
>
> V.3.292-3

Their 'present business Is general woe' (ll.318-9): after the shattering of many loves and many hopes, a new community of feeling may be seen to arise between those who stand together, almost bereft of words.

In the comedies, moments of interplay using the briefest dialogue are sometimes more tentative and less essential to a play's development, as if it were entirely up to the actors whether the invitations are accepted or not. In *Twelfth Night*, Sir Andrew's 'I was ador'd once too' (II.3.170), Viola's 'I pity you'(III.1.120), and Olivia's 'Most wonderful!'(V.1.217), can be deeply felt and sensitive reactions, or they can be spoken lightly as part of a strongly developing group reaction. But the effect of interplay can also be sustained so deeply that the character can seem almost unable to escape from a situation in which feeling outstrips words. In *As You Like It*, a sense of physical arousal goes far beyond the primary meanings of the words of the text; here understanding on a very personal and instinctive level is almost everything: 'I protest, her frown might kill me.' — 'By this hand, it will not kill a fly...' or 'I will.' — 'Ay, but when?' — 'Why now;...' (IV.1.96-8, 115-7).

Interplay between Shakespeare's characters is presented by a great variety of means. Words provide seemingly limitless opportunities with their multiple meanings and associations: words that are spoken in one sense and heard in another; words that prove unsatisfactory and so lead to further errors or unnecessary explications; words that seem to have an energy of their own or to release unexpected energies in the minds of those who use them. Images, rhythms, sounds, phrasings and syntax all communicate in ways that are beyond the intentions of the speaker; and so do silences and silent actions. Crucial shifts of intention represented by the simplest words are only one of the more noticeable signs of this incessant engagement between speakers. Even a sustained exposition, narrative, description, debate, or argument, which is spoken towards one specific and limited end, can awaken conflicting reactions in those who listen, and occasionally in those who speak. Few passages of dialogue in any but the earliest plays do not portray an interchange between the speakers at several levels of consciousness. Characters use both words and actions with confidence, but they are also at the mercy of them. The play is a kind of contest or game, in which skill and accident are inextricably mixed; it is so deft and complicated that each time it is re-played new discoveries are made, and it is not always clear who will emerge the stronger, or more in control of the game.

Sometimes two speakers are highly aware of interplay as a contest and so they use every opportunity to exploit advantage. Hamlet brought before Claudius, after he has killed Polonius and met with his mother, is startlingly at odds with the king. Claudius begins the interview with a 'Now' which alludes to the fact that Hamlet is 'guarded' and at his mercy:

> CLAUDIUS: Now, Hamlet, where's Polonius?
> HAMLET: At supper.
>
> IV.3.17-8

Pressed for an explanation (but of course, he knew that Claudius could do no less; and Claudius knows that Hamlet intended to confuse), Hamlet plays with the idea and develops it so that he seems to threaten the king; or, in another way of playing the scene, he may seem to be obsessed with disease and death, and perhaps touched with madness or pretending that he is:

> CLAUDIUS: At supper! Where?
> HAMLET: Not where he eats, but where 'a is eaten; a certain convocation of politic worms are e'en at him. Your worm is your only emperor for diet: we fat all creatures else to fat us, and we fat ourselves for maggots; your fat king and your lean beggar is but variable service — two dishes, but to one table. That's the end.

CLAUDIUS: Alas, alas!
HAMLET: A man may fish with the worm that hath eat of a king, and eat of the fish that hath fed of that worm.
CLAUDIUS: What dost thou mean by this?
HAMLET: Nothing but to show you how a king may go a progress through the guts of a beggar.
CLAUDIUS: Where is Polonius?

Claudius pretends to make nothing of this, by returning to the comparatively simple question with which he had started. Hamlet, aware of this, is now less constrained; he mocks openly, while continuing to threaten. So Claudius has to take charge:

HAMLET: In heaven; send thither to see; if your messenger find him not there, seek him i' th' other place yourself. But if, indeed, you find him not within this month, you shall nose him as you go up the stairs into the lobby.
CLAUDIUS: (*To Attendants*) Go seek him there.
HAMLET: 'A will stay till you come. *Exeunt Attendants.*
CLAUDIUS: Hamlet, this deed, for thine especial safety —
Which we do tender, as we dearly grieve
For that which thou hast done — must send thee hence
With fiery quickness. Therefore prepare thyself;
The bark is ready, and the wind at help,
Th' associates tend, and everything is bent
For England.

The unnecessary word 'fiery' and the short emphatic phrases that follow may show more than Claudius intends; they are fleeting signs of the deep unease which Hamlet has provoked and of which Claudius speaks as soon as he is left alone: 'For like the hectic in my blood he rages'(l.66). They may also betray that he has already planned the 'present death of Hamlet'(l.65). Both are now fully aware of danger and try to test the other's knowledge:

CLAUDIUS: For England.
HAMLET: For England!
CLAUDIUS: Ay, Hamlet.
HAMLET: Good!
CLAUDIUS: So is it, if thou knew'st our purposes.
HAMLET: I see a cherub that sees them. But, come; for

England!

This face to face, eye to eye, word for word encounter cannot be broken off without further interplay; neither can leave without some further, more probing, contact:

> HAMLET: ...But, come; for England! Farewell, dear mother.
> CLAUDIUS: Thy loving father, Hamlet.
> HAMLET: My mother: father and mother is man and wife; man and wife is one flesh; and so, my mother.

On 'Farewell, dear mother', they both may laugh at an intentional "misunderstanding"; yet this may be Hamlet's most obvious aggression, so that Claudius pauses before giving a very slow and mocking reply. Or perhaps Hamlet is so deeply wounded that he speaks rashly at last, without forethought. Or perhaps he may be so sure what the odds are and who his enemy must be, that these are conclusive words, spoken with deep bitterness. What is certain about this interchange is that the actors must take their cues not from words only, but from the way each one is spoken, and from the physical and emotional distance between the two adversaries. When Hamlet has gone, Claudius' strange mixture of polite mockery and deep concern drops away entirely, and urgent commands take over.

This short encounter is neither intimate nor sustained, but in its confusing and fiery interchanges — its orders and submissions, questions and answers, taunts and withdrawals — the confrontation is alert and fateful. Two of the principal persons in the play are meeting for the last time before events change their relationship entirely, and yet they hardly meet except in a very literal sense of that word. They react strongly to everything that is said and done, but with willful unpredictability. They make skillful use of words and, as it were, lie in wait behind them, looking for advantage. In performance any one of several speeches can seem to reveal the action most clearly, but which one this is could hardly be identified ahead of time from a study of the script alone, or even from performances by the same two actors on previous occasions. 'Farewell, dear mother.' — 'Thy loving father, Hamlet' is a single exchange which can oscillate widely, and perhaps wildly, between sarcasm, pain, madness, and precise, coldly considered aggression. Then how does Hamlet speak of his 'cherub' — with what assurance, or wishful thinking, or outrageous impertinence? The joke about Polonius' rotting corpse has time to register with Claudius while the theatre audience laughs, and so he has time to chose how his following words show or conceal his own reaction to the joke. Does Hamlet's comparative loquacity seem to weaken his stance before Claudius, and does the king's restraint strengthen the impression he makes? In all these matters the text supplies no answer; its function is to provide the means for an interchange between these two characters which actors can explore until they find a way of playing it which suits their parts as they have evolved throughout rehearsals and performances.

*

Actors must be free, open and generous if interplay between characters in Shakespeare's plays is to be realized in good measure and with a fitting sense of adventure. The words of the text will set their imaginations working and then the individuality of each actor and the conditions of each particular performance will be brought into play. Everything that happens can be reflected in some way as the text is enacted: what sort of audience, what kind of staging, what personal preparation the actors have made; and the place of performance, season of the year, day of the week and time of day, company organization and support, critical reaction to previous performances, news in the world outside the theatre. An accidental change in the timing of a single line, or in the awareness or posture of speaker or listener, or in the audience's response, can throw a scene off any prepared course and release a new kind of interplay.

Actors should be ready to respond to their varying opportunities, feeding their imaginations on whatever happens between them in each performance and on the new possibilities revealed in the text. But it may often seem easier, safer, and more immediately effective not to do so. (The ability to be so free is not a common gift, nor can it always be relied upon.) Therefore actors are often told to choose only one clear interpretation for each character; and to decide on one "intention" for each scene which they must then play as strongly as possible; in this way, they will be sure to create an impression of individuality and purpose at every appearance, especially if the other actors are all geared up to work against them, according to their own decisions and abilities. Freedom of response, it is said, threatens the shape of a whole production and weakens the excitement and forward drive of the play's action.

Much of the advice given to actors today militates against the open interplay which Shakespeare's text invites. *An Actor Prepares* and *Building a Character* by Constantin Stanislavski, translated in 1936 and 1949 respectively, provide a terminology and method of training which can inhibit interplay and isolate actors. The Russian actor and director, intent on developing strong performances, advocated an intellectual consistency in performance. Actors should discover a "through line of action" for each role and play it without disruptive inconsistencies. They should provide themselves with a "super-objective" for each character, and use it to give an impetus to every detail of a performance. Each time he or she sets foot on the stage, the character should have an active "intention," and an objective to realize. So in *Building a Character* the student is told:

> In every phase of our work, whether we were speaking of inventions of the imagination, proposed circumstance, objects of attention, units and objectives and the other steps, we constantly had occasion to speak of *logic* and *continuity*. I can only add that these are elements of prime importance in relation to all the others and to many gifts which actors possess.
>
> p. 287

Such exhortations have been applied to the acting of Shakespeare's plays in ways which work against their inherent openness and against that amazing authenticity of personal encounter which can so enliven their action and catch the audience's closest attention.

Robert Cohen's *Acting in Shakespeare* (1991) teaches how to define performance and to set the "speech acts" of the various characters in opposition:

> In acting Shakespeare, your need to pursue a goal (a victory, an objective) for your character, to interact vigorously with other people (other characters), to use a wide range and variety of tactics in pursuit of your goal(s), and to allow your character to be drawn by expectations of victory (and shaken by fears of defeat) is every bit as important as in acting Arthur Miller or David Mamet.
>
> p. xiii

The emphasis is not on freedom and improvisation, but on individual preparation and consistency; not on interplay, but on conflict. The actor must decide to make this or that happen through each "speech act": "It is necessary to understand for what reason the character says the word or line to the person addressed"(p.9). Or again, "Shakespeare gives you an extraordinary portfolio of characters who are defined, primarily, by the plans and choices they (and you, playing them) will make"(p.13). Of the Messenger who tells Claudius, in *Hamlet* Act IV scene 5,

> Save yourself, my lord:
> The ocean, overpeering of his list,
> Eats not the flats with more impetuous haste
> Than young Laertes, in a riotous head,
> O'erbears your officers...

Robert Cohen says:

> The problem for the actor is not merely to make sense of the image, which is difficult enough, but to make sense of a messenger who would, at a moment of life-or-death crisis, compose an extended literary nicety.
>
> p. 35

The notion that the text is animated by interplay with other persons in a particular situation, that a speech happens as an event of a drama in which the actor as character is caught in a situation that releases unexpected responses, has not entered the mind of this teacher. Actors must "try to calculate the effects of their actions... [and] seek to *plan* their acts" (p. 12). When urged to attempt variations in how a scene is acted, the actor is told to choose "gestures that help you convey your meanings and win your goals" (p. 203).

Certainly such advice helps young actors to concentrate their attention, and to discover "intentions" which will banish a lot of unnecessary, trivial gestures and will eradicate stumbling speech, but it stands in the way of the mettlesome excitement that Shakespeare's plays can give in performance, that authentic sense of persons meeting in unpremeditated interplay. Stanislavski himself was aware of this, for he viewed his "system" of training as strictly limited in application. It was an introduction to acting that would get rid of a "forced, conventional untruthfulness" found in most stage representations of life, and also the "embarrassment, stage-fright, the poor taste and false traditions which cramp our natures" (*Building a Character*, pp. 287-8). It was only "a companion along the way to creative achievement,... it is not a goal in itself" (p. 197). He was increasingly skeptical of his own teaching and confessed his own "powerlessness to achieve the greatness of creative nature" (p. 300). In later years, Stanislavski said that "no formulas" could show how to play any part, and that a truly creative actor needed four qualities:

(a) he has to be physically free, in control of free muscles;
(b) his attention must be infinitely alert;
(c) he must be able to listen and observe on the stage as he would in real life, that is to say to be in contact with the person playing opposite him;
(d) he must believe in everything that is happening on the stage that is related to the play.[1]

All four of these qualities help to release that interplay between characters which can bring Shakespeare's plays to varying and appropriate life.

Actors in Shakespeare's plays must not be islands to themselves, making decisions about their performances in isolation and fighting their own corners. Interplay requires companies whose members are open to each other in performance; and also open to audiences. For these reasons, training and rehearsals should not be directed so that answers are found for every "problem." Neither rehearsal nor performance should be governed solely by a desire to get matters "right"; both should be an adventure, an opportunity for discovery, a game in which everyone may be a winner. Actors must be able to listen, to receive, and then to allow the play to work within themselves, so they may express, by whatever means seems true at that moment, whatever their character and the drama evokes.

Many stories could be told to illustrate how Shakespeare's plays can come alive in interplay, and many teachers — Peter Brook notable among them — could be quoted on various means to encourage this necessary openness. But Michael Redgrave's account of his youthful performance in *As You Like It* in 1936 at the Old Vic Theatre, London, with Edith Evans as Rosalind, contains many of the essential ingredients:

> The majority of actors act for themselves or for the audience. I believe that the only way to act is to your partner. As a partner Edith Evans was like a great conductor who allows a soloist as much latitude as is needed, but always keeps everything strict. It's strict but free. Never is anything too set, too rigid. The stage relationship always leaves enough room to improvise. For the first time in my life, acting in *As You Like It*, I felt completely unselfconscious. Acting with her made me feel, oh, it's so easy. You don't start acting, she told me, until you stop *trying* to act. It doesn't leave the ground until you don't have to think about it. The play and our stage relationship in it always had the same shape. It was entirely well-proportioned and yet, in many respects, it was all fluid. In the forest scenes

> between Orlando and Rosalind, she would encourage me to do almost anything that came into my head. Yet, if I had done anything excessive she would have stopped it by the simplest means. Somehow it didn't occur to me to do anything excessive. For the first time, onstage or off, I felt completely free.[2]

*

From the beginning to the end of his career, Shakespeare continued to develop new ways of encouraging a sense of authenticity in each performance. But perhaps no play relies more strongly on interplay between its two leading actors than *Macbeth*, where from their first meeting the charge which each derives from the other's presence seems to run through almost everything they say and do:

> LADY MACBETH: Thy letters have transported me beyond
> This ignorant present, and I feel now
> The future in the instant.
> MACBETH: My dearest love,
> Duncan comes here to night.
> LADY MACBETH: And when goes hence?
> MACBETH: To-morrow — as he purposes.
> LADY MACBETH: O, never
> Shall sun that morrow see.!
>
> I.5.53-8

With these few lines, understanding and communication move rapidly ahead: in ways that each actor must discover in rehearsal and performance, they know now that they both have decided that Duncan is to be murdered. After Macbeth has been crowned, however, he draws apart into a world of his own, using her presence only for reassurance:

> Thou marvell'st at my words; but hold thee still:
> Things bad begun make strong themselves by ill.
>
> III.2.54-5

But he still needs and uses her presence for reassurance; after this final couplet, he adds the short line, 'So, prithee go with me'; and they exit then together, the actors showing whatever degree of mutual consent has arisen from the action they have played so far. By the Banquet scene, he knows that the 'strange things' that he has in mind must not be 'scann'd' (III.5.139-40), and the two can now be seen drawing further apart: if he were to think of her too much, he might withdraw from those deeds to which he is now committed. Man and wife conclude the play totally separated, but Lady Macbeth's sleep-walking shows that she is still obsessed by his presence; after that scene, she leaves the stage calling for his hand and leading him, in her imagination, to bed (V.1.64-6).

Macbeth is provided with a further moment of remote contact with his lady, in 'the cry of women' which precedes news of her death (V.5.8). Perhaps their interplay is at an end, for his reply to that cry is

> I have almost forgot the taste of fears....
> Direness, familiar to my slaughterous thoughts,
> Cannot once start me.
>
> V.5.9-15

But these words may be hiding a deeper response which he cannot name, for, when her death is reported certainly, he has to hold back from direct comment. He seems to recall the whole course of their life together before he speaks of the future, and of the daunting emptiness of the stage on which he must now act alone:

> She should have died hereafter,
> There would have been a time for such a word
>
> V.5.17-8

How Macbeth responds to this new isolation will depend on the whole progress of the play until this moment. Some indication of the width of possible interpretations can be found in the different interpretations given to 'Out, out, brief candle!'(V.5.23). Is that candle the spirit of man, or the light and hopes of one man's waking hours, or the light which one person can lend to another, giving both meaning and purpose? Or is it a representation of the dying Lady Macbeth, 'the effect of her death on his thought'?[3]

It would be a rash actor who tried to perform Macbeth without establishing an intimate relationship with his Lady. She must possess his mind totally at times, and her presence must remain part of the inner life of his performance to the end. Perhaps she should have power to revive his spirits when he needs every faculty of mind and body, and every nerve, in order to fight in the last moments like a baited animal tied to a stake. In her very first scene, Lady Macbeth had been aware of a need to resist a voice that she heard in her "transported" imagination:

> Come, thick night,
> And pall thee in the dunnest smoke of hell,
> That my keen knife see not the wound it makes,
> Nor heaven peep through the blanket of the dark
> To cry 'Hold, hold!'
>
> I.5.46-51

In most performances, Macbeth does not hear these words because he enters after they are spoken, as the Folio text directs. But we cannot be sure that this original printing of the play placed this stage direction in the right place; the compositor may have moved it to a convenient space which he had provided on the page by setting one iambic pentameter as two half-lines. Suppose Macbeth was directed to enter earlier in Shakespeare's manuscript of the play, so that he hears these lines or the last of them. Or suppose he overhears the very last words as he enters where the Folio text says he does. Or suppose Lady Macbeth's thoughts become known to him through intuition. In any of these ways, Macbeth's last words in the play can be an echo of her thoughts, a last interplay between them:

> Lay on, Macduff;
> And damn'd be him that first cries 'hold, enough!'
>
> V.8.34

I am not saying that many Macbeths consciously echo Lady Macbeth in their last words — I do not know for sure that any one has done so — but I do argue that this is possible, unconsciously — together with many other possible readings of the line. The actor has to draw upon whatever strength he can at this critical moment, so that he tries 'the last'(l.32). Little in the words of the text will tell him how to speak any words now, or how to give himself up wholly to the final fight. Here he faces the one enemy who is fated to kill him, but Shakespeare has left the actor free to find and use whatever shaping and informing influences have arisen as he has journeyed through the text and action, and has interacted with other characters. The lived and shared experience of the play itself gives meaning to performance at this critical moment, rather than any conscious "intention" or "purpose": only this can give the authenticity the text requires.

PART TWO

Action and the Stage

NINE

Narrative and Focus: Richard II

SO far I have considered the actor's contribution to performance, but already I have drawn attention to relationships between performances, shifts of interest from one character to another, effects of movement on stage and changing modes of illusion. Now the stage picture must come to the forefront. As a play is performed, a dramatist is controlling the audience's view of its action, now towards a single character, now a group, now a dead body, or an empty throne, or nothing.

An audience is aware of the physical objects displayed before it, as well as the words it hears. Shape, size, color; contrasts, numbers, distance; movement, organization, and lack of organization are all influencing the audience's response. There are moments when a number of figures seem to stand within a realistic perspective in calculated relationship to each other, and moments when they form a two-dimensional frieze (no figure more important than another), or when a small eccentric detail dominates the whole, or when an empty space is more impressive than the rest of a crowded stage. We need to speak of the changing picture on the stage as of a composition; as we might speak of the formal characteristics of a painting. This deployment is part of the performed play and strongly affects what it does to an audience; it is part of the theatrical language which Shakespeare developed during the course of his career.

Two warnings are needed. First it will not be sufficient to list the contents of the stage-picture and their relationships. We must try to describe how the audience perceives that picture. In a picture gallery we recognize that there is an appropriate way of looking at any picture. It would be absurd to stand all the time within a foot or two of a French impressionist painting, a Monet or a Degas. That would be appropriate only if we were considering the painter's technique. In order to see the effect that his picture is able to transmit, we would automatically step back a few paces and so become aware of the relationship of the brush-strokes to each other, of the whole effect of light, color, movement and space. The picture is made for such a wide focus. Other pictures — some Dutch realists for example — invite, and require, a minute scrutiny: one needs to step up close to the canvas. So it is in the theatre: the right focus, be it wide or intense, is necessary for seeing the masterpiece. Without this adaptation in our attention we may see only what appears to be incompetent brush-work, or an inability to give distinction or emphasis.

In watching a play in a theatre — any play, in any theatre — we sometimes sit forward in our chair, head forward and eyes intent on one particular point in the arena or picture which is the stage; this kind of dramatic focus is intense, concentrated. We observe or watch for the minutest action or word; we often see only one particular person or hear only one particular sound, even though the stage may be crowded or noisy, or disorderly. The opposite extreme is a wide dramatic focus. Instead of sitting forward we are sometimes relaxed, sitting back, and responsive to the whole picture. At such a time no one person or sound, or action dominates the impression we receive; we are sitting back and 'taking it all in'; we are conscious of the overall effect, of the interweaving of pattern and the range of color. It is a wide focus. We can become aware of a changing dramatic focus by marking these two extremes.

We must also remember constantly that the play exists in time; the stage picture is always developing from one form to another and at varying speeds. One momentary grouping may gain emphasis or meaning because it echoes an earlier grouping, in a different setting or with another dominating figure. A single figure may be more eloquent of loneliness because just before the stage had been crowded and animated. The changing visual impressions are also modified by narrative. So a sudden liveliness may appear to be little more than a meaningless disturbance, because the audience is wholly unprepared for it and so it shocks rather than elucidates. When narrative expectation is thwarted by a movement to some other part of the fable, an apparently static, formal scene may lose its impression of stability, or a brief descriptive scene take on an unusual air of deliberation. The stage picture is always changing and the audience's reaction to it can be controlled by dramatic narrative or a necessary response to character and situation.

The stage picture cannot be assessed easily; but if we do not discover the appropriate focus for each moment we may misread the dramatic text — and that is done all too easily.

*

I shall consider first, *Richard II*: an early play, written, for the most part, in a particularly lucid style.

It begins with the stage set formally. Richard is enthroned and surrounded, as the Quarto edition of 1597 says, with '*nobles and attendants*'. Richard commands the center of the stage, but he is seen as a king in relationship to his subjects, rather than as a person interesting in his own right. He speaks in set fashion to his uncle, John of Gaunt, and requires precise, official answer. When Gaunt's son, Henry Bolingbroke, and Thomas Mowbray, Duke of Norfolk, are called to the King's presence, they bitterly accuse each other of treason. Richard fails to reconcile their demands of honor and appoints a day for trial by combat at Coventry. The whole stage empties at once, and on the outcome of that future event the audience's attention will wait.

So the first scene would appear if it were played on its own merits, with each word spoken as simply as possible. But if the audience has some previous knowledge of Richard's history, or if the actors try to give consistent portrayals of their roles, there will be further and conflicting impressions. Richard's formal protestation of impartiality, his 'Forget, forgive; conclude and be agreed', and his comments on 'bold' Bolingbroke, may carry subtextual impressions of irony, apprehension or antagonism. Bolingbroke's accusations may seem aimed at the King rather than Mowbray, and Mowbray's confidence to stem from royal support rather than his own innocence But even if these impressions are missed, the audience will be made to question the scene's textual and visual impressions by the simple duologue of the next scene. Mowbray has been accused of murdering Thomas, Duke of Gloucester, a son of Edward III and so Bolingbroke's uncle and the King's, but now, in contrast to the visual elaboration of the first formal picture, a quiet, still, intimate scene shows Thomas' widowed Duchess appealing for revenge, and his brother, John of Gaunt, refusing because:

> correction lieth in those hands
> Which made the fault.

The King and judge of the first scene had been responsible for Mowbray murdering Gloucester, a fact to which no overt allusion has hitherto been made. Now the audience must question the earlier picture in retrospect, or find their unease strengthened. The new information is given unemphatically, for Gaunt does not have to persuade his hearer of its truth, but just before the audience's interest is redirected to the lists at Coventry, the Duchess is shown alone, believing that she goes to die.

For the third scene, at Coventry, the full stage is again 'set' (as the Quarto has it) formally. The King enters in procession to the sound of trumpets, and personal feelings are subdued within the larger gestures and more fluent responses of public ceremonial But now the focus is changed, for the audience will watch both sides closely, and 'God's substitute' also, as he stands as judge on a higher level of the stage. The excitement of the duel itself is quenched before it begins, when Richard, with a single movement of his hand, stops proceedings. This is unexpected and so draws all the alerted attention to the King who holds attention by wise words about civil strife and his own duties, and then pronounces the judgement which he and his council have agreed upon: Bolingbroke is to be banished for ten years and Mowbray for life. But this is not all: the newly watchful audience may discern a brief sign of complicity or shame as Richard with 'some unwillingness' passes sentence on Mowbray, and a covert accusation as the banished man claims a 'dearer merit': a single hesitation can now sharpen the audience's perception of signs of subtextual motivation. Bolingbroke's submission with:

> Your will be done. This must my comfort be,
> That sun that warms you here, shall shine on me....

may seem to veil a rivalry with the King himself. Richard dominates the stage as he gives judgement, but at the close of the scene Bolingbroke is left alone with his friends and, as he fails to acknowledge their farewells, the course of the drama waits upon the expression of his personal and private feelings. So a newly clarified interest is balanced between Richard and Bolingbroke.

To sum up the visual effects so far, we can say that Shakespeare has introduced the action with a wide focus so that the audience is made aware of the patterns of the King's relationship to nobles and officials, and of father to son and fatherless nephew. But a more intimate focus is then induced with a short scene which adds notably, but quietly, to the exposition, and so when the next crowded, formal scene follows there are momentary intensifications of focus; but these never lead to direct narrative statement. Sometimes the audience's curiosity is aroused by some action or speech after it has been completed; or one character, by his words, provokes a closer scrutiny of another, or of relationships between several other characters. But the moments of close interest are sporadic and always lead back to a comprehensive view of the stage, or to a quick review of the preceding action. The audience's intense interest is not engaged for any single character or event, and yet, since the wider issues have been resolved in judgement and banishment, it is these insights which arouse most of the audience's expectation of further development. We can say that the stage-picture is at once comprehensive and subtle, that the focus is potentially intense over a wide design.

More informal scenes follow which complicate the audience's view, extending their interest and knowledge without coordinating individual impressions. While the splendors and proprieties are still alive in the memory, Richard is seen disrobed and at ease with his intimates. Now he is sarcastic about 'High Hereford' and answers the national threat of rebellion in Ireland by deciding to lease his royal estates and exact subscriptions from wealthy subjects. When news comes that Gaunt is sick, Richard wishes his uncle were dead so that he might seize his possessions, and then goes to visit him: 'Pray God we may make haste, and come too late', he says, and 'Amen' respond his companions. In all this the pious and responsible solemnities of the first regal scenes are mocked: is this erratic informality a truer picture of Richard and of his country?

In a solemn, static scene that follows, the dying Gaunt speaks of the 'scepter'd isle' of England with a reiterative eloquence that lends fire to patriotic commonplaces and has made the speech famous out of its context: this is a self-contained, largely verbal episode. Next Richard enters, and Gaunt denounces his husbandry and openly accuses him of the murder of Gloucester. Gaunt leaves the royal presence and, as York tries to placate the King, his death is announced. Immediately Richard confiscates Gaunt's possessions and York is no longer patient but denounces Richard as Gaunt had done: his remonstrance is breathless, not so imposing but more pitiful than Gaunt's, yet the King does not listen; rather, with surprising decision, he makes York governor in England during his own absence in Ireland, and then again hurries from the scene. As Gaunt and York have taken the center of the stage in denunciation, Shakespeare has ensured that the King prevents a prolonged close focus by jests and rapid decisions and movements. Verbally the situation is clearer, but the focus is still predominantly wide; it has only become more insecure, more uncertain and more frequently disturbed by momentary clarifications and intensities.

As soon as Richard has left the stage, the Earl of Northumberland and the lords, Ross and Willoughby, agree together that the King 'is not himself' but transformed by his flatterers, and then they hasten to join Bolingbroke newly returned at the head of an army to redress all wrongs. Here is a simpler, stronger interest in the narrative development, but before the audience is allowed to follow it, there is a quiet moment in which the Queen mourns the absence of her 'sweet Richard' — an entirely new reaction to this baffling figure. When she hears of Bolingbroke's arrival she despairs and York is unable to reassure her: 'Comfort's in heaven', he warns, 'and we are on the earth'. He has little confidence in his resources or decisions: and, as he leaves with the Queen, the audience sees Richard's lesser friends count their chances and promptly decide to save their own skins, two fleeing to Bristol and one to Ireland. So from this gentle and then hesitating and shifting scene, the audience will turn with relief to Bolingbroke who now appears confident in arms and attended by Northumberland. They are joined by other nobles and all speak courteously, as if in homage to the new central figure. Bolingbroke's speeches are both strong and relaxed, so that the stage picture is at last ordered and assured (as it had seemed to be at the beginning), and the action steadily developing. York enters to denounce the rebel, but then declares himself neutral. There is a brief scene recounting the dispersal of the King's Welsh army on hearing rumors of his death, and then the action moves to Bristol where Bolingbroke, now accompanied by York as well, condemns to death Bushy and Green, Richard's cowardly friends. He takes charge of the realm as if he were the king of it, and holds the center of the stage; again echoing the first 'set' scene.

The narrative encourages the audience to expect the uneasy focus to settle on the opposition of two main figures, two potential centers of the stage. But when Richard returns as from Ireland with Aumerle and the Bishop of Carlisle, after being absent for some four hundred and sixty lines (over one sixth of the whole play), he does not meet Bolingbroke at once. The scene of his return (III.2) is antithetical to that of Bolingbroke's: Richard is joined by other friends, as his rival had been, but they bring bad news and not an easy courtesy; and, whereas the rebel's course was clear, the King's is makeshift. Yet from this point to his death the dramatic focus grows more and more intent upon Richard for his own sake, whenever he appears; the audience sees progressively deeper into his consciousness. Sometimes the more stable Bolingbroke is a potential rival for attention in the center of a crowded stage, but after his opponent has surrendered he says very little: he assumes the crown, but never mentions his intention to do so; he deposes Richard, but leaves most of the business and persuasion to Northumberland and York. The audience is continually aware of Bolingbroke's presence, but he seems to stand farther away from them than Richard, or than he himself had done formerly. Such is the cunning perspective of the stage picture.

The focus is intensified on Richard by huge transitions of thought and feeling, and by silences. He easily dominates the stage on his return because all the ill-tidings are known to the audience before they are told to him, and so there is no competitive narrative interest. Moreover he is eloquent and the other characters dependent upon him. But the focus is so narrowly intense because of his silences— it seems as if the extremes of his spoken despair and hope are impelled by some unexpressed fear, some knowledge or state of being which he cannot escape and cannot fully meet. He tries many ways to hope or despair, to some stable and 'true' reaction: at first plain fantasy, then affirmation of trust in God, then meditation on the oblivion of death, then renunciation of his duties. But his friends on stage cannot believe or join in any of them, and silence always follows — as if none of his words were valid the moment after they have been spoken. Richard himself is aware of this ineffectiveness and directs attention to it verbally: he thinks he will be mocked for 'senseless conjuration' and that he has been 'mistaken all this while'.

At the end of the scene he discharges his army and hurries offstage, 'From Richard's night, to Bolingbroke's fair day' and forbids anyone to speak further. He seems to know that it is from the expression of his own thoughts that he tries to escape at the end, rather than from physical or political danger. Between the rhetoric and the silences, the audience's attention is drawn towards Richard at the center of the stage and towards the unexpressed insecurity and suffering at the center of his being.

The scene in which Richard confronts Bolingbroke's army provides a wide stage-picture organized, for the first time, on two opposing centers. As Richard speaks and looks royally, claiming the power of 'God omnipotent' and prophesying war as the result of Bolingbroke's treason, he seems once more to justify his position on the upper level of the stage at the center of the picture. Yet when Northumberland promises that the rebel claims only his own inheritance, Richard suddenly changes and agrees to meet his demands: it is as if the focal point of the composition suddenly lost its substance. As his message is carried back, Richard acknowledges:

> O that I were as great
> As is my grief, or lesser than my name!
> Or that I could forget what I have been!
> Or not remember what I must be now!
>
> III.3.136-9

Then again his insecurity is made apparent by the extremity and variety of his reactions: he speaks openly and fluently of future defeat, a life of pious poverty and an obscure death. As Aumerle weeps, Richard retreats still further into the fantasy of 'two kinsmen' digging 'their graves with weeping eyes'. Mildly he submits to Northumberland's request that he should meet Bolingbroke in the base court; but before he descends from his dominating position in the picture, his mind flashes to his former power and glory:

> Down, down I come, like glis'tring Phaethon,
> Wanting the manage of unruly jades.

To his enemies it seems that:

> Sorrow and grief of heart
> Makes him speak fondly [foolishly], like a frantic [mad] man;
> Yet he is come.

The visual submission is criticized, as it were, by Richard's words, which he cannot wholly control. He cuts short all argument by placing himself in the enemy's power before that is demanded of him; and, as before, he hurries to conclude the scene. From now on, the picture will tend to be dominated by Bolingbroke and his agents, but the focus is still intent upon Richard whenever he speaks or moves. Borrowing phrases from the criticism of paintings, we may say that the whole composition is static, at rest; but it is disturbed by the figure of Richard which is mobile and restless.

A wholly static interlude follows, of wide focus. It is set in a garden where Richard's Queen overhears two gardeners talk of affairs of state. They speak solemnly and pityingly of the 'wasteful king' who has not 'trimm'd and dress'd his land' as they their garden, and repeat the news that he is to be deposed. They are not Shakespeare's usual comic characters impressing their own personalities or points of view. Their quaint, slow-moving dialogue acts as a fixed point of reference like Gaunt's talk of a 'sceptred isle', an unequivocal statement of the widest dramatic issues from outside Richard's personal dilemma.

Then the action moves to London, with Bolingbroke in full control. The Bishop of Carlisle boldly denounces the rebel and prophesies 'Disorder, horror, fear, and mutiny' to future generations. He is arrested by Northumberland and at this tense moment Richard is brought on to the stage. He has already decided to resign the crown — Shakespeare does not use this incident to argue about political issues — and now gives effect to his decision step by step, as if obeying instructions or as if seeking to re-create the ceremonial solemnity of the early scenes. But he is now aware that his words and actions do not reflect his inward nature, neither his 'regal thoughts' nor his deep sorrow. And his audience, both on stage and in the auditorium, is made aware of this disparity. When he cries 'God save the king', no one dares respond 'Amen', and when he calls Bolingbroke to stand opposite him with one hand on the crown he is forced to protest that he cannot resign his cares with the resignation of his office. As he tries to speak of this, his words have a new authority: they do not express conflicting extremes and do not issue from nervous silences. The man who submits now dominates the scene: he draws all attention to himself and, within the pattern of ordained events, he controls the nature of the action and denounces his enemies. Yet this new strength derives from weakness: he speaks more firmly and steadily because he now knows he cannot speak of his own crimes nor alleviate his grief; he cannot tell 'what name to call himself'. It is at this point that Shakespeare introduced an incident for which his sources gave not the slightest suggestion: Richard calls for a looking-glass and when he sees few signs of his suffering in it, he dashes it to pieces. The true image of Richard is not in his appearance, nor his words. Again the scene is quickly finished: he asks for leave to go and is conveyed to the Tower. Shakespeare has at once presented a wide picture and led the audience's interest intently towards a single figure standing to one side of the composition; and as the focus intensifies, the drama becomes abruptly disturbed by subtextual realities and the whole wide picture is disturbed and rapidly dissolved.

There is a brief scene as the Queen greets her husband on his way to prison, not recognizing the royal lion in his meek submission. There is no nervous alternation of mood now, nor anxious silence. They exchange short rhymed speeches, and then part with a kiss, in accepted silence. But the audience whose interest has been so intensified upon Richard may see the very fluency of the scene as a deliberately external manner of valediction; Richard communicates his inward grief by trying to conceal it, and in performance the dialogue can sound tender and precarious, as well as controlled. Richard yet again hurries from the stage, lest they 'make woe wanton with this fond delay': he is still afraid of what he might say; for all the verbal formalism of this scene, the center of the picture is still mysterious, still lacking a defined and static quality.

The audience hears of further indignities that Richard is made to suffer, but it has to wait through two bustling, half-comic scenes before he is presented again. Then — and this is for the first time in the play— he appears alone. In soliloquy the audience's attention is drawn wholly to him. The focus is now undeniably intense, and yet Shakespeare introduces a considered, reflective, almost literary tone:

> I have been studying how I may compare
> This prison where I live unto the world....
>
> V.5.1-2

In due order Richard now describes his disordered thoughts—religious, ambitious, flattering — and acknowledges that he is content in none of them. As music is played off-stage, he speaks of 'wasting' his 'time', and of his recompense in being 'wasted' by time and being forced to 'mark the time' of Bolingbroke's progress. Grief, folly, faults, defeat and insecurity are all acknowledged; he no longer tries to escape from such thoughts but seeks to tame them by expressing them thoughtfully. The tone is almost unvaried and the pace almost steady: not quite, for still the balance is not easy. The change has left him helpless, expecting that:

> Nor I, nor any man that but man is,
> With nothing shall be pleas'd till he be eas'd
> With being nothing.

Yet music, played out of time, threatens this composure. Only when he remembers that it is meant for his comfort and is a sign of love, can he bear that too, and the scene is once more composed. Then comes a quickening of interest in an unexpected entry: he is hailed as 'royal Prince!', and Richard answers the visitor quickly with a sharply ironic 'Thanks, noble peer!' He is a groom of his stable, and tells Richard of his horse, the roan Barbary, and of this creature's pride in bearing Bolingbroke in triumph. Richard curses the horse, but then stops to consider: because the animal was 'created to be aw'd by man' he begs its forgiveness, and remembers that he himself has been forced to bear a burden and submit as if he were an animal. Immediately a warder enters with food and orders the groom away; the focus is sharpened by the unknown, and by an attendant sense of immediate danger. Richard, however, thinks of his servant — 'If thou love me, 'tis time thou wert away' — and a silence can be held in performance, despite the excitement, by an undefined and unexpressed sympathy between master and groom. The latter replies: 'What my tongue dares not, that my heart shall say'. Such a silence does not require utterance; momentarily there is intimacy and understanding, and even, perhaps, a deep peace.

After this intensely focused moment, Shakespeare returned to his primary sources with the warder's harsh words asking Richard to eat. The warder refuses to taste the food to guard against poison, saying that Bolingbroke's order forbids this, and then Richard leaps at him with:

> The devil take Henry of Lancaster and thee!
> Patience is stale, and I am weary of it.

There are cries for help and Exton and his assistants rush in. Action is violent and general: Richard kills two men, and then is overpowered by numbers and struck down. Suddenly the stage is fully alive with his anger, authority and physical strength, with a struggle and then defeat — all in an instant. The deep, necessarily static focus has been broken, and then when the violence is past— violence can sustain interest in the theatre only for comparatively short times—Richard speaks his last, presumably faint, words (again wholly Shakespeare's invention) that are all the more impressive by contrast with the tumult:

> Mount, mount, my soul! thy seat is up on high;
> Whilst my gross flesh sinks downward, here to die.

Richard had often longed for death because it would bring oblivion and perhaps pity, but as he faces assassination he finds new aspiration: royal anger and, then, hope in a world beyond death and change, spring from his deepest being.

Shakespeare's Richard talks a great deal about himself — some critics have called him a poet rather than a king — but an understanding of his part in the play cannot be found by simply analyzing what he says, weighing the word against the word; his stage reality depends also on subtext, and on the changing picture as it directs the audience's attention progressively towards the thoughts behind the words and the thoughts of silence, and towards his last unthinking, physical reactions. By simple quotation it can be shown that Richard is a man who talks 'too idly', one 'who wastes time' and is then 'wasted' by it; or that he is a king who must uncrown himself and yet cannot escape the cares that 'tend the crown'. But such formulae do not embrace the whole experience the play provides in a theatre.

*

In a tragedy, after death there is always more to say. If only the eyes are closed and pious ceremonies performed in silence, the audience is shown that death affects other people besides the protagonist. A hushed drum, a bowed head, or a moment without sound or motion is enough to establish death as a fact for others' comprehension; the hero may have unpacked his heart with words but this must still be presented, his death must have this consequence. Many dramatists have made the further communication explicitly, in a chorus which tells the men and women of Thebes that no one can be called happy until he has died in peace, that there is always an end to tears, that wisdom is taught by suffering. Some authors, more busily, have recounted death's manifold implications through a group of women tidying their thoughts aloud; others have announced a long-kept secret through the mouth of some wise, experienced man — how he who has died had been true to his heritage, or had been struck down by some hidden guilt. Authors who prefer to maintain a full dramatic illusion have presented retaliation or submission, praise or blame, in continued action, or have concluded with a prayer that begs some god to appease man's misery and remorse. In Shakespeare's day the standard procedure was explicit comment, a statement of the play's meaning or significance. Elizabethan tragedy usually drew a firm line after the death of the hero, and then totalled up good deeds and bad. In this play, Shakespeare's method is to give another scene, another picture with different figures: after the death of Richard, when the focus has been more intense than ever before, Shakespeare transferred attention to Bolingbroke seated in Richard's throne; a formal 'set' scene, with a predominantly wide focus.

The transference is, however, long prepared for: the wide focus of the early scenes had not been invoked needlessly. The first stage pictures with Richard as judge of Mowbray and Bolingbroke, were repeated half-way through when Bolingbroke stood as judge of Bushy and Green, and then of Aumerle and Surrey against the charges of Bagot, Fitzwater and others. In his second judgement Bolingbroke dealt with the same offense as had concerned Richard: the murder of Thomas, Duke of Gloucester. But there were significant differences: the contestants were more numerous and more quick-tempered; the judge said far less than his predecessor, his most arresting contributions being his silence, his repeal of Mowbray and then, on hearing of this old enemy's death after fighting in the crusades, his praise and prayer for him. All these scenes are echoed in the last formal scene, and so strengthen it; once the momentary surprise has passed, it seems the inevitable close to the play as a whole.

Again, between Richard's farewell to his Queen and his last appearance, Shakespeare elaborated on accounts in his sources by introducing two scenes showing the Duke of York's discovery that his son, Aumerle, is engaged in conspiracy against Bolingbroke. The audience need not know these events in order to follow Richard's story — indeed, almost invariably the scenes are cut from modern productions — so Shakespeare must have had other reasons for inventing them. Firstly they demonstrate the effects of revolution; and, secondly, their comic details of calling for boots to a loquacious wife, provide a release from the tension of following Richard's story. And they also affect the dramatic focus. By introducing these scenes Bolingbroke is again seated as judge. At first he seems well able to manage the danger to his person, reducing the stature of both Aumerle and his mother with an ironic: 'My dangerous cousin, let your mother in' (V.3.81). But, as the Duchess kneels in supplication and refuses to obey Bolingbroke's thrice repeated 'Rise up, good aunt' until he has promised, and doubly promised, pardon for her son's life, the audience is shown both the new king's power and his subject's tendency to doubt the effect of his commanding words of friendship and forgiveness. The irony touches Bolingbroke closely, for as the suppliant rises she cries (and this is all she says): 'A God on earth thou art' — the rebel, the silent king, has to hear himself called a god by those he favors. To this salutation he answers nothing: but his tone changes and, ignoring the agonized and flustered woman, he speaks directly of tracking down other conspirators and swears that all of them shall die. The episode ends when the Duchess leaves with her pardoned son and places such revolutions of fortune in another perspective: 'Come my old son; I pray God make thee new'.

I have dwelt so long on this scene because the final scene of the play is again, for the fourth time, Bolingbroke enthroned as king and judge. The picture including its central figure is now quite familiar, so that despite its wide focus the audience may give particular attention to small points of difference, or imprecision. York, Northumberland and Fitzwater bring news that his enemies are defeated and slain; only the Bishop of Carlisle is brought a prisoner before him, and he — strangely perhaps — is pardoned because Bolingbroke has seen 'sparks of honor' in this implacable enemy. Then there follows another, more impressive entry into the royal presence: Sir Pierce of Exton with Richard's body in a coffin. At least four men are needed to bear this burden on to the stage, and they must move more slowly and ceremonially than the eager messengers who have preceded them. Bolingbroke does not speak, but as the coffin is deliberately placed before him, Exton announces:

> Great King, within this coffin I present
> Thy buried fear.

The answer is:

> Exton, I thank thee not; for thou hast wrought
> A deed of slander with thy fatal hand
> Upon my head and all this famous land
> ... Though I did wish him dead,
> I hate the murderer, love him murdered.
> The guilt of conscience take thou for thy labor,
> But neither my good word nor princely favor;
> With Cain go wander thorough shades of night,
> And never show thy head by day nor light.

He turns from Exton, to address his silent, watching noblemen:

> Lords, I protest my soul is full of woe
> That blood should sprinkle me to make me grow.

And the play ends with self-assumed penance:

> Come, mourn with me for what I do lament,
> And put on sullen black incontinent:
> I'll make a voyage to the Holy Land,
> To wash this blood off from my guilty hand.

A reader of the play might claim that Bolingbroke's last words expressing guilt are prompted by his practiced political intelligence: to dash Exton's hopes, or to announce new business to employ the energies of fractious nobles (following such counsel as, in *Henry IV*, Shakespeare was to put in Bolingbroke's own mouth). But in performance such interpretations are not fully satisfying, for the picture, the visual impression, qualifies and in this example re-inforces the words. On the crowded stage all are silent and intent upon their king, so that if he attempted dissimulation he would scarcely be content with the continued silence which is the only response to his words (compare Prince John and the Lord Chief Justice talking together after Henry V has made a similar announcement of foreign wars at the end of *II Henry IV*). Moreover this moral note has been heard before where it could serve no political purpose: as Bolingbroke prayed for Mowbray, as he spoke of his son's irresponsibility hanging like a plague over him, and perhaps as he pardoned Aumerle 'as God shall pardon me', and as he pardoned the Bishop of Carlisle. Possibly Bolingbroke's silence when he heard his subjects accuse each other of treason and when he heard the Bishop denounce his assumption of the throne, should be viewed as earlier attempts to conceal a subtextual guilt. These moments passed quickly and without emphasis, but the repetition of the picture of a king crowned and surrounded by his nobles directs the audience attention progressively upon variations and movement: slight tensions beneath formal poses can thus become impressive.

As at the end of a sonnet, the last line can send the reader back to the first, till the experience which the sonnet gives is viewed whole and complete, contained and understood, so at the end of this tragedy, the audience's visual sense will retravel to its beginning, to a group of ambitious, striving, related and insecure human-beings. To ensure this response the awakening of a new Richard in his death-scene has been presented so briefly; Bolingbroke has been held un-communicative within the wide picture of the drama while the intense focus was directed more and more upon Richard; and the early scenes were allowed no single dominant interest. Instead of concentrating the drama upon a hero's story, Shakespeare has presented a man in isolation and defeat who overcomes fear and learns to recognize guilt, responsibility and courage in himself; and has off-set this with a man who knows little of fear and recognizes guilt only when he assumes the responsibility he has continually sought. The last scene presents Bolingbroke in a new way, verbally: and Richard is there in his coffin, eloquent of his own story, visually.

Both Bolingbroke's and Richard's last words are about their souls, and of Heaven or the Holy Land; and this also completes a series of scenes, still moments when an isolated figure appeals to a state of being outside the world of the stage. In the second scene, the Duchess of Gloucester is told to 'complain' to 'God, the widow's champion and defense', and this resource is again invoked by the unexpected report of the banished Mowbray fighting in the crusades, by York reminding the distressed Queen that 'Comfort's in heaven, and we are on the earth', and his warning to Bolingbroke:

> Take not, good cousin, further than you should,
> Lest you mistake. The heavens are over our heads.

The last scene, in a moment of piety, lightly draws these moments together too.

The surest and most comprehensive effects of the conclusion are carried by the stage picture: viewing the wide picture the audience may see deeply into the characters and the society portrayed, and even into a timeless perspective associated with traditional religion. This visual and formal language is not so precise as words, but it can affect the audience subtly and without its conscious knowledge; it can suggest vast implications and sensitive psychological reactions; it can awaken a response without limiting it by definition, declaration or propaganda.

TEN

Setting, Grouping, Movement and Tempo: Hamlet

No Elizabethan would have thought of constructing a series of stage sets to imitate or suggest the appropriate locale and mood for each scene. Nevertheless, the setting for a Shakespeare play was important then as now. Perhaps the main difference was that Elizabethan actors could never forget it, never construct an ingenious piece of scenery and then perform in front of it with no further regard for its mood or form. Setting and acting were necessarily in accord, because the most common means of changing the stage-picture were the actors' costumes, properties, bearing and behavior. In addition, there were a few larger properties and sound effects that could be used, and music. But actors, by their very presence, could completely change the picture, its mood, line, color, form. Many effects were obviously beyond them — the suggestion of a particular house or a particular landscape — but we should not underestimate the range or effectiveness of their method of setting a play.

Consider the change from an interior to the open air. Fine clothes would be cloaked as for a journey, or light clothes exchanged for more durable ones. Distances would seem to be greater, as the actors call instead of speak, or crowd together to hear a confidence that could be exchanged at ease within doors. In the open they would perhaps look farther off, and leave the stage with a greater sense of resolution and purpose. If this change took place during winter or at night, all these effects would be greatly accentuated; the relaxed behavior of a sheltered interior would contrast with the quick movements and huddled forms appropriate to the cold air, the apparent openness of a well-lit interior with difficult recognitions in the dark. The fact that snow was not represented on the stage, nor darkness, great height or distance, would serve only to accentuate the means whereby the 'scene' was suggested: long, heavy and dull-colored cloaks, close groupings, the alternating stillness and rapidity, whispers, sudden calls. Some changes of setting were even more impressive: from a court scene with costly, crowded costumes and formal groupings to the low-pitched colors and relaxation of servants' quarters, or the countryside; from a public room to a private, from a domestic scene to a military, or to a religious. These are some of the settings which Shakespeare used in Hamlet and which any staging of the play should try to represent, no matter how complicated or simple the scenery may be.

To consider these changes in due order is to view an element of the play which Shakespeare controlled with care:

> It begins high up in the open during a bitterly cold night, with only a few cloaked figures and a silent, questing ghost: and the ghost alone does not feel the cold nor, until the end, move with any neglect of formal majesty.
>
> Then, with a great and unheralded change, there is a crowded interior, ample in words and gesture, formal and colorful for a royal celebration. Soon the stage almost empties, but remains an interior until a return to the battlements, night and the ghost.
>
> Then it is the court again, and will remain so for more than two consecutive Acts. But now there is less formality and much coming and going, hearing and overhearing; and Hamlet is for a time alone, and for at least a few moments, silent and defeated. Within the interior, the action moves forward but the stage twice empties completely, once after Hamlet's new resolve to watch the King, and once after Claudius' to watch Hamlet; and then it fills steadily towards a second formal scene, the crowded play-scene. This time there is a double formality, that of Elsinore and that of the play within the play. It ends suddenly in disorder and, as lights are called for off-stage, with a new impression of darkness, the more alert for being indoors where entrances can be made in an instant. Short, broken episodes follow, still in the interior and at night, with one long emotional scene played intimately as in the Queen's private chamber; and there the ghost reappears to be seen only by Hamlet. It is still night when, after a brief pursuit, Hamlet appears guarded before Claudius, and is ordered to leave the court under escort.
>
> Then, after this long sequence in the interior, the stage is again the open air, the change accentuated by the introduction of the new marching figures of Fortinbras and his army; they belong to a different nation, as well as introducing a full military setting. Just as they are going, Hamlet enters attended and dressed for travel. He is soon alone again but now as if in a vast stretch of open country; and then he walks off-stage.
>
> The release to the wider, relaxed setting was brief, for at once the scene returns to an interior for further action at court. But Hamlet is no longer there, and no more than three or four people are on the stage at any one time; and they repeatedly move apart from each other. A wider setting is, however, suggested by the

freedom of Ophelia's madness which disregards court and domestic proprieties, by the entry of a sailor and, most strongly, by the noise and shouts of an angry crowd twice heard off-stage when Laertes returns from France.

Then there is a fourth move to the open, for the gravedigger, Hamlet's return to Denmark and the funeral of Ophelia. This ceremony, with procession, bell and priest, is the only elaborate religious setting in the play, but in the presence of the mourning King and Queen it echoes the formalities of Elsinore. And, like the large court scenes, this also breaks into disorder as Hamlet and Laertes have to be parted from each other by force. Then the stage rapidly empties.

The scene is once more the interior with Hamlet and Horatio alone, and twice visited by single messengers. The stage fills for the duel, and this new formality, with the King and Queen enthroned, leads, like the previous two, to an uproar; but this time the disorder leads not to hurried partings and an empty stage, but to the stillness and quietness of death. At once drums are heard in the distance and Fortinbras enters the scene, its splendor now in ruin at his feet. He is attended by his soldiers and dressed as for his earlier appearance outside Elsinore in the country, and he is accompanied by the English Ambassadors, entirely new figures who also come as from a journey. This entry from the world outside effects a last formality, so that in procession the bodies of Hamlet, the King, the Queen and Laertes are taken out of sight, borne aloft to be placed 'high on a stage' in view of the 'yet unknowing world'.

If we borrow terms from the criticism of the visual arts, we may say of the changing impression of the 'scene' that the stage-picture is alternately an 'open' and a 'closed' composition: sometimes it is a self-contained whole, bounded by apparent limits; at other times it is limitless and flowing, suggesting continuations beyond the bounds of the stage. And in these changes, the picture is eloquent: the court is a prison from which escape can be made, an established pattern that is broken, an arrangement, with a clear center and interdependent elements, which gives place to one isolated figure within its emptied frame, and later to disorder and forced actions at night, and finally to carnage and a new central authority. Or in its open form, with distant views obscured at first by darkness, it is a place free for visitations and for movement.

This contrast between open and closed compositions was accentuated by the form of Elizabethan playhouses — a fact that performances in an auditorium of the same shape and size will quickly reveal. If an actor stood close to the tiring-house façade he was viewed by all the audience in relation to an architectural background with regular, centralized form and decoration: this would give a closed dramatic composition. (See Figures 2 and 3.)

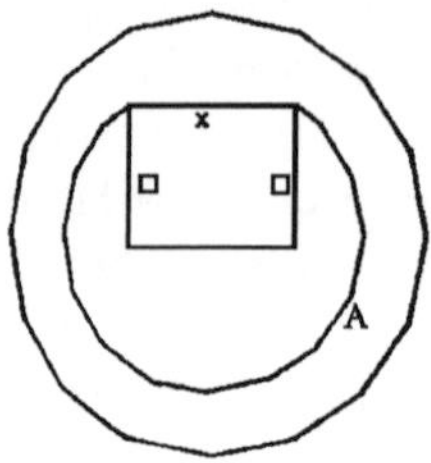

Figure 2.

Figure 3.

But if he stood near the outermost edge of the platform-stage a large portion of the audience, including those in the most expensive seats, would see no background to his figure except the anonymous audience at the other side of the theatre, backed by the continuous, horizontal lines of the galleries in which they sat or stood: this would give an open dramatic composition. (See Figures 4 and 5.)

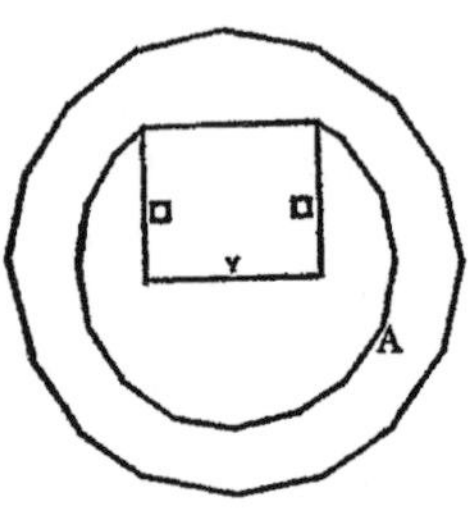

Figure 4.

Figure 5.

These two extremes were modified in many ways, particularly when a crowd of actors or, perhaps, large properties were introduced to remove the sense of isolation natural to the extreme forward edge of the stage; but the eloquent contrast between them is the reason why so many Elizabethan plays, besides *Hamlet*, involve an alternation between interiors and open country so frequently and so confidently. *Macbeth* and *King Lear* offer clear examples of its use.

The *dramatis personae* are meaningful as soon as they appear in these varied settings, before they have spoken a single word. Hamlet himself starts with a long silence in a formal set scene, watched and watching; he is drawn into the pattern and then moves apart and is left alone; he leaves on talk of the ghost, and subsequently waits for the ghost on the battlements, and then follows it; returning to the interior, he plans his own formal scene and then in darkness and rapid movement seeks his mother; he is pursued and escapes to the open; he is absent from the court to return, at first unrecognized, for the funeral; then after some preparation he takes another formal position stripping himself of his doublet and signs of rank for the duel; in the last rapid and extended disorder he assumes control and dies in silence; and then his body is honored as it is carried off-stage.

Or, for example, Laertes: dutifully taking his time and place in the formal picture and then dressed and ready for a journey from court; returning to an emptier court with an insurgent, disordered crowd off-stage; the King and Queen following him outside in mourning; taking part in the duel and helplessly dying in the final static picture.

Or, Claudius and Gertrude: leaving Elsinore only for the funeral. Or, Ophelia: moving circumspectly, until she is the only person to act within the court as if she were anywhere, or nowhere, free from all restraint. Or Horatio who goes to the court from the battlements, who greets the sailor and then appears at the graveyard: never at the center of a formal grouping until at the end when he is with the dying Hamlet.

The story, or sequence of events, also gains relevance from the settings. This is chiefly effected by the device of repetition, so that each return to Elsinore catches reflections of its earlier manifestations and is given significance by them. The last formal grouping for instance, contains memories of earlier ones: the first when Claudius expressed his purposes unopposed, until disturbed by the black figure of Hamlet; the second when the court watched an acted intimacy and then an acted murder; the third when the court honored Ophelia's corpse; the fourth which is to witness a duel.[1] 'Atmospheric' effects are repeated too: the impression of darkness in Elsinore after the Play Scene recalls that of the battlements, so that the ghost's return may be almost expected. Such repetitions also tie the various elements of the action together and, in the last scene, give a clear sense of completion, a strength very necessary for such an episodic narrative with ambiguous characterization and almost continual verbal elaboration. When Hamlet finally controls the disordered formality the audience will sense through the setting that a new pattern has been established from the old: the very thrones used in the first scene are now empty, probably in the same place, and the same courtiers are merely 'mutes and audience' to a frightening act. This may be the most powerful impression of the last scene, for it is visual and, therefore, rapid, complete and unquestioned. And, when Fortinbras and the Ambassador enter from without and in foreign costumes, the audience will know that Elsinore is no longer a restricted and threatened enclosure; the scene is open, if not freed.

The changing setting is a valuable means of expressing story, themes and characters, and of giving coherence to many elements. Its impressions are conveyed visually, by objects and behavior, and affect an audience without it realizing what is happening, and swiftly and largely; in performance they can carry and shape the play.

*

For all its broad effectiveness, the setting contributes to the subtlety of the play in performance, by the interaction of closed and open stage-pictures, and by repetitions. And subtleties, together with robust eloquence, are also communicated by the movement of the figures within the scene.

Here, the most unquestioned effect is the dominance and unusual independence of the hero. Sir Tyrone Guthrie has said that:

> *Hamlet*, oddly enough, is a play which can be rehearsed very quickly.... If the producer and the actor who plays Hamlet are well prepared and in full agreement, the production can, in my opinion, be put together in two weeks. The reason for this is that none of Hamlet's scenes demand a very close *rapport* between the participants. Most of the psychological material is conveyed in soliloquy; to a unique degree the *rapport* is not between actor and actor, but between Hamlet and the audience.[2]

Hamlet is alone for his soliloquies of course, and throughout the play he voices thoughts which are almost soliloquies within the dialogue; he first speaks in an aside; he watches and is watched. He repeatedly moves apart from the other figures and they must 'seek my Lord Hamlet': the ghost, Horatio and the soldiers, Rosencrantz and Guildenstern, Polonius, the 'tragedians of the city', Claudius, Laertes, Osric and the second messenger who follows him—all these, on separate occasions, seek out Hamlet, and force an encounter. Once Claudius and Gertrude avoid an encounter with him, but Ophelia is 'loosed' to him and later his 'mother stays' for him. Hamlet does not need to seek others, but Horatio, the actors, the musicians and the Norwegian Captain come when he calls. Only the gravedigger, the memory of Yorick and Ophelia's funeral procession are encountered by Hamlet without being summoned or seeming to wait for him.

Many scenes conclude with movements directing attention towards Hamlet: the stage first empties so that Horatio may seek him and, despite many new characters and interests, it does not empty again until Hamlet is shown alone preparing to see his father's spirit. Every one of his exits arouses strong expectation for his subsequent action: he has to follow the ghost, return to court with a new and compelling duty, prepare *The Mousetrap*, fight apparent madness, confront his mother, the King, treacherous friends, his own apparent lack of resolution. In the last scene but one, after a general climax, he walks off-stage before its conclusion; but here he goes in defiance and afterwards there is a marked hiatus in dramatic development in which Claudius briefly reorganizes the stage-picture before a general exeunt. Even on this occasion, when he leaves the stage for no expressed purpose, the groupings are disturbed and rapidly displaced

Hamlet dominates so obviously that the figures among whom he appears can be underestimated, not least by those who have to produce and perform the play without sufficient time or patience to discover the qualities inherent in the text. This hero Shakespeare has placed among characters who are subtly strong, and subtly related to each other. And this achievement is not fully revealed until the play is allowed to grow and establish itself in production on the stage. First, there is a concerted effect, the impression of Elsinore as a dangerous and involved society. In both court and family, sudden arrivals are discovered to be foreknown; even casual re-entries are often expected. Other figures, besides Hamlet, are watched or shadowed — Ophelia, Laertes, the players, Claudius, Gertrude. Public occasions and general celebrations have private implications; what seems leisurely is truly hurried, and sudden orders have been long deliberated. At the very beginning, a spirit visits Elsinore who is unconfined by darkness and bitter cold, and who fades on the 'crowing of the cock' and the tender light of matin. And throughout the play there are moments, without movement, when characters remember 'our Saviour's birth', 'the burning eyes of heaven' or 'heavenly powers'; when Claudius begs help of 'angels'. The figures on stage move carefully, with hidden urgency or reluctance, with an awareness of each other and of another, spiritual reality.

Secondly, the strength of individual movement or gestures cannot be judged from the text alone; their eloquence is often achieved without words or where words seem unimportant. Here indeed is their unique contribution, for movements speak in association with words to represent reactions which are consciously hidden or beyond the conscious grasp of the characters. This may be seen in Claudius and Gertrude.

Their first appearance together with a public celebration of marriage is a large and simple visual effect, and Gertrude's close concern for her son suggests a simple, and perhaps unremarkable modification. The only movement which is obviously strange here is the speed with which Claudius leads her off to celebrate a reconciliation with Hamlet and at the same time leaves him, apparently unnoticed, behind. From this point until after the Play Scene, Claudius and Gertrude always enter together, and remain together except when the King wishes to spy on Hamlet. Their movements seem to represent a comparatively singleminded relationship. But Claudius enters without Gertrude for his 'Prayer Scene' (III.3) and, for the first time, Gertrude enters without him for the Closet Scene (III.4) and is left alone, again for the first time, when Polonius hides behind the arras. Thereafter earlier accord is revalued by an increasing separation, often poignantly silent, and unexpected. When Claudius calls Gertrude to leave with him after Hamlet has dragged off Polonius' body, she makes no reply; twice more he urges her and she is still silent. But he does not remonstrate or question; rather he speaks of his own immediate concerns and, far from supporting her with assurances, becomes more aware of his own fears:

> O, come away!
> My soul is full of discord and dismay.
>
> IV.1.44-5

Emotion has been so heightened that it is remarkable that they leave together without further words. The audience has been made aware of a new distance between Gertrude and Claudius, of her immobility and silence, and of his self-concern, haste and insistence.

From this moment onwards their movements on leaving the stage become increasingly eloquent. When Claudius has set a watch on Ophelia, he appeals to Gertrude for sympathy, telling what he can of the dangers that threaten; but she says nothing and, if Claudius pauses, she will draw attention away from him to her physical withdrawal. When Laertes enters, supported by insurgents, Gertrude instinctively tries to hold him back and protect Claudius; but he, in contrast, faces

Laertes' sword, assumes command, and after curt assurances, forgets his Queen in immediate concerns. At the end of the scene, after Ophelia's second appearance, Gertrude has to leave the stage without a word from Claudius or to him. Danger had brought them together for a moment, but the spectacle of Ophelia's suffering separates them further than before: this is the first time that the Queen must leave entirely alone. The visual point will not be lost in performance, for as the King moves with urgent purpose, she will leave slowly with silent grief and helplessness; there will be a contrast of tempo, and quite simply, her exit will take much longer to complete, so that she must be seen alone on the empty stage. (An actress will be tempted to wait and then make a separate exit expressing her own unappeased grief.)

When Claudius returns with Laertes, he momentarily departs from duologue for a kind of soliloquy:

> Not that I think you did not love your father;
> But that I know love is begun by time,
> And that I see, in passages of proof,
> Time qualifies the spark and fire of it.
> *There lives within the very flame of love*
> *A kind of wick or snuff that will abate it;*
> *And nothing is at a like goodness still...*
>
> IV.7.110-14

His new isolation from Gertrude supplies a motive for this digression from immediate and dangerous concerns; and will strengthen its effect. If Claudius moves apart, or merely breaks his contact with Laertes, the stage picture will lose definite focus with the absence of explicit motive, and the audience's sense of time, relevance and perspective may become insecure. It may hear echoes of the Player King:

> What to ourselves in passion we propose,
> The passion ending, doth the purpose lose....
> This world is not for aye; nor 'tis not strange
> That even our loves should with our fortunes change....
>
> III.2.189-97.

and even of the ghost himself:

> O Hamlet, what a falling off was there,
> ... to decline

> Upon a wretch whose natural gifts were poor
> To those of mine!
>
> I.5.47-52

These are refinements which may not be realized in performance, but because of the movements of the figures in the later passages of the play, Claudius can at least seem far removed from the immediate context of persuading Laertes, and appear to consider, momentarily, his new isolation. The audience will note an effort as he recalls himself with 'But, to the quick of the ulcer', and once more seeks 'desperate appliance'.

Nothing stops the physical and emotional separation of King and Queen and some movements express it more sharply. After Gertrude has told of Ophelia's death, Laertes leaves precipitously and it is of him that Claudius is thinking as he follows, not at all of Gertrude still rapt in her evocation of Ophelia's death, and her helpless admission of 'Drown'd, drown'd'. When Hamlet has left the graveyard, Gertrude is ordered in a single line to 'set some watch over her son;' now Claudius can easily dismiss her and be free to ensure an immediate attempt on Hamlet's life and take a kind of pleasure in the prospect. At no time has Shakespeare caused either of them to comment directly on their progressive separation, yet the audience's awareness of it develops; and so strongly can this be fostered in performance that it may seem at last that, in failing either to speak or to make a complete break, these characters are unable to understand all that is happening, and powerless to help themselves. The audience is encouraged to observe more deeply than either of the *dramatis personae*. Their dying cries gain ironic force and clarity from this long preparation: Gertrude calls on her 'dear' son and implicates her husband in murder; Claudius, with 'O yet defend me, friends; I am but hurt', appeals for a response he has never considered and tries a desperate lie. The audience may sense, without further information, that these few words express what has been progressively implied by movement and gesture, and that the subsequent immobility of death marks a true termination.

Shakespeare has ensured that the audience of *Hamlet* views its characters in depth. Yet this metaphor is hardly adequate; for what he has added to the stage picture is a fourth, or psychological dimension in which the hidden and subconscious reactions of each character can be presented, by movement as well as words.

Although movement should be viewed in its large impressions, its components can be identified most readily by following individual figures through the play. By making Rosencrantz and Guildenstern move together at Claudius' command, Shakespeare ensured that their minds seem mechanical and undistinguished: so much so, that theatre directors often assume that the two characters are indistinguishable.[3] Their unspoken thoughts are first clearly indicated after Hamlet's direct questions, when their mutual silence and then the whispered 'What say you?' draw close attention to their instinctive need to keep together. Their eagerness to play safe is also manifested when Hamlet dismisses them with brief courtesy on three successive occasions, for, as they murmur quick civilities, bow or exchange looks, the audience will see an unspoken embarrassment and, as they go out, a drawing together. When Claudius calls Guildenstern after the Closet Scene, *both* of them enter at once, silently. Guildenstern has the smarter mind, smoothing over awkward moments and being quick to question, with 'Prison, my lord?... In what, my dear lord?... A thing my lord?', and yet when action is needed for pursuing and guarding Hamlet it is Rosencrantz who assumes the lead without discussion. They at last drop all pretense of friendship and appear with the 'guard' as Hamlet's captors and warders: they leave that scene at one with the silent soldiers who move impersonally, under orders. Their natures are progressively revealed, one brusque and one watchful; and the consequences of having become the tools of Claudius are progressively manifested, without their choice or knowledge.

The audience's view of Horatio changes less, but deepens in the same way and widens. In the first scene, although he 'trembles and looks pale', he holds back his judgement until he can speak in an ordered way:

> Before my God, I might not this believe
> Without the sensible and true avouch
> Of mine own eyes.
>
> I.1.56-8

And in the course of the play he has no sudden movement or impulse, or immediacy of speech, to draw attention to him. Yet he is often on stage silent and watchful, and ready with a brief reply when such is required by Hamlet. Before the Play Scene, he enters with an unassertive promptness when Hamlet calls. Perhaps the audience's view of him is more ambiguous when he proves unable to keep 'good watch' over Ophelia; but this is not made an issue in the dialogue nor emphasized by a return to the stage. It could be sensed only as an unspecified uneasiness, and it would not prevent 'Now cracks a noble heart. Good night, sweet prince…' from sounding with a steady, deeply felt assurance. It is for such moments that his static and always unembarrassed physical presentation was chosen. This figure has been made remarkable and strong by the lack of movement and by silent attentiveness, as well as by brief speeches.

The comic aspects of Polonius' speech and behavior ensure that the audience views him with a measure of detachment; yet Shakespeare has also presented him as an isolated figure and this can draw sympathy. After *The Mousetrap* has manifested something like the full danger of the situation, Polonius comes to Claudius and his busy insistence on his original plan for trapping Hamlet is neither welcomed nor heeded by his master whose thoughts are elsewhere; the eager Polonius must pause and then leave without any response commensurate with his purposes. His urgency to Gertrude meets with an almost equally slack response, as though she too has other thoughts than his. By contrasts of movement and tempo the audience will view Polonius less simply than at first: after it has been shocked by disregard for his daughter's feelings and, perhaps, has laughed at misplaced confidence in his own intelligence and petty cunning, it may recognize in hurried, surreptitious, isolated movements the limitations of a self-centered mind; there may be a quickening of sympathy for his blindness and clumsiness. His death, as he fusses helplessly in the toils of an arras, seems an unalterable conclusion.

On his return to the play in Act IV, Laertes is an important contrast with Hamlet, not only in his reckless and outspoken attitude to revenge, but also in the way that his independent action yields to movements alongside Claudius, even at his sister's funeral and between the bouts of the duel. Ophelia, on the other hand, has an effective isolation. She is presented as of key importance to Hamlet, but is not shown with him until she stands as a speechless decoy during the 'To be, or not to be' soliloquy. When she has to make a decision, her brief speeches — 'no more but so?... I shall obey, my lord... My lord, I do not know... No, my lord.... Ay, my lord... I think nothing, my lord' — cannot answer the audience's curiosity: she might evade or misrepresent; she may seem to have considered deeply, or to live only for the moment, lightly. The audience will intently view her young, untried body for some further sign: her silences and brevity of speech, contrasting with the volubility of her brother and father, and her passive waiting for Hamlet to 'affront' her, ensure that, if she speaks her lines with the studied care that their versification, syntax and vocabulary seem to suggest, she will appear to have a painfully private, uncommunicable consciousness.

When she exposes herself to Hamlet's scorn ('you made me believe so.... I was the more deceived') and then lies to him about her father, a strong hidden conflict of sensations will be keenly felt. She sits at *The Mousetrap* taunted by Hamlet and then trying to enter the world of the play he has prepared; but he does not notice her departure and probably the audience does not either. She returns for the two mad-scenes in which both words and movements express her helpless thoughts at last, in all their range: sexual, pitiful and wilful. But her isolation is greater than before, for no one can contact her or restrain her, not even Laertes. Without her actual presence, her influence upon the play continues as Gertrude reports she died making a wreath for the dead, supported and then lost in flowing water. The movements of this slight figure express the limits of her being and so add to the impression of the effects of time and accident in the play. Most characters move towards a single-minded utterance and gesture, but the spirit of the young and beautiful Ophelia is expended wastefully, and, until she has become a corpse, she is out of reach of others.

Hamlet is often seen as a hero who through uncertainty seeks to 'end his part in peace' like a perfect actor, with his cause 'rightly' known, to accept his role of 'scourge and minister', to be 'ready' for his 'end' and accept heaven's 'ordinance' in its timing and planning. But he does all this in a world which is also progressively revealed and progressively caught by processes which are not controlled by the characters' conscious thought. Hamlet's passage through the play differs most significantly in his attempt to understand this process; he has not won a 'special providence' for his particular cause but, rather, a thoughtful and difficult concern about that providence. While his courage, affection and deliberation, his anger, pain and despair for the 'harsh world' are all revealed, the other characters move with equal certainty towards an unwilled revelation of their deepest natures. The end of *Hamlet* is the end of a world, of Elsinore as well as its prince. It is a general doom, like the last scene of *Lear*; perhaps more thoroughly, for the dead bodies must be removed by foreign captains at the command of a foreign inheritor.

The staging of the last episodes can illustrate how individual and group movements are coordinated. Obviously, careful direction is required merely to keep the picture changing in this crowded scene. The King and Queen must enter together, with spectators and assistants for the duel; Laertes must choose the poisoned rapier so that the audience may see, but not Hamlet; a cup must be taken to Hamlet, and 'set aside'; Gertrude must be able to cross to Hamlet, give him a napkin, drink from his cup and wipe his brow, and the cup must again be put aside so that it is not spilt in the uproar that is soon to follow, and can be found quickly by the wounded Hamlet; Laertes must be able to speak aside to Claudius and then, on his return to the combat, to himself; the duel must become an 'incensed' fight; Gertrude must swoon and be attended out of reach of Claudius; Hamlet must be able, rapidly, to take command of the whole scene, order doors to be locked, kill Claudius with his rapier, reach for the cup, force him to drink from it, and put it down again so that Horatio may find it later, still with some wine in it; many voices must shout 'Treason', yet Claudius must be helpless during Laertes' eight lines of explanation. In all this, movement and positioning must be clearly fixed, or 'shaped', by the stage-director during rehearsals, so that 'rashness' and 'indiscretion' as well as considered 'plots' all work together on the crowded stage towards a certain end. The actors could not perform the scene, simulating the various passions called for by the text, without this hidden control and co-ordination. But after Hamlet's duologue with Horatio:

> There's a special providence in the fall of a sparrow. If it be now, 'tis not to come; if it be not to come, it will be now; if it be not now, yet it will come — the readiness is all ...
>
> V.2.211-13

we may judge that Shakespeare knew this, and calculated upon its effect. The complicated difficulties of stage-direction will mean that a plan can be sensed behind the most hurried and unconsidered movements; and this, in turn, adds to the impression in performance of fate or 'divinity' controlling the interrelated movements of the characters, an inevitability something like that of the last stage in a game of chess, without any speech to direct attention to it. The attentive presence of Horatio and the precisely timed entry of Fortinbras are further movements which place Hamlet, Elsinore, Denmark and the world outside in a theatrical reality with a large and sweeping impression of men motivated from deep within themselves and drawn to their final positions by an unseen, unheard control or providence: a reality that reveals at last men's inward truth, through the operation of accident and intention, falsehood and truth, villainy and virtue.

*

The effectiveness of the changing stage picture is partly controlled by variations of tempo which are caused by both speech and movement. Anyone who has acted or directed a play will know that a change of tempo can affect mood, clarity, size, force and even meaning and character, and that an acceptable, workable tempo is often the most elusive element in a production, the one that must wait for the latest rehearsal for proper adjustment. Associated with tempo is rhythm, and both are at once general to each scene, Act, and play, and particular to each incident and character. A single character may have one timing for his outward behavior and another for his inward thoughts and feelings. Stanislavski felt the need for a conductor to give the beat to actors during a performance as if they were a complicated kind of orchestra. For some acting exercises he introduced numerous metronomes, all ticking at different but related speeds. He relegated these matters to the end of his course of instruction, because of their importance and their difficulty.[4]

Tempo is, then, a continual concern of all responsible for a performance and is capable, at all times, of affecting the audience's reaction. But to consider its large effects that present the play forcibly to an audience, the striking contrasts, which are frequent in *Hamlet*, are the most important features.

The slowest tempos are in reflective passages, where feeling and thought are not immediately expressed in purposeful action. Among these are parts of the longer soliloquies, the disquisition on a 'sterile promontory' and 'brave o'erhanging firmament', the instructions to the players and the following talk of a man that 'is not passion's slave'. All these passages are centered on Hamlet himself and while he is absent from the stage only Gertrude's account of Ophelia's death, evoking a regard for suffering and helplessness, has anything like the same restrained tempo, or rhythms so unresponsive to other influences, so completely dictated by the speaker alone. Later there are passages between Hamlet and the gravedigger, allowing the prince to consider the 'noble dust' of an emperor with a curiosity which looks before and after the dramatic event. These moments sustain a slow tempo, but with them should be linked others in which this co-exists with a more urgent tempo beneath words or outward behavior: in such passages the state of Denmark is considered deliberately while waiting for the ghost, or the formalities of Elsinore, the dumb-show, the funeral procession and preparations for the duel are presented as a cover to thoughts and inclinations which are more alert. Their main effect is the same: to encourage the audience to deliberate with Hamlet in preparation for some new action; often they ensure that the audience is precisely and carefully involved with him immediately before some of the most rapid passages of the play.

Rapid tempo, as far as Hamlet is concerned, usually comes with action after some new understanding has been, far more slowly, achieved: such are his 'wild and whirling words', his strange jests and behavior to his friends after seeing the ghost, the 'rogue and peasant slave' soliloquy as soon as he is alone after the player has wept for a 'mobled queen', his elation after *The Mousetrap* has caught the conscience of the King, his conflict with Laertes at Ophelia's grave in which he 'forgets himself' and reveals 'something... that is dangerous' from deep within (V.1.256). There are a few brief passages of swift words and action when Claudius or his servants move with 'deliberate' suddenness (V.3.8-9), but, as a slow tempo was mainly used to show Hamlet's deliberations, so a rapid tempo shows the flame, or as one might say 'the whirlwind' (III.2.7-8), of Hamlet's passion. It marks his instinctive and emotional reactions: first to his mother's marriage and Claudius' succession, then to his father, his mother, Ophelia, and, in his rapid jesting when Claudius pursues him after the killing of Polonius, to danger and gathering opposition. Slow tempo for Hamlet's deliberate involvement with himself and an ideal world; rapid for his instinctive and passionate response to the world around him: so tempo impresses an important polarity within Hamlet and within the play.

This is a simplification, a first view of the extremes. In performance large impressions may also derive from a device which brings strong and contrasting tempos into obvious conflict. This is used mainly for the presentation of Hamlet's response to women, Ophelia and Gertrude. Other stage-techniques like the exceptional use of a sustained and simple slow tempo for the account of her death, suggest that Shakespeare was more concerned with the presentation of Ophelia than her words alone can imply, and the conflicts of tempo in Hamlet's main scene with her support this. First, the encounter is delayed until Act III, so that the audience is particularly attentive. In soliloquy Hamlet has considered 'enterprises of great pith and moment', but seeing Ophelia he is drawn away, simply and immediately. She acts an anonymous courtesy, and he gives a similar stumbling performance:

OPHELIA: Good my lord,
How does your honor for this many a day?
HAMLET: I humbly thank you; well,...

There is no need to suppose that Hamlet knows that Polonius and Claudius are overhearing because the tempo of this meeting is both slow *and* watchful: as he is drawn towards her, they both deceive each other, or try to do so; and, searching her eyes with 'are you honest?... Are you fair?', Hamlet could sense the prevarications. From this intimacy he is stung to abuse her, himself, man, woman: he loved her, and then, rapidly, he loved her not; she is fair and honest to him, yet she is no longer so; this is and is not Ophelia. His mother had left 'Hyperion' for a 'satyr' and now Ophelia becomes associated in his imagination with this betrayal; and now he is passionate in rapid denunciation. The suddenly direct 'Where's your father?' probably brings a break in the action and then comes Ophelia's lie: 'At home, my lord'. But even in his mounting anger there is conflict: as he attacks her, he leaves her; as he abuses her as whore and enemy, he repeats the one escape he can offer and, probably, again holds back to scrutinize her face:

> Get thee to a nunnery. Why wouldst thou be a breeder of sinners?

In the whirlwind of abuse he impulsively repeats 'To a nunnery, go' five times, until he rushes from the stage: in the new rapid tempo, a more deliberate, lingering reaction, the slower one of care or irony — whichever way the actor takes these words they will be slower — is still maintained as a rock among currents, an under-surface tempo emphasized by its rhythmic repetition. The existence of this stillness within the tempest is proved on Hamlet's exit, for as Claudius and Polonius hold back, Ophelia is able to speak her controlled and elaborate regret for the 'courtier's, soldier's, scholar's eye, tongue, sword; The expectancy and rose of the fair state', in a following calm.

The Closet Scene, between Hamlet and his mother, has something like the same handling of tempo and rhythm. From the first passionate interchange which makes Gertrude suppose that he will murder her, its development is strong, but there are at least three moments of contrasting calm: following the death of Polonius, on the ghost's entry and then on Gertrude's response as Hamlet drives his meaning home. At first his compulsive denunciation of his mother's 'compulsive ardour' cannot be halted by her admission of guilt and her calls for 'no more'; but when the ghost has deflected the course of the scene so that he 'temperately' proceeds (l.140) and she forgets her own defense in concern for his apparent madness, then there is a certain calm. Now she can speak slowly and with the impression of a deep-seated truth: 'O Hamlet, thou hast cleft my heart in twain.' This is, indeed, the heart of the scene: assured in his relationship with his mother, Hamlet now looks forward and outward, seeing himself with settled deliberation as heaven's 'scourge and minister' (III.4.175). From this point tempo once more increases; for now he mocks the 'bloat king', his schoolfellows and politicians; he mocks at death too, and 'lugs' Polonius from the room. But in the rising tempo and more savage involvement of the end of this scene, Hamlet retains a contact with its calm center; this is made apparent in his intimate, five-times repeated, 'Good night' to his mother. Like Ophelia, Gertrude remains in the slower tempo. She is left alone and speechless, and when Claudius finds her, she is still rapt in silence. Twice, with Ophelia and with Gertrude, Hamlet's passionate and rapid reactions are held, or harnessed, by a fixed slower response which is also deeply felt and instinctive.

Tempo in the last two scenes indicates a new control. When the memory of Yorick brings a flash of earlier denunciations of women, this is subdued at once. Hamlet cuts short the struggle with Laertes after his mother's final interventions, reasonably asking for understanding; but control is still precarious and Hamlet immediately leaves the stage. The last scene begins with sustained deliberation, easily rising to the rapidity and finesse of the water-fly Osric and then answering his more weighty seconder. Immediately before the court enters for the duel the tempo is slow, but with an inward excitement. Then the duel gives a new mixture of tempos, both alert and slow, and sometimes rapid; timing follows a regular pattern in the formalities and intermissions; it quickens, as one of the combatants makes a thrust, and is held back with their mutual wariness; it is circumscribed by the rules of the art of fencing and also unpredictable in its precise movements and sequences. Speed and forcefulness increase as the fight becomes 'incensed' (l.293); and suddenly, with blood, all is still. Disorder at once follows, with sharp moments of recognition and then Hamlet with passion *and* deliberation is the central, dominating figure; and once more stillness follows, weighty with both pain and consideration. Yet, even now, the action is quickened once more by the steadier, gentler tempo of affection and responsibility, in an interchange between Hamlet and Horatio. Then, from a distance, is heard a soldiers' march and the reverberations of a 'warlike volley'. This is to be the tempo and rhythm of the conclusion: regular and impersonal.

The duel and concluding moments of Hamlet's role provide both stillness and excitement; the extremes of deliberation and passion are expressed, and the quieter impulses of affection and trust; and then there is a new and comprehensive control of tempo.

*

A study of the techniques of stage presentation provides an opportunity for describing the effects of the whole play. We may say, perhaps, that Shakespeare has ensured a threefold reception. First, he has presented man in society and in families and personal relationships. The settings and groupings and movements of the last scene ensure that the audience views every character on the stage, separately and together, judging their responsibilities and fulfilments, and the future of those that remain. Secondly, to a deeper view, there is the completed drama of human consciousness seen in all the characters but in Hamlet preeminently; having followed the hero through the play the audience will hear and see him as a man, not miraculously redeemed or purified, not executing an elaborately prepared revenge or process of justice, not suffering hopelessly, but acting with deliberation and passion, fully known according to his conscious, subconscious and physical being. Thirdly, there is a growing impression of inevitability and complicated control: so the play can be received as a public ritual. The hero, who has made a solitary journey through hardship and across the sea, returns to the single combat, death and acceptance; and, in all, in the final presentation of all the characters according to their inward truth, the heavens seem 'ordinant'.

One of the advantages of the theatrical view is that it can show us how the play is able to be *all* this, in the brief time of its lengthy performance, and how it involves the audience in many ways: a performance of *Hamlet* is an intellectual, sensuous, passionate, instinctive and strong experience.

ELEVEN

Stage Shows

SO far in this book, every chapter has demonstrated that Shakespeare enjoyed working with and for actors. He exploited their talents to the full, and the development of his art depended on the development of theirs. Shakespeare's finest poetry was written for actors to perform; speeches, which a reader can study for days at a time, or skip over, grasping little of their various meanings, they would animate, release, color, express, and make comprehensible, as part of their entire impersonations. Only in performance by a company of skilled actors can the plays be appreciated in appropriate form, full images of life.

But Shakespeare sometimes spoke by other means as well. We have seen already how a coffin is made to represent a dead character at the end of *Richard II* and in the graveyard scene of the last act of *Hamlet*. The same stage property, together with other signs of pomp and circumstance, starts off the play of *Henry VI, Part One*:

> Upon a wooden coffin we attend;
> And death's dishonourable victory
> We with our stately presence glorify,
> Like captives bound to a triumphant car.
>
> I.1.19-22

But Henry V, as represented by the coffin, is not 'so dreadful... as was his sight,' and almost at once the mourners turn into rivals in search of power, breaking up the ordered show which had started the scene and turning their backs on the coffin which, of course, has no power to stop them. Royal pageantry lent itself to visual presentation and Shakespeare grasped this opportunity, as a means of accentuating his characters' various responses to what these signs represent. In the history plays and several of the tragedies, throne, crown, sceptre and other marks of kingship represent potent forces and call for particular responsibilities.

Elizabethan theatre companies held considerable stocks of other large properties — arbors, beds, grassy banks, tombstones, altars, and so forth — and Shakespeare utilized a number of these to set his scenes. Tables, chairs and stools, in variety, were also used to suggest indoor locations and so played their part by representing a change of scene. They also called for distinct kinds of behavior and posture, and for changes of rhythm; to 'sit down', was for Shakespeare a cue for a new engagement, a shift in the dynamics of the action. So Hamlet insists, to his mother:

> Come, come, and sit you down; you shall not budge.
> You go not till I set you up a glass
> Where you may see the inmost part of you.
>
> III.4.18-20

Antony and Octavius are awkward until they decide to sit down together, at the same time; and then they can talk:

> CAESAR: Welcome to Rome.
> ANTONY: Thank you.
> CAESAR: Sit.
> ANTONY: Sit, sir.
> CAESAR: Nay, then. *They sit.*

Perhaps Caesar does sit first; but either way, Antony takes advantage of his yielding to speak in a different style:

> ANTONY: I learn you take things ill which are not so,
> Or being, concern you not....
>
> II.2.28-34

However played, the action of sitting and the physical changes involved alter the characters' involvement with each other.

The theatres of Shakespeare's time had various openings in the structure to the rear of their stages, which could be used to represent a study or some private chamber, or the gates of a city, or a tomb; and in the floor itself a trap door could open up to be a grave, a cellar, or the entrance to hell. The upper level of the structure behind the stage could provide hill-top, castle wall or bedroom window. All these resources Shakespeare used, but perhaps equally important to his mind were the large stocks of small properties which could be handled by actors in many different ways, all expressive of their characters' moment-by-moment involvement in the drama: swords, pikes, flags, fans, ewers, dishes, goblets, rings, chains, purses, coins, masks, skulls, pictures, books, documents. Every play makes very considerable demands on the property department of a theatre because each of them is very specific in its requirements. Costumes too, in great variety, made visual statements, adding to the actors' powers of expression: they showed at once a character's social and political status, and the time and place of the action; and they modified behavior.

These physical elements of stage production we have already considered along with the actors' performances, but there were times, especially in his later years, when Shakespeare gave them special importance, using purely visual means more boldly, in elaborate displays, to create a significantly different image of life. Such stage shows are important in their own right and also as indication of how the staging of other plays might have made visual statements which are not immediately apparent in the printed texts. Sometimes spectacle takes over from the actors.

*

The most spectacular of the plays is *The Tempest* of 1611. Prospero, the magician, or *magus* who has studied the properties of man and nature, is placed in control of the stage so that he seems to be in control of the world around him. At his bidding, without other human intervention, the stage is filled with amazing visual shows which mark the progress of the play's action. The first is a storm at sea, activated by repeated thunder and lightning, roaring winds, and other loud noises, together with some means to ensure that 'Mariners' enter '*wet*'. Dialogue indicates that there may have been much play with rigging, either on stage or just off. Everyone assembled can lurch and turn, as if they were on the deck of a ship in violent tempest, on the point of splitting and sinking. The second show-piece is the presentation of a banquet by '*several strange shapes*' accompanied by '*solemn and strange music*' (III.3.17, S.D.); a dance and '*gentle actions of salutations*' invite the assembled people to eat. This 'show' uses costumes and stage properties to make a 'dumb discourse' (III.3.39). As the audience on stage is about to partake of the food, thunder and lightning intervene, and a harpy — half bird, half woman — appears, claps its wings and, '*with a quaint device, the banquet vanishes.*' The amazed on-stage audience is then addressed, and convicted of the sin of driving Prospero from his dukedom; to enforce the message, drawn swords are rendered harmless by a spell. More thunder accompanies the harpy's disappearance and then the '*shapes*' re-enter, '*with mocks and mows*' to remove the table. Prospero has been watching, from '*above*', and applauds his spirits for the show — 'a grace it had, devouring': he believes that his enemies 'now are in my power'(ll.83-90). A silent spectacle and single speech have accomplished all that he had wished, commanding attention and awakening the intended reactions.

Very shortly afterwards, Prospero is in charge again as his spirits present yet another show, this time an elaborate entertainment with three goddesses who 'enact [his] present fancies'(IV.1.120-1). When nymphs and reapers join together in a dance celebrating the wealth of nature at harmony within itself, it provides an image of a perfect world. All is sweetness and light, fit offering for the betrothal of Miranda, Prospero's daughter, to Ferdinand, the Prince of Naples. The show's master has made the theatre-within-the-theatre seem to be 'Paradise' (l.124), but only moments later Prospero starts '*suddenly*' and, with '*strange, hollow, and confused noise*', everything disappears. The delights of fantasy, which he had called into being in an amazing stage show with an unmistakable message, had caused Prospero to forget that his life was threatened by his resentful servant, Caliban, together with a drunken fool and butler.

As this spectacle is disrupted — the stage-direction says that the spirits '*heavily vanish*' — it is evident that Prospero finds such visually rich and supra-human pleasures of no use in the real-life situation which has been developing unseen during the performance; indeed the spectacle has been a distraction. We may think that Shakespeare has used stage show only to assert its triviality.

But yet another visual display follows immediately, as those who have plotted against Prospero's life are pursued around the stage by spirits in the shape of various hounds. Once more Prospero is in command, but this time he urges his creatures on, as if wishing to take part in the show on his own account; he tries to augment its force: 'Fury, Fury! There, Tyrant, there! Hark, hark!', he calls out (IV.1.256). Although there is again little actual dialogue, the stage is filled with violence and noise, cries of human pain and bewilderment mixed with breathing and yelping of spirits. As his victims 'roar', Prospero orders that Caliban and the drunken fools shall be 'hunted soundly' and reassures himself that:

> At this hour
> Lies at my mercy all mine enemies.
> Shortly shall all my labors end....
>
> IV.1.261-3

His power to create a spectacle, reinforced by violent action and sounds, has led Prospero to believe himself to be invincible.

Performances of *The Tempest* in the Banquetting Hall at Whitehall were recorded on November 1st 1611 and again in the season of 1612-13. On these occasions the demands of Shakespeare's text may have been answered by the use of costumes, stage-machinery and music which had been provided in the first instance for the costly masques which were the most notable entertainments at the court of King James I. Especially when written by Ben Jonson and designed by Inigo Jones, these celebratory spectacles were astonishing in their fantasy and innovating in their technique: they must be the source for the masque in *The Tempest* and for its other spectacular episodes.

In modern productions of this play designers have worked with much the same intentions, creating illusions which exceed ordinary expectations and transform the entire stage into a world of wonder demonstrating its creator's power. John Conklin's set for the production by Mark Lamos at Hartford Stage in 1985 used lighting that was both unreal and unusual, and transparent gauzes; it also revealed a further depth behind the main acting area of the stage (see plate 9). G.W. Mercier's design for the production by Julie Taymor, for the Theatre for a New Audience in New York in 1986 and at Stratford, Connecticut in 1987, used masks, puppetry, revolving bobinet screens, a black scrim, flowing silks and projected images, together with an open, unlocalized space. The actor-spirits moved fluently and magically, appearing and disappearing at will. Photographs show black-clad figures manipulating the puppets which created some of the magic, but these were invisible to the audience: (see plates 10-11). In Shakespeare's time more solid devices than these could also awaken wonder, and remove the action on stage far from any imitation of ordinary reality. By such means, *The Tempest* represents, in Shakespeare's age and ours, a wise man who re-made the world in an attempt to render it more potent for good and more responsive to evil. By using stage shows Shakespeare has created a drama which is unequivocal in its statements, and almost irresistible in its effect..

In other plays written at about the same time Shakespeare used similar shows on a smaller scale to further the narrative and action of a play with unmistakable statements. Jove appears on his eagle in *Cymbeline* and Time enters as Chorus in *The Winter's Tale*. In *Henry VIII*, Queen Katharine is given a 'Vision', with '*solemnly tripping... Personages*', which goes beyond what an individual actor can realize:

> Saw you not, even now, a blessed troop
> Invite me to a banquet; whose bright faces

Cast thousand beams upon me, like the sun?
They promis'd me eternal happiness,
And brought me garlands, Griffith, which I feel
I am not worthy yet to wear.

IV.2.87-92

But these are all fleeting moments, of value only to single characters or to the audience in the theatre. They are part of the play's narrative, not visions summoned by one person to affect the course of the action or express his own thoughts. The masque-like elements of *The Tempest* are Shakespeare's furthest development of the stage show both in elaboration and in contribution to the developing drama.

Yet while Prospero controls his spectacular effects, this 'most potent art' has limitations. Right up to the last moments, Prospero believes that by its means all his enemies are within his power. By his spells he has drawn them into a circle around him, and their minds and bodies are no longer able to resist. They are assembled like figures in a masque, ready for its concluding dance; as they recover their senses, solemn music sounds and Prospero dresses himself as Duke of Milan, ready to confront them. But now nothing magical happens; instead of spectacle, Shakespeare relies on individual performances. Prospero weeps in 'fellowly' sympathy with the old counselor, Gonzalo, and he embraces Alonso, King of Naples who had helped to dethrone him. To Sebastian and Antonio his own brother, who are the chief disturbers of his peace, he is almost silent; he 'will tell no tales', even though to call one of them his brother 'would even infect my mouth'(V.1.126-34). The only further show Prospero can provide now is that of Miranda and Ferdinand, playing chess together; and it is this very human vision — their first words are 'Sweet lord, You play me false'(l.72) — which serves to mark the consequences of the peace that has been patched up between Prospero and his 'enemies'.

The only dance in this conclusion takes place off-stage: after being wakened by 'strange and several noises', the crew found their 'royal, good, and gallant ship' in such good trim that their Master was seen 'cap'ring to eye her'(ll.230-39). For Prospero, the play ends when he invites the assembled company into his cell to listen as he tells 'the story of my life' and then to take their rest 'for this one night'. In effect, he promises to put himself on show; there will be no magic displays now. So Shakespeare concludes his most spectacular play with very human and understated stage business; the overwhelming effects of masque-like show yield to a number of actors crossing the stage, speaking very little but attentive to each other and shouldering the entire burden of the drama. Prospero invites them all courteously, 'Please you, draw near', and then watches them proceed him off-stage, his most 'wicked' enemies along with all the royal party.

The Winter's Tale, a slightly earlier play first performed in 1610-11, had already made much the same point, but in a less forthright way. Besides Time, as Chorus appearing alone on-stage, there is a Sheep-shearing Feast in which twelve countrymen have 'made themselves all men of hair' in order to dance for the assembled company. They are out of the ordinary:

> One three of them, by their own report, sir, hath danc'd before the King; and not the worst of the three but jumps twelve foot and a half by th' squier.
>
> IV.4.329-31

The show which they enact may effect some chemistry essential to the plot, for Polixenes, as he watches, becomes ready to challenge his son, Prince Florizel who dressed as a shepherd is wooing the Queen of the Feast, Perdita. But the truest magic in this play — and its most astonishing spectacle — is arranged by Paulina, and there is little to explain how she has produced it. For fifteen years she has kept the Queen, Hermione, alive in a secret retreat; this followed a highly dramatic crisis in which Hermione fainted when Apollo's oracle vindicated her chastity and her husband, King Leontes, refused the divine revelation. At the end of the play, when Leontes is penitent, and his daughter, Perdita, has been restored to him, Paulina invites the king to her 'gallery' to see a statue of his late wife. The thrill of this stage show is accentuated in that Shakespeare has broken his own rule and kept the audience in the dark about Hermione's survival; indeed, with several deft touches, he has encouraged belief that she is dead. With considerable powers of stage management, using music, curtain, and pedestal placed in a 'chapel', and with a carefully controlled audience, Paulina summons the statue to come to life. It is an astonishing visual surprise, but it effects something which is absolutely and markedly real: as Leontes takes his wife by the hand he cries out 'O, she's warm', and then she 'hangs about his neck' (V.3.110-3) in silence.

In effect, the stage show of Hermione's 'statue' is a hoax, and ultimately it achieves little more than one more demonstration of Hermione's patience and Leontes' penitence and sorrow. As a result of the show, Hermione has nothing to say to her husband, speaking only to Perdita and to the gods. Paulina is then given a husband, somewhat unceremoniously since neither she nor he has anything to say in the matter. After some brief introductions and some more begging for pardon, Leontes calls everyone to leave the stage: 'Let's from this place...Hastily lead away'(ll.146-55). As in *The Tempest*, a stage show does not provide a full conclusion in which the characters or audience can participate freely. Its chief contribution to the play's action is to lead towards the moment of reunion, when man and wife clasp each other in silence and make by means of that physical contact whatever reconciliation they can. This intimate moment has no further explication: here is the essential mystery at the ending of this play, not in its highly expressive visual show.

*

But visual show, for all its limitations, is part of Shakespeare's plays in performance from first to last. It takes over from lively encounter between individual characters in two contrasted ways, which sometimes work together: it holds up the action to establish a wider and clearer view of its implications; and it creates its own statement alongside more immediate concerns, in parallel with them or more completely intertwined.

In *As You Like It*, the last scene has '*still music*' and the strangeness and wonder of the appearance of Hymen, god of marriage. He comes unannounced, without explanation or any sign of human involvement. (In performance he may be impersonated by Corin or another of the minor characters; but even if this actor stumbles or is obviously inadequate to his role, all the other characters accept the spectacle at its intended value.) Hymen's 'Wedlock Hymn', which echoes the words of the marriage service in the Elizabethan Book of Common Prayer, is announced in a way that suggests the god has his own attendants who sing, while mortals stand in amazed silence:

> Whiles a wedlock-hymn we sing,
> Feed yourselves with questioning,
> That reason wonder may diminish,
> How thus we met, and these things finish.
>
> V.4.131-4

Hymen has already paired off the four couples in the play, promising their future happiness, and is now ready to withdraw or ascend back into the heavens over the stage. But Shakespeare has not yet finished the comedy: the philosophical Jacques has his own tribute to make to the lovers, which is neither so simpleminded as Hymen's, nor so content to celebrate the present moment. Jacques speaks only to the men, and his tone is both superior and discriminating; his message is clearest to Silvius, to whom he bequeaths 'a long and well-deserved bed', and to Touchstone whose 'loving voyage Is but for two months victualled'(V.4.182-6). Then Jacques walks off stage before the dancing which follows immediately. As he leaves, the Duke has to call the others to

> begin these rites,
> As we do trust they'll end, in true delights.

As the dancing begins, the play is once more only a show, but the audience has been alerted to the variety of individual engagement in the wordless spectacle.

A few other times the action of *As You Like It* is held up for a stage show which silences talk and stills the lively interplay between its characters. The first is the 'good sport' in which Orlando fights with Charles the Wrestler who has entered the stage having just killed three men in three successive bouts. Here the play's romantic hero is shown stripped of his usual clothing, alert and decisive, and in great danger; and Rosalind can do little more than watch, and show how greatly she is involved with Orlando's safety. The strangely tense interlude is soon over, for when Charles is thrown he is killed instantly, and his corpse is removed with little attention paid to it. Afterwards Rosalind can joke about what she has witnessed, but at the same time she realizes that what she says falls hopelessly short of what she has experienced. When she and Orlando do face each other after the event, they are both almost tongue-tied. Perhaps in this encounter there is a visual echo of the two wrestlers facing each other before the match only moments before. As she leaves the stage, he cries out, 'O poor Orlando, thou art overthrown!'(I.2.238). On this occasion, the spectacles of confrontation hold up the progress of the drama to suggest more than words alone can witness or contain.

Another strongly visual moment comes in Act IV, as the comedy draws towards its end. A deer has been hunted and killed, and the event is celebrated on stage with song. Jacques and the Lords, dressed as foresters, resolve to honor the one who has killed the deer, presenting him to the Duke 'like a Roman conqueror'(IV.2.3), dressed in the deer's horns and skin. Then they all sing a song:

What shall he have that kill'd the deer?
His leather skin and horns to wear.
Then sing him home:

Take thou no scorn to wear the horn,
It was a crest ere thou wast born.
  Thy father's father wore it,
  And thy father bore it.
The horn, the horn, the lusty horn,
Is not a thing to laugh to scorn.

IV.2.10-18

Pride, laughter, mockery, bawdy, and noise are all suggested by the words of the song and perhaps that is all Shakespeare intended here. But theatre directors have often staged the celebratory procession along with the song. Sometimes the corpse of a deer is paraded around the stage, with some show of dignity. But the spectacle is more in keeping with the words of the text when one of the lords is actually dressed in the horns and the still-bloody skin of a slaughtered deer, and the dance-procession is staged with a show of sexual and violent involvement. So this scene, which can be cut without any damage to the plot or action of the play, becomes a sustained spectacle which displays the effects of triumph and death; it establishes a sense of horror and wonder, and also provokes laughter, shortly before the whole cast puts on its finest forest clothes for the seemly conclusion of the play under the guidance of Hymen.

Processions around the stage always take time to complete and so they can be used to hold back more individual issues while the audience is responsive to visual show. Shakespeare used this potential repeatedly. In *A Midsummer Night's Dream* both Titania and Oberon have their own attendants who act as presenters for the King and Queen of fairies, at each entry establishing their special reality. At the end both troops join together to take mysterious and beneficent possession of Duke Theseus' palace, so that, alone among the comedies, the *Dream* takes the lovers beyond the moment of their betrothal.

In *Much Ado About Nothing*, the scene in church when Claudio denounces his bride has dialogue which begins abruptly with the congregation fully assembled. This may seem odd, until the simple stage direction for entrance to the stage is converted into a suitable procession, so that the scene itself starts without words. First of all the parties of bride and bridegroom take up their separate and appropriate positions, accompanied with music. Only when everyone is settled, and perhaps after an expectant pause, Hero will appear on her father's arm, her hair flowing freely as was the custom of brides: she presents an instantly recognizable picture of innocence and it is after this statement has been visually established that the words of the text take over and swiftly lead the scene in a contrary direction. This show is one of several processional entries in this play, but two of the others are more immediately mysterious, with masked figures which cause the persons already on stage to receive the show with suspicion and careful words. Since masquers sometimes chose 'beetle brows' for their vizors (see *Romeo and Juliet*, I.4.32), a performance of these masked entries might be in extreme contrast to that of the wedding scene. Perhaps the last entry of the ladies in Act V should be very wild or forbidding, because this show proceeds the peace which concludes the contentious wooing of this comedy.

Other scenes of spectacle are assemblies rather than processions. In the penultimate scene of *Much Ado* everyone is wearing mourning as they enter and take up their positions in front of a tomb in the monument of Hero's family. It is night time, and, in further contrast to the wedding-morning scene, whole hours seem to pass, between 'midnight' (l. 16) and the first touches of dawn:

> Good morrow, masters; put your torches out;
> The wolves have preyed, and look, the gentle day,
> Before the wheels of Phoebus, round about
> Dapples the drowsy east with spots of grey.
>
> V.3.24-7

Here the stage show has been static as a 'solemn hymn' is sung, and its slow representation of sorrow and pain seems intended to help the audience to receive Claudio back into the comedy without feeling that he has too easily shrugged off the enormity of his treatment of his bride. Here, for this character, words alone might have sounded too glib or too ambiguous.

Perhaps Shakespeare's use of spectacle is most closely tied to his presentation of the inner drama of human consciousness in the witches' scenes of *Macbeth*. These become more and more elaborate as the play proceeds, even if Hecate in III.5 and the three further witches who enter with her in IV.1 are considered spurious additions to

Shakespeare's text. The various apparitions called up by the first three witches in their last scene (IV.1), culminating in the procession of crowned heirs of Banquo, make an undeniable effect. Even when a production employs an absolute minimum of stage trickery, the slowly emerging figures, or puppets or shadowy projections, can enforce attention and demand explication. When the stage effects are ineffective, or even laughable, the solemnity with which they are received can establish an eerie calm in the midst of clumsiness or chaotic ineptitude. Moreover the action of the play before and after this moment is in absolute agreement with the messages presented through these visual signs or demonstrations.

But Shakespeare follows the apparitions with yet another visual show which concludes the staged part of the witches in the play. This is not meaningful in the same explicit way as the apparitions, but is a dance which can seem entirely purposeless, except as an expression of triumph;

> FIRST WITCH: ...But why stands
> Macbeth thus amazedly?
> Come, sisters, cheer we up his sprites,
> And show the best of our delights:
> I'll charm the air to give a sound,
> While you perform your antic round,
> That this great king may kindly say
> Our duties did his welcome pay.
>
> IV.1.125-32

The following stage-direction, '*Music. The Witches dance, and vanish*', provides no clue to the nature of what is shown on stage. Some editors believe the whole incident is an unauthorized interpolation into Shakespeare's text, but theatre directors and designers have sensed that they must avoid any sense of anti-climax at this point; even without these lines (or the three extra witches), the full resources of their actors and stage devices must be employed in order to give a strong exit to the witches who have established such a presence in the play. Macbeth's next words show that it is the witches and not the apparitions which take possession of his mind, as he realizes that he is now alone:

> Where are they? Gone? Let this pernicious hour
> Stand aye accursed in the calendar!

A concluding dance for three or six witches can be staged so that it sums up the whole scene with mere spectacle, impressive in part because it alone is without specific meaning. Evil and insatiable power are here manifested in their own way.

Macbeth's next actions may explain more. Knowing that all are damned who trust the witches, he nevertheless sets in motion the slaughter of Lady Macduff and her children. The witches' departing show has overwhelmed any thought of pity, whether what he had seen was a grotesque and almost laughable celebration, or whether it was some sixty witches who danced and flew in the air to the accompaniment of a full orchestra, as in Henry Irving's production.[2] The wordless show of evil, as it takes its leave and celebrates its own triumph, commands Macbeth's obedience, even though he knows the consequences are both 'pernicious' and 'accursed'.

*

The stage shows in Shakespeare's later tragedies are presented subtlely, so that they seem to be part of the developing action and a necessary element in the interaction of characters. In *King Lear*, when the old king is carried on stage to be awakened slowly by music, a still moment is created by Cordelia's kiss: everything is still and quiet, and her action is so delicate and visually impressive that it has been recorded in paintings and in sculpture to greater effect than any other incident in the play. Later, the dead bodies of Goneril and Regan are brought on stage without any further reference to them in the dialogue; they are needed to create a large visual display which echoes the opening scene in which Lear had demanded that his children should declare their love for him in public. But then, as Lear attempts to speak, attention is drawn away from this wider picture to fasten more closely on Cordelia and Lear. He insists on one last and very different visual show:

> Do you see this? Look on her. Look, her lips.
> Look there, look there!
>
> V.3.310-1

But there is no sign of life to be seen, and it is his own weakened and tortured self that captures the audience's attention. The following dialogue shows that those persons grouped around him ignore the illusory visual evidence which he had tried to bring to their attention.

In *Antony and Cleopatra* a number of entries and one exit are presented as if they were stage shows produced for an audience on stage and, through this device, to the audience in the theatre:

> PHILO: Look where they come!
> Take but good note, and you shall see in him
> The triple pillar of the world transform'd
> Into a strumpet's fool. Behold and see.
>
> I.1.10-13

> ENOBARBUS: Hush! Here comes Antony.
> CHARMIAN: Not he; the queen.
>
> I.2.73

> ALEXAS: My lord approaches.
> CLEOPATRA: We will not look upon him. Go with us
>
> I.2.83-4

> ENOBARBUS: There's a strong fellow, Menas.
> MENAS: Why?
> ENOBARBUS: 'A bears the third part of the world, man; see'st not?
>
> II.7.87-9

Towards the end of the play there are staged shows which are more static, the first in Act III, scene 9, when Cleopatra is forced to observe the almost silent Antony sitting alone, oblivious of her presence. Then in Act IV scene 15, the wounded Antony is drawn up slowly to Cleopatra's monument, to receive her last kiss. Finally, in the last scene of all, Cleopatra takes time to dress in her royal robe and crown before taking to her breast the asp that will kill her: this pose is held after her death until Caesar enters, as Dolabella says,

> To see perform'd the dreaded act which thou
> So sought'st to hinder.
>
> V.2.329-30

In *Coriolanus* the hero is often on display, in different guises: as civilian, as Roman soldier (before battle and after), as conqueror, as petitioner ('in the gown of humility', II.3.39), as consul, as traveller; and then surprisingly he appears '*in mean apparel, disguis'd and muffled*'(IV. 4. Entry), and as Volscian commander. In this last guise he is the center of his new associates' attention, and is frequently described by them and by Romans who go to visit him:

> I tell you he does sit in gold, his eye
> Red as 'twould burn Rome...
>
> V.1.63-4

> He wants nothing of a god but eternity, and a heaven to throne it in.
>
> V.4.23-4

Theatrical spectacle is here at one with individual performance. The star actor holds center-stage, a sight to stare at in amazement; but the audience's gaze will also try to penetrate to his inner self and the thoughts and passions that drive him.

Further stage spectacles in this tragedy are entirely silent. The first when Coriolanus holds his mother '*by the hand, silent*' as the stage direction in the Folio text insists (V.3.182). The next when the women return to Rome having won mercy from Coriolanus; here the senators cry out a welcome and Volumnia is identified with 'Behold our patroness, the life of Rome!'(V.5.1), but neither she nor any of the accompanying women speaks a word. The last spectacle is in Corioli, with the hero dead. A command holds back the violence:

> Tread not upon him. Masters all, be quiet;
> Put up your swords.
>
> V.6.134-5

The half verse-line suggests a pause for everyone to take in the sight, and then Aufidius speaks. Seeing what he has done, this enemy finds that his 'rage is gone', and he is ready to help bear and honor the corpse with other soldiers.

In each of these three late tragedies, Shakespeare seems to insist that the actor as character is the most potent silent spectacle theatre can produce. The crowded stage, the imperatives of action or narrative, and even the flow of words that shape the drama and give to it that sense of immediate and individual life which is the essence of Shakespeare's art — all this he has occasionally held back, so that the audience may wonder at the silent human being then on display. Each member of the audience is free to confront the center of the tragedy and to make a response in his or her own terms. In *King Lear*, Albany refuses specific comment:

Bear them from hence. Our present business
Is general woe.

V.3.316-17

The close of *Antony and Cleopatra* sustains the last visual impression of the dead queen by means of detailed description, each phrase precise and many of them objective:

...she looks like sleep,
As she would catch another Antony
In her strong toil of grace.
Here, on her breast,
There is a vent of blood, and something blown;
The like is on her arm.
This is the aspic's trail; and these fig leaves
Have slime upon them, such as th' aspic leaves
Upon the caves of Nile.

Even the conquering Caesar has no words except for his adversary and the effect of her death:

High events as these
Strike those that make them; and their story is
No less in pity, than his glory which
Brought them to be lamented. Our army shall
In solemn show attend this funeral,
And then to Rome. Come, Dolabella, see
High order in this great solemnity.
Exeunt omnes.

PART THREE

The Play and the Audience

TWELVE

Plays in Performance

IN Shakespeare's own day the drama of human consciousness was the newest and most admired element in plays. Lifelike, accomplished and temperamental performances encouraged audiences to identify themselves with the 'star' actors, to wish the character portrayed, in the words of Thomas Heywood, 'all prosperous performance, as if the personator were the man personated.'[1] Robert, Earl of Huntington declares, in a play by Anthony Mundy concerning his *Downfall* (1598), that he will be a tragic actor:

> And thou shalt see me with a lofty verse
> Bewitch the hearers' ears, and tempt their eyes
> To gaze upon the action that I use.
>
> ll. 265-7

And here is Polymetes in Thomas May's *The Heir* (1620), a play with extensive borrowings from Shakespeare:

> Has not your lordship seen
> A player passionate Hieronimo?
> — By th' mass, 'tis true. I have seen the knave paint grief
> In such a lively color, that for false
> And acted passion he has drawn true tears
> From the spectators. Ladies in the boxes
> Kept time with sighs and tears to his sad accents,
> As he had truly been the man he seem'd.
>
> I.1

Even the new form for theatre-buildings that was developed in London during the last two decades of the sixteenth century, with galleries surrounding a platform stage at two or three levels on at least three sides, would have encouraged a single point of focus. What we call today the 'up-stage' position from which an actor can best control his audience would have been more nearly central to the theatre. The dramatist, John Webster, depicted an 'Excellent Actor' at the center of a circle:

by a full and significant action of body, he charms our attention: sit in a full theatre, and you will think you see so many lines drawn from the circumference of so many ears, whiles the Actor is the Centre.

Characters, 1615

In these conditions, Shakespeare's ability to write acting parts, in which the psychological basis of character could be slowly revealed and passionate or deliberate speeches sustained by rhythm and metre, established fully the star actor's hold over his audience. Within a few decades of their first performances, *Much Ado About Nothing* was sometimes called '*Benedick and Beatrice*' and *Twelfth Night* re-christened '*Malvolio*'. And since that time, romantic actors and critics have still further established the predominance of the characters.

But Shakespeare requires more from his audience. In some plays, as *Julius Caesar* or *Coriolanus*, his theme was obviously political and social, and, as we have seen, he frequently provoked a wide focus upon the stage. His devices for ensuring this more comprehensive view are more remarkable when they are seen as counterstrokes to the newly established and creative influences that made the star actor so dominant. They are endlessly resourceful, changing from play to play to give appropriate presentation to their imagined 'worlds'.

We have seen how Exton's entry with the dead body of Richard II provokes the audience to attend more closely to Bolingbroke's words and actions, and then to observe the attendant but silent nobles. In *Romeo and Juliet*, after the death of the lovers, attention is deflected to all the 'parties of suspicion' and the families grouped on the stage; and the audience is forced, during the Friar's long explanation, to consider all the actions and motives that have led to the catastrophe. In *Julius Caesar*, the minor attendant figures are not so significant but, here, two suicides follow each other so closely that the audience is encouraged to compare. Brutus says that Rome will never breed a 'fellow' to Cassius (V.3.101), and then Antony enters and claims that Brutus was 'the noblest Roman of them all' (V.5.68). By the side of Antony stands Octavius Caesar, who gives the last command:

> So call the field to rest, and let's away
> To part the glories of this happy day.

The contrast of this cold, efficient voice, exemplified in the phrase 'happy day', sharpens the double view of the play; the audience may remember Octavius's earlier remark that 'some that smile have in their hearts, I fear, Millions of mischiefs' (IV.1.50-1). Certainly, after twin suicides and succeeding tributes, Shakespeare's presentation of Octavius is calculated to rebuff an intense scrutiny. The audience will view the respect paid to Brutus' body as the soldiers file off stage with a concern for political consequences.

Before the end of *Richard III*, a play always performed for the opportunity it gives to a star actor, the audience's interest is widened by the Ghost Scene, in which all whom Richard has murdered move regularly across the stage cursing and then blessing: Richard is 'devil', 'butcher', 'boar', and Richmond is associated with 'good angels', 'peace', 'offspring'. But after this Richard continues to draw the closest attention, especially in the revealing and nervously intense soliloquy on awakening from his dream. In this psychological aspect of the play, Richmond is a minor contrast only: looking to the future, trusting in God, rather than looking to the past and present, judging and revealing *his own* life. But the contrast in presentation is an active stimulant in ensuring the widest dramatic view after the hero's role has reached its brilliantly enigmatic conclusion in blindly fighting and calling for the means to fight. Although 'A horse, a horse! My Kingdom for a horse!' has stayed longest in the memory of audiences, Richmond's long concluding speech, that announces his marriage to 'unite the white rose and the red' and the nation's purgation, invites the audience to reconsider the whole action and relate, as best they can, their experience of Richard's suffering and courage to Richmond's dismissal of him as a 'bloody dog'.

The end of *Macbeth* is a development from this technique. Malcolm also has a sustained verbal statement to offset the intensity of Macbeth's last scenes. But he has the advantage of the England Scene (IV.3), the longest in the play, which establishes his political ability and association with Macduff, Ross, and the holy English King. He is also convincingly young, so that his less mature, less practiced voice will accentuate the turning forward of dramatic interest. Moreover, Malcolm's political and military initiative is made theatrically more obvious: drums beat only for him; thanes are shown deserting Macbeth to join him; and his army carries green boughs that are emblems of renewal and a fulfillment of the last prophecy of the Witches. Old Seward's expression, and then suppression, of grief for his son's death immediately after Macbeth's last exit from the stage fighting, has an intensity that is sufficiently sudden and unprecedented to draw attention for a moment to what is, in terms of narrative, a minor incident; this, too, helps to free the audience from the hold Macbeth exerts, so that it can turn more freely to the moral, political, royal and religious aspects of the tragedy that are stated by Malcolm in the conclusion.

Two plays in which the transference to a wider interest is effected by ensemble playing against the strong attraction of a single star role, are *Henry V* and *The Merchant of Venice*. In the first, the star part is restricted during the final Act, and in the second it is omitted altogether. After the audience has centered its attention on Henry in thoughtful prose speeches to the three soldiers and then the soliloquy which identifies his subtextual guilt and tensions, the battle fills the stage with various business. In the wooing episode of the last Act, Henry has to speak plainly and repeatedly in order to be understood and so the focus is narrowed; but the climax of this scene is a silent, shared kiss, and immediately the stage picture is widened as the French and English courts re-enter and take up formal positions. Henry has now comparatively little to say, being shown as one of many on whom responsibility for continued peace must rest. Queen Isabella of France is given new prominence for the penultimate speech which likens peace to a 'spousal' that can be threatened by jealousy. There is a general 'Amen' and all Henry does to conclude the play is to arrange for oaths to be taken and ask for prosperity: here, again, the audience will view the whole assembly of recent enemies and look for signs of good faith. The last moments provide a trumpet call and a silent exeunt of French and English together, and then the Chorus enters to remind the audience that France was subsequently lost, and England made to suffer with blood.

The conclusion to *The Merchant of Venice* is often considered a failure, for, unless stage-business is tactfully managed and the acting of the whole company well judged, the intense focus evoked by Shylock's suffering and destructive impulses will not yield to the wider issues of the last Act; the lovers' behavior can seem wantonly light, a shallow game of hide and seek. Obviously Portia has stood over against Shylock in the Trial Scene, but her wholly successful disguise and the sustained eloquence of her 'Quality of Mercy' speech did not encourage the audience to attend to her in the same way as to Shylock. (Indeed, it is hard to imagine a drama that could present two roles as deeply realized as Shylock's in one episode.) The fifth Act, which moves back to Belmont, can only satisfy the interest that has been awakened if, first, the music called for by the text provides a relaxed and dignified harmony appropriate to the associated talk of the music of the spheres, and, secondly, if the quick, glancing wit and the rapid encounters and lively spirits of the lovers are played as surface excitements covering an inner assurance of mutual love, a private and as yet untried enjoyment, that can respond to the harmonious music. In this way the formal grouping of the final exeunt can have a subtextual basis — as Shylock's impassioned performance and last exit must have had — and thus carry appropriate conviction. So the last Act is revalued in performance: for example, the sober willingness of Antonio to hazard, even now, his soul for his friend is heard as a brief textual expression of the usually unspoken trust, generosity and love which underlie the temporary excitements and are the beginning of the only answer that can be attempted to Shylock's remembered pleas for judgement

*

Generally the comedies, by reason of their multiple plots, evenly matched roles and general liveliness of action, maintain a predominantly wide focus. Laughter depends on release from too narrow concerns — as Feste, the professional fool in *Twelfth Night*, knows when he takes Olivia's mind off the immediate cause of grief in order that she will laugh and then be able to see her own predicament in a wider context. (The man who slips on the cunningly placed banana-skin does not laugh so soon as those who set the harmless trap and so, from the first, observe the whole scene.) 'Humour', said Cazamian,

> demands the freedom of an unattached mind... [and] lives in the relativity that is fair to all creatures.[2]

The very titles of Shakespeare's comedies demonstrate a broader interest than either the histories or tragedies. When Shakespeare adapted Thomas Lodge's novel, *Rosalynde*, he kept the heroine and her name, but called the play *As You Like It*; at its conclusion Rosalind and Orlando are only one out of four pairs of lovers and celebrate not only their journey's end but also the return of her father to his dukedom.

The Church Scene in *Much Ado* (IV.1) illustrates the dominant width of view for the comedies. It presents an incident which told simply could scarcely avoid an intensification of interest. But, first, Shakespeare ensured that the audience knows all the story, that Hero is truly faithful and her enemies already apprehended. Then he gives Hero, who suffers most, very little to say and little opportunity to provoke or hold attention. Claudio speaks with clear, strong sentiment and compelling imagery as the situation demands, but the fluent and sustained rhythm of his verse (not equalled elsewhere in the play) cannot represent passion with an impression of either immediate sensation or subtextual feeling. And, even while he holds the center of the stage, attention is deflected by supporting speeches from Don Pedro and by three interruptions, one from Don John whose compact, cold utterance easily attracts attention by contrast. Benedick's abrupt and unnecessary comment, 'This looks not like a nuptial', may be intended as a forced joke, relaxing the tensions of the scene as well as deflecting interest. By these means, even during Claudio's powerful denunciation, the audience views the whole stage.

All the comedies end with general celebration, often involving music and grouped movements across the stage. In *Much Ado*, news comes of Don John's capture, but the *dramatis personae* take pleasure in not thinking about him — and so will the audience — as the pipers strike up for the final dance. After Marcade's entry and a more searching focus than elsewhere in the play, *Love's Labour's Lost* closes with songs which celebrate Spring and Winter, and tell of all married men, and Dick, Tom, Joan and Marian. Indeed, in the comedies, Shakespeare's cunning manipulation of the stage picture is most remarkable in providing moments of intense focus, so that his characters are progressively revealed in scenes separated by much other lively and shared business. The predominant focus is so broad and the dramatic material so abundant, that the plays might have become superficial and their general conclusions slick and mechanical.

Soliloquies and climactic revelations of character in extended speeches where the comic situation releases unusual and fantastic reactions are the main ways of presenting the drama of human consciousness in the widely focused comedies. For example, in *A Midsummer Night's Dream* the contrasts of wood and city, and of experienced courtiers, young courtiers, mechanicals and fairies have so influenced the dramatic structure and complicated both plot and theme that the widest aspects of the comedy have continual fascination. But the audience is also closely involved with individual characters and this depends on moments of surprisingly intense focus. Bottom, in particular, is presented before appearing at court with increasing freedom and a progressive revelation of his innermost nature. When he first enters with an ass's head on his shoulders, his fellows run away at once, like 'wild geese' frightened and 'distracted', and he is left alone in ignorance of what has happened. As he tries to be realistic and to rouse his own vanity and bravery, his words have the rhythms and progressions of actual thought and fear; the focus is intent on him:

> I see their knavery: this is to make an ass of me; to fright me, if they could. But I will not stir from this place, do what they can; I will walk up and down here, and I will sing, that they shall *hear I* am not afraid.
>
> III.1.109-13

There is a still more sustained intensity when he wakens from his 'dream' (IV.1.197-217). Here Bottom is revealed as the actor who wishes to be glorious in great company, even if it means singing a ballad about his own unbelievable, foolish and unsubstantial dream. Shakespeare has interwoven echoes from earlier talk of rehearsing so that this soliloquy begins and ends with amateur theatricals and is thus a convincing development from the less heroic Bottom of the first Acts. These successive moments of revelation and intimacy mean that when he absurdly performs the part of Pyramus before the Duke, the audience will not laugh like the courtiers on the stage; it has thought of Bottom as he does of himself and after that, as Theseus explains, even such 'shadows' as these 'unfitted' actors may 'pass as excellent men' (V.1.210-15).

*

Changes between wide and intense dramatic focus are elements in what happens when a Shakespearian play is performed. The varying focus controls, on the one hand, the social relevance of the action and, on the other, the opportunities for actors to reveal the emotional and intellectual strength of their characters, especially where a train of subtextual impressions is progressively developed and at last stated more directly. To the customary discussions of a play's language, themes, plot, situation and characters must be added a consideration of these techniques. They are not so easy to describe, being untouched by literary criticism and needing a full response to visual and temporal, as well as verbal, elements; but, along with the other theatrical devices that we have examined in this book, they can account for characteristic effects in performances of Shakespeare's plays.

In the theatre each play offers a kind of encounter, an invitation to move into a play world, to see it generally and with the eyes of particular characters; and then, perhaps, to be led to see from a different viewpoint, or with more penetration, or to be cheated of firm understanding when that had seemed to be offered. At times

Shakespeare thwarts his audience, but more frequently he *seems* to allow its members absolute freedom, to imagine further or more precisely in their own terms: at moments of fullest or sharpest realization, the dramatic facts may be left behind — the actual stage, setting, actor, even the words that are spoken. It seems to me that this is because the most deeply felt moments are not strongly textual: they rely on subtextual exposure or intensity, on changes of tempo, rhythm, texture or weight, on 'large and sweeping impressions of scene and the movement of figures', on the release of laughter or grip of expectation, or on a close, particular *view* of the whole stage of characters after sequential changes of the stage picture. The audience is encouraged to respond by less precise means than words alone, but means that have a developing strength and relevance through consecutive and complete performance, and in no other circumstance.

There are two important consequences of this dramatic strategy. First, actors and directors must learn to discover and use the opportunities Shakespeare has provided, and this will involve close textual study as well as patient, imaginative and experimental rehearsals. And, secondly, critics and students must recognize that Shakespeare's art can never be represented by the printed text of his dialogue, his intentions never explained by simple quotation. The complex and subtle setting for any speech, and the speed, rhythm, weight or body of its words, as well as their meanings and allusiveness, must also be described in terms of an actor's performance and in relation to the changing stage picture. Only so can Shakespeare's plays be considered, as he intended, as if being performed in a theatre.

To try to discover the stage life that suits the text of any one of the plays is a fascinating pursuit, and to try to describe it only less interesting than its re-creation.

APPENDICES

i

The Theatrical Element of Shakespeare Criticism

"It has taken more bookish Shakespeareans many generations to understand the controlling importance of stage performance," wrote Harry Levin in *The Question of "Hamlet"* (1959).[1] In his view, criticism had recently made a determined attempt to consider Shakespeare's plays in the theatre, as well as on the printed page. I think that this is so, and that persuasion directed to initiating this practice is now unnecessary; at this stage in our approach to Shakespeare's plays, it is more profitable to ask what effect this renewed theatrical consciousness has had.

Levin's own book exemplifies one common way for a critic to remember the theatre. Three times he refers to actual performances to demonstrate a critical attitude. Sarah Bernhardt's acting of Hamlet is said to be part of the "romantic legend of a weakling, too delicate for this world" (p. 5). Edwin Booth, identified as "a romantic actor," is held to be typical of those who found "congenial" the assumption that "Hamlet was really the victim of the mental disease he claimed to be simulating" (p. 111). This critic has little time for these notions and his theatrical instances are presented with overtones of ridicule. In support of an attitude that Levin considers more important, a reference to an actor introduces a paragraph and is given a vague puff of recommendation. So Tommaso Salvini, said to be "one of the most celebrated Hamlets of theatrical history," is quoted as being able to sum up this part "in a single trait: *il dubbio*" (p. 74). But having provided the entrance for a new theme, theatrical criticism retires and the paragraph proceeds with a long quotation from Erasmus, who is said to be borrowing from Plato. On each of these three occasions the critic is using particular theatrical references, none too precisely, as a kind of exfoliation of his discourse on the play; they are by no means essential to his purpose.

Far more ambitiously a sensitivity to the theatrical nature of Shakespeare's writings has led critics to look as well as read. On all hands in contemporary criticism we can find attention paid to what happens onstage as well as what is said. For example, the section on *Macbeth* in John Arthos, *The Art of Shakespeare* (1964), opens boldly with the comment:

> The play began with the supernatural in obvious and fascinating theatrical devices, and it ended with as preposterous a one, the fulfillment of the last of the prophecies.
>
> (pp. 36-37)

The usual difficulty is how to make use of such observations: if there is a great deal of spectacular drama, how is that to be related to the verbal life of the play that is finely and allusively explored according to critical methods designed for wholly literary texts? The main argument in this consideration of *Macbeth* in *The Art of Shakespeare* is centered on the words; the eloquent peroration to Arthos' study makes no mention at all of what is seen, of the theatre, or of the "preposterous theatricality" of the play.

Attention to the visual elements seems most germane to a critic's purpose when they are minutely related to speech. Again Harry Levin's book exemplifies this. It is divided into four parts, called "Presuppositions," "Interrogation," "Doubt," and "Irony." Its structure, as these headings suggest, is determined by verbal and literary concepts, nothing clearly theatrical or visual. But this is how the critic's mind is based and how it works; it is when his "understanding of the controlling importance of stage performance" is most closely allied to this basic way of thought that it brings greatest interest and illumination; then it seems genuinely necessary to his discourse and not, merely, the means to import individual jewels of theatrical reference.

For example, Levin makes much of the drinking in the last scene of *Hamlet*, relating this activity to the words used earlier in the first court scene (I.2) and in Hamlet's talk with Horatio before seeing the Ghost. He notices the contrasted actions involved here, so that one reflects on the other and gives definition: Gertrude, he says, "sips" the poisoned drink (p. 98), but Hamlet makes sure of Claudius' "union" by "forcing the cup to his lips." A fourth reference to a particular performance in Levin's book does relate to his interest in specific words, and has the same kind of usefulness. In reading Hamlet's scene with Ophelia, the simple words, "I was the more deceived," may well make no more impact than those that come before and after; but Levin reminds us that in these words Mrs. Siddons is "said to have concentrated the essence of her role" as Ophelia (p. 28). Levin believes that doubt is central to the theme of the play, and this theatrical reference helps him to give more than usual importance to a single line.

Levin's book on *Hamlet* shows theatrical understanding working best when it is in step with his basically verbal analysis. Is this as far as the new theatrical criticism should go? Levin himself seems to think so. The quotation with which I began should be continued:

> It has taken more bookish Shakespeareans many generations to understand the controlling importance of stage performance; now that such understanding has been reached, there may be some danger of over emphasis.

Five years after Levin's book, another book on the same play, called *An Approach to "Hamlet,"* was published by L. C. Knights. In this I can find only one theatrical reference. It comes in considering descriptions of the Ghost in Act 1, scene 1:

> None of this [Knights notes] provides any very clear answer to the question that an audience is likely to ask—What sort of a ghost is this? Is it good or bad?
>
> (p. 44)

The remembrance that this is a play to be performed is a little oblique, and it raises pure supposition. Would an audience ask this question? Would an audience, gripped or at least led forward by what *is* being said and done on the stage, ask any question at all, particularly if it is not posed in the play? What does chiefly affect the audience's mode of response in this first scene, where do they look, what do they listen for, and how do they do this? These are important considerations, but if a critic wishes to raise them he must do so responsibly, with some care.

No critic writing today could be unaware that some attention has been paid to theatrical matters and, clearly, some have decided not to take this very seriously. Who is right? Is there "some danger of over emphasis"?

I have already implied my own view: I think the "understanding" has not gone far enough. This is not because great revaluations have been effected already, but partly because theatrical criticism has made such little headway. The first critics to take this path with purposeful intention seem to have done the best. We still look back to Granville-Barker, writing as much as sixty years ago. If challenged on the usefulness of theatrical criticism, we remember how Granville-Barker vindicated the structure of *Antony and Cleopatra* by pointing to the stage effects of the juxtaposition of short scenes. We think too of his championship of *Love's Labour's Lost* when he showed the theatrical effect of its elaborate language. Yet even here there is no complete vindication of his critical bias: *Antony and Cleopatra* is still considered in much the same critical terms as it was fifty years ago, and recent productions have not shown the play to be any more certain of theatrical conviction; *Love's Labour's Lost* is now established in critical favor, but often for subtleties unnoticed by Granville-Barker. If this early criticism of Shakespeare's plays in a fully theatrical context gives hope, it is of revaluations with limited or temporary relevance.

Yet none of this persuades me that the theatrical course is ineffective. In the theatre everything is subject to revaluation, every time a play is performed; this is the nature of the medium. An assurance that this or that interpretation or mode of performance is the only one that is appropriate to a dramatic text will not come easily: for a start, no mode of performance will be easy to describe. After trying to consider Shakespeare's plays in their theatrical element, I have become almost incapable of "evaluative criticism" in any usual sense of those words. I discover only possibilities, forgotten details, unobserved correspondences, potentialities; I open questions and rarely am able to close them. In some conditions of performance, one opinion about Shakespeare's writing and imagination seems useful and, even, correct; but when conditions change, that opinion is often discarded.

Among the usual metaphors or analogies used to describe a critic's task, certain ones are dominant. The critic is said to judge, to weigh, to define, to assess or even to "fix." He sometimes seems to be "taking sights," or measuring or estimating height, depth, or width. He "looks for a pattern" and "plucks out," or "dissects," the "heart of the mystery." He "places" a work of art in a perspective or a background. I see the appropriateness of all these metaphors, but they do not correspond to my basic activity in trying to understand one of Shakespeare's plays in a theatrical context. I am then acutely aware of the temporary nature of every judgment, because each moment of understanding is influenced by many accidental circumstances of embodiment and confrontation. On no two occasions does a play seem the same; it cannot be held still for "examination."

Sculptors sometimes say that a block of marble has a figure within it, waiting to be released. I think a play-text is like that: there is something that has to be discovered, in three dimensions, in time, sight, sound, words, rhythms. And each sculptor—each actor, director, and theatrical critic—will find a different figure within the living, idiosyncratic block of theatrical raw material. Each time he tackles a play he will make a new start, find a new structure, and unintentionally discard elements that had seemed important before. If the critic's encounter with a play is like that, how can he construct an argument that will establish an inescapable revaluation? If any critic of Shakespeare attempts to "fix" a play, he will do so most readily by ignoring its theatrical element—that is, by wholly unwarranted simplification.

The most obvious way to start considering the theatrical aspects of a Shakespeare play is to study a production of it. But this is easier to say than to do. If the critic detaches his mind at performance, so that it is free to question, compare, and analyze, the production immediately changes, because the forward pressure of events is lost. The critic must see the same production many times, and ask most of his questions afterwards. Then more problems arise: why did he fail to hear certain words that in reading had seemed highly significant? Going back to check, he may find that they were indeed not spoken by anyone, but were cut from the acting text—why?—or he may discover that they were spoken, but now he wonders why they escaped his notice at first. Questions proliferate: why did certain words sound unusually impressive? why did the empty stage on one particular occasion seem so meaningful? why did the critic look only at one of the many persons onstage? Talking about the performance afterwards with other members of the same audience seldom brings more assurance, for what has taken possession of one imagination may have failed to register with another. The critic will frequently reflect that the production he has seen cannot possibly be like a performance envisaged by Shakespeare; audience, theatre, staging, performances, all are very different. He will often be annoyed by what is obviously makeshift or meretricious in the productions he sees.

All this is common experience for anyone who tries to analyze a play in the "understanding of the controlling importance of stage performance." Two courses seem open. One critic will give up, and argue that these accidentally varying emphases come from misunderstanding and irresponsibility in actors and directors—and he should add in audiences—and take us further away from "the words themselves," which is all that Shakespeare has tangibly "left us." Another critic will continue his quest and bring scholarly method to his problem. He will go to still more productions, so that he can compare one with another. He will read all available dramatic criticism in order to check his reactions against others, especially those of theatregoers familiar with theatrical tradition and procedures. He will study the stage history of his chosen play, so that the fashions and predilections of this time and age can be offset by those of previous generations. So this critic will not only gain a historical perspective on any one production but will also be able to give some consideration to those performances that were, in their own time, judged to be preeminently revealing of Shakespeare's achievement.

Such scholarly activity brings rewards. Some elements in audience reaction to a play are consistently present, or almost so; some lines seem particularly memorable, though capable of diverse interpretations. Such facts the critic will collect and consider. He will also become a theatre historian, for the evidence of past performances will be more meaningful if he knows the conditions in which the play was staged, the lines that were cut (and added), the habitual manner of individual actors. For example, Harry Levin's reference to Mrs. Siddons would tell us more about the play if we knew the particular kind of power that she possessed as an actress: "when such-and-such a kind of actress is portraying Ophelia," we should say, "these words about deceit can seem tense and weighted with significance."

The critic will now go to the theatre himself with more awareness, and he will have opened up many precise considerations. How is the performance governed by casting problems within the company, by the kind of setting used, by the intensity or variability of the lighting? What influence, if any, has the director had over the acting? Do some incidents stand out by accident rather than design, because they are out of style with the rest of the production? Do others disappear because the actors cannot respond to some of the demands of the text, lacking vocal, physical, or emotional resource, or simply because they are not aware of them? By this time the critic is in danger of being overwhelmed by his own curiosity, and he will again reconsider his procedures. This time, I think, there are three courses open to him. Again he may give up: he seems to be still further from direct contact with Shakespeare's words, and at this stage has gained only perplexity. Or he will start "working in the theatre" for himself, either by taking part in actual productions or else by rehearsing and producing the play in his own mind, in the theatre of his mind.

From the beginning of criticism the theatre of the mind has attracted attention. In so far as a critic "hears" lines and "sees" actions and gestures, he is staging the play there; Harry Levin must have "staged" the business with the goblets in the last scene of *Hamlet* in his mind. But there is a world of difference between such occasional "realizations" and the difficult and complicated activity which takes place after the critic has given some detailed and prolonged study to actual productions and theatre history. For example, is it true to say, with Levin, that Gertrude "sips" from the poisoned chalice? In her brave concern to identify herself with her son in the presence of her second husband, to reassure him, or perhaps to reassure everyone and not least herself, would she "*sip*"? Surely the gesture should be stronger than this word implies. In any case, *when* does she drink: when she says "The queen carouses to thy fortune, Hamlet"? or after Hamlet has said "Good madam"? or while the King says "Gertrude, do not drink"? or after the first or second phrases of her own "I will, my lord; I pray you pardon me"? All these moments give a practical opportunity for the actress to drink, and each will probably suggest a different kind of drinking; each, with the accompanying words, will have a different effect upon the audience's understanding of the play. (I am inclined to think she drinks as early as possible, because one line after the words I have last quoted, Hamlet is ready to say "I dare not drink yet, madam—by and by.") It is one thing to consider the visual effect of this gesture in the theatre of the mind, and quite another to relate that to the infinite possibilities and the limiting practicalities of a whole play in performance. Momentary attention to imaginary performance is arguably worse than disregarding it entirely; it is so easy to be pleased with the glimpses caught of possible meanings and possible excitements without proceeding to relate that incident with the complete, continuously changing stage picture and the continuously sustained and developing impersonations.

Even when the critic can begin to work responsibly in the theatre of his mind, needing just as much imagination as he did at first, but bringing also a meticulous particularity and a full view of the stage, there are traps in this procedure. The imaginary stage is not easily kept constant in size; it often has no dimensions at all. It has no individual actors, to whom some things are technically impossible and who once onstage cannot be forgotten. It is not controlled by time, but is liable to have several differing and unpredictable clocks, so that time goes with varying paces and can often be forgotten entirely. In a word, it is hard to keep one's eye on the object—the full play—in the theatre of the mind. Keeping the play in continual rehearsal in this theatre is a stimulating, exploratory, necessary activity; but it is not easily a responsible or scholarly investigation. If he wishes to understand the "controlling importance of stage performance" the critic has no choice: he must also work—in some way—in a "real" theatre, no matter how inadequate or how fortuitously contrived. He must meet facts, some facts at least.

I used to think that the critic needed a theatrical laboratory where he could make "research tests" and observe or even measure the effects of different interpretations of the textual evidence. But a fragment of a play suffers out of sequence and out of the developing context of the whole play in performance. Moreover the contents of the experiment can never be adequately controlled: individual actors bring with them so much that cannot be fully understood and cannot be discarded; stages, audiences, and ensemble effects are not easily made to measure, even if the critic-researcher could contrive an adequate measure. The theatre is an art form in which accident and preconditioning have irradicable influences. They are, indeed, essential ingredients, and their effects over a whole play are endlessly and subtly revealing.

The theatrical critic will certainly be tempted to change his mind, to believe that he had been mistaken about the "controlling importance" of this elusive reality. The words on the printed page are each fixed there in due sequence of regular type: would it not be more responsible to concentrate attention on them, knowing that they are not *all* the play, but, at least, a definite and significant part of the play? But by this time it is, I find, too late to turn back. So much has been seen and heard, so many theatrical potentialities of the text have been discovered, that the words simply will not lie down again, in their original place; once a play is alive in its theatrical and variable element it will not easily die. The true choice is not between a verbal reading and a theatrical one, but whether or not to allow Shakespeare's words to awaken—to create, as it were, on their own account. In the theatre, which is its element, his text is the originator and energizer of all that we see and hear.

I think that becoming involved directly, at firsthand, with the process of a play in rehearsal and performance is an inevitable step that must be taken by the responsible critic of Shakespeare's plays. I know this is an extreme view, but for firsthand (if not original) work, nothing less will do. We accept this in editorial matters: a critic can take his text on trust, making some effort to find out what is the best-regarded edition to use and prefacing his work by some clear disclaimer; but a responsible critic will want to be his own editor in the last resort. So, too, he must meet the play he studies in the theatre, actually and for himself, or else he must acknowledge that he takes certain facts on trust or on secondhand authority, or ignores them altogether. Shakespeare wrote for the theatre—that is his medium, the element in which his art is designed to live—and therefore, for all its difficulties, theatrical reality is also *the* element of Shakespeare criticism.

If the theatrical critic of Shakespeare is occupied in discovering possibilities and questions, this should be an accepted condition of much of his work. We should not look for rapid revaluations, or conclude that we have been overemphasizing the basic condition of "stage performance" merely because the object we are viewing seems to change every moment before our very eyes—that is its natural condition. Perhaps the main task of a critic is not to evaluate, fix, place, or penetrate, but to write commentaries that encourage a full engagement with the text in varying conditions of performance; certainly such activity must be a prerequisite for any responsible revaluation.

Besides this basic and exciting work of discovery, other tasks await the theatrical critic. The one that has chiefly engaged me recently is an attempt to outline a "method" for reading a play.[2] I wanted to examine the way I work in the theatre of my mind and, by describing the processes I find most useful, try to understand one stage in critical awareness more precisely and so help myself and, hopefully, others to read Shakespeare with greater consciousness of theatrical potentialities.

Another task is to observe and describe the constants between many productions, and also the theatrical cruxes where any particular play seems most open to varying realization in performance. In *The Tempest*, for example, the moment when Prospero stops the masque is wide open to different interpretations. The character battles with himself in silence, so words cannot define the struggle. Prospero says that he has

> forgot that foul conspiracy
> Of the beast Caliban and his confederates
> Against my life. The minute of their plot
> Is almost come.—Well done! Avoid! No more!—
>
> IV.1. 139-42

but he does not say *why* he remembers it now, nor why it is important, seeing that he is almost godlike in percipience and controlling power. Why break the dance, in which four elements mingle, just before its completion? Comments on his behavior speak of wonder and alarm, and his own next speech is addressed to the dismayed onlookers, only indirectly concerned with himself. In my experience, no two Prosperos have here expressed the same kind of involvement; yet here, clearly, is a major crux in plot, action, character presentation, thematic development, and even in the spectacular impression of the play. Why did Shakespeare fashion it thus, with only inference as guide?

The critic will all the time relate theatrical possibilities to the text, and seek to judge each effect in the widest context that can be held in his mind. He will find that no speech or gesture has its meaning alone. For example, in *Hamlet*, when Polonius talks of "The best actors in the world, either for tragedy, comedy, history, pastoral... " and so forth (II.2.405 ff.), he has just been outrageously mocked as if he were a "great baby," with Hamlet leading two student-friends (whom he has just learnt not to trust) in a zany attack upon his dignity and good sense. As Polonius calls the prince "My lord," the echo comes back from Hamlet, "My lord," and Polonius replies with yet another "my lord" (but at the sentence end this time): thus repartee is the stuff of this dialogue. It is immediately after this that Polonius launches into his long speech, and the actor may well find psychological justification as well as technical control by stressing the longer rhythms of the new sentence over against the running, thrusting, echoing badinage. After the first long sentence of Polonius' speech, the structure and rhythms then shorten; after an antithesis that is comparatively brisk, the last sentence starts with an adverbial phrase and then a short statement:

> For the law of writ and the liberty, these are the only men.

It sounds as if Polonius has won attention by his elaboration and so can bring the speech clearly to a halt. If he has turned away from the mocking and abusive young men, he will be tempted to regain contact with these last words and look them straight in the eyes. Hamlet and his friends may well be silent now, and so Polonius' words "the only men" may thus gain sharp attention and sound like a reproof: these coltish clowns are no men. In performance at this point I have been abruptly reminded of Hamlet's elaborate and careful speech which has just been listened to in silence by Rosencrantz and Guildenstern, the speech about "What a piece of work is a man"; if Polonius gains silence here, his words will seem to touch Hamlet's consciousness at just this point. Something appears to have stirred in his mind, for the prince's next words are rather theatrical, assuming impersonation, but concerned, nevertheless, with judgment, a "fair daughter," and death by sacrifice. *How* Polonius times his speech and speaks the last word in it; *how* the three young men have responded immediately before (are they still laughing?); whether there is a short silence or not; whether Polonius catches Hamlet's eye; *how* Hamlet speaks the following lines: all these elements of the drama in performance are interrelated and together control what the audience sees and hears, and what it understands.

The critic will also look again at the evidence about Elizabethan performances, and use his practical understanding of present-day theatre to try to reconstruct the modes of stage realization that are most natural to the text as Shakespeare contrived it. This will involve continual reappraisal, prompted as much by the lack of similarity between today and then as by the similarities. For example, the repertory system of the Elizabethan theatres ensured a particular kind of preparation by the actors. When a play is put on for one night and then dropped for a week, a fortnight, or even several months, some previous rehearsal will be necessary on each occasion. Clearly the timetable of productions in the busy Elizabethan theatre season would allow, at the most, one rehearsal onstage; and I do not know any evidence to suggest that they invariably took advantage of this. Each performance of a play under these conditions would have an air of improvisation, of danger, of actors watching carefully for what exactly will happen next, a tone and tension that are entirely absent from our well-drilled, well-oiled productions that run with frequency and often continuously. Elizabethan productions must have been precarious, and must have varied from night to night in over-all effect as well as in incidental force or clarity. If an actor has prepared some words with a large and slow delivery, it would matter very much to him at what pace, pitch, and volume the words immediately before his are spoken: he must respond to their rhythms or else his impressive delivery will sound affected, or ponderous, or funny, or unconvincing. The Elizabethan actor needed a more continuous watchfulness than we can easily imagine, for not only was there little group-rehearsal or developed habit of performance, but he could not possibly gain for himself a precise knowledge of what he was to hear and see; he did not have a copy of the text of the whole play from which to study, only the words of his own "part" and the briefest of verbal cues on which he was due to speak. Elizabethan performances were alert, if not precarious. Whenever Shakespeare was in the audience, or an actor in the play, he must have expected to hear the words he had written in ever-new forms; he must have been used to discovering new possibilities.

A critic who works in the element for which Shakespeare wrote will not always command the assurance which will enable him to argue conclusively for major revaluations of Shakespeare's plays. For much of his time he may well cease to be a critic to become an explorer, a patient collector of questions, possibilities, and potentialities. He will also run the risk of being hooked for life, and he may well spread the habit of never knowing for sure what is *in* Shakespeare's plays waiting to be realized.

I do not think this prospect is disquieting, but what anyone used to theatre work would expect. I remember a conversation with T. S. Eliot recorded by Nevil Coghill:

I think I saw you at Rupert Doone's production of *Sweeney Agonistes?*... I had no idea the play meant what he made of it... that everyone is a Crippen. I was astonished.

So was I.

Then you had meant something very different when you wrote it?

Very different indeed.

Yet you accept Mr. Doone's production?

Certainly.

But... but... can the play mean something you didn't intend it to mean, you didn't know it meant?

Obviously it does.

But can it then also mean what you did intend?

I hope so... yes, I think so.

But if the two meanings are contradictory, is not one right and the other wrong? Must not the author be right?

Not necessarily, do you think? Why is either wrong?[3]

In its theatrical element, a play reveals more of its potentiality all the time, the human implications, the emotional, physical, and intellectual possibilities which belong to its original words, the "meaning" of the whole play. A critic will remain open to these varying realizations by meeting the play in its proper element; and then he will evaluate the play with considerable hesitation.

Beyond this he may speculate. Shakespeare is only a special case, an obvious and superbly complicated example: do we, then, know for sure what is *in* any *play*? Beyond that, do we know what is in any work of art created for us to perceive? The theatre may be only the most varying, the least stable, the most endlessly surprising of literary and artistic media; in which case it will be the most accommodating of media, the one most able, in the hands of a master, to speak to any age, through any filter of misunderstanding and inattention—so long as it is perceived in its full and actual theatrical element.

ii

The Nature of Speech in Shakespeare's Plays

The two words "Shakespeare's plays" can signify many things. They may cause us to think of a single, fat, and familiar volume or of a row of uniform paperbacks, some more thumbed than others. There, in small space, is "the text," one of the most fabulous treasure houses of the past; there we can roam at will and appropriate whatever catches our fancies. We take speeches from this great hoard of words and reflect upon them, changing them according to our own individual thoughts and desires. Of course, we are troubled by problems of obscurity, authenticity, punctuation, and spelling, and by doubts about reference, definition, and interpretation. But "Shakespeare's plays," in this physical sense of type on the page, is a palpable, basic, and limited thing, a constant point of reference.

But in another sense "Shakespeare's plays" is much less manageable. The phrase can awaken a whole world of still-breeding thoughts: teeming theatrical images that have been introduced to our minds, selected not by ourselves but according to opportunity and chance. Shakespeare is not solely responsible for his plays in this sense. He has many collaborators who create in our day—and not in his—effects of their own by a variety of means: designers of set, costumes, sound, and light; carpenters, technicians, and stage managers; together with the actors who take his words upon themselves and the directors who control each evolving production. The plays in performance provide a multitude of interlocking sensations, all highly variable in origin, means, effect, and stability. "Shakespeare's plays," in this sprawling and spawning sense, cannot be defined or confined; they are shadows of the mind that resist our predatory grasp.

Between these two extremes of meaning, there is a great divide. On one side, it is proper to speak of the plays' language, vocabulary, images, gestures, style, syntax, dialogue, text. On the other side, other words can be added to our critical discourse: *delivery*, *action*, *play*, *performance*, *personification*, *perception*, *reception*, and *interplay*, together with *entertainment*, *celebration*, and *discovery*. *Interpretation* does not offer a crucial distinction between the two opposed meanings of "Shakespeare's plays," because the text and its theatrical enactment are equally hospitable to many different readings; both await our differing attempts at decoding. Nor does *speech* or *dialogue*, *discourse* or *speech-act*, with reference to words allocated to particular characters in a certain sequence, take us decisively away from the comparatively secure world of the printed word. Only *Speech* as the act of speaking and a part of performance provides the crucial distinction. Speech, in this sense, identifies an element of Shakespeare's plays that is close to the text and yet also releases a seemingly unfettered theatrical life.

Speech originates from words on a page, but it also introduces the individual performer, idiosyncratic, specific, and always changing. Speech involves us as members of an audience and not as independent readers. Of course, speech does not account for all that happens in a theatrical event, but it is such a crucial element, dividing and yet connecting a text and its performance, that we should think as clearly as we can about its nature. Such inquiry might help us to respond more fully and perhaps more suitably to the plays as they lie inert and ready for our reading on the printed page.

There is no need to call for more study of Shakespeare's speeches in a textual sense. The words spoken by individual characters have been studied with great finesse, especially in recent decades. We have become increasingly interested in what words *do*. We can now understand how rhetoricians in Shakespeare's day manipulated the minds of their auditors by varying their methods of exposition, the structure of their speeches, and choice of words, figures of speech, and modes of address. We have learned how Renaissance poets were aware of subtle influences of meter, rhyme, assonance, and all the musical effectiveness of sound, how silence can be given meaning over against the spoken word, how text can suggest subtext, how words mask and disguise thoughts, how questions may be answered by avoidance of direct response. We have studied, too, how speeches in Shakespeare's plays imply gestures and actions that add visual effects to the auditory operation of words. We have begun to understand how meaning is never fully present in any utterance but depends also on what is not said, on the difference from other possible words and sets of words. We look beyond an editor's annotation that offers a single definition or paraphrase and would like to know what words Shakespeare did *not* select. We recognize that a subversive use of ordinary means can effect huge changes of understanding; and so familiar words have become as interesting as those "hard" words which Shakespeare forged for the very first time or borrowed from obscure sources. Personal pronouns—*us* and *them*, and, particularly, *she* and *he*—auxiliary verbs, exclamations, the most routine modes of address and reference, now seem to leap forward for our attention and signal innovative thoughts.

Words swim in our minds, assemble together, and break apart. They change as we study them; they float and sink and get carried downstream into other regions. Words are stimulating and elusive, mocking and bewildering. We realize now that we shall never pin down the effect of Shakespeare's text in our minds or in those of other readers and audiences.

This new awareness is changing our view of Shakespeare's plays while older methods of study continue to grapple with the words in print. Verbal and visual images, ambiguities and associative subtleties, repetitions, variations, and other devices to refine and extend meaning; semantics, syntactics, pronunciation, and morphology all are being considered and reconsidered. In calling attention to the nature of speech in Shakespeare's plays, I may well seem to be redundant, because so much investigation is in hand at present that few people can keep up-to-date with all that is being discovered.

But speech is an individual human activity as well as a collection of printed signs to be listed, described, and decoded. Speech is physiological and therefore as complex as a living organism, and in each manifestation it is therefore unrepeatable. Even when an actor has prepared for speech with the utmost care and efficiency, he or she will respond in a highly instinctive, unconscious manner to the exigencies of each moment in each new performance. Speech in theatrical terms is part of a continuous activity in space and time, within the speaker and without; and every single sound has special qualities not shared by any other.

For example, it is not enough to disentangle by temperate study the signs encoded in the words "To be or not to be...." What that speech communicates in performance depends a great deal on the set of mind and body in the actor who speaks it. To whom does he speak? In what direction or at what distance? Is it to himself, or to a real or an imagined audience, or to a mixture of all three? Where does he breathe in the course of uttering all those words? What quality of sound is natural to his voice, and how is this altered by his speaking within this particular dramatic context? How loudly or quietly does he begin and continue and conclude? What is his pulse rate, how steady his tempo, how insistent or hesitant his inflections? Beyond all this, what happens within the actor as he attempts to present Prince Hamlet at this point in the play? How the actor has fared in the performance before this moment will influence very strongly—and sometimes in unexpected ways—the game that he now plays with the text, with his fellow actors, and with his audience.

(A crude indication of what is involved physiologically in the performance of such a speech can be obtained by memorizing it and then speaking it loud and clear for at least one auditor some thirty feet away. Four or five attempts to make the speech work and communicate will demonstrate an actor's need to gather and control the expenditure of energy, to choose moments for emphasis, to maintain an intelligible phrasing of the words, to follow through from one moment to another, to make the speech his own. Such speech is a challenge, and the chance of winning or losing in that game is part of the excitement and meaning of the play.)

All attempts to evaluate the nature of speech in Shakespeare's plays that do not take into account the actor's contribution to the exigencies and pleasures of performance are grounded solely in textual matters and confined to the page. Studies with titles such as *Littérature et Spectacle*, *The Semiotics of Theatre and Drama*, or *Reading the Signs* promise to engage with this problem. But they exact a large price by insisting on specialized jargon, parenthetical references, and exhaustive enumeration, and then these scholarly works deliver very little to our purpose. Keir Elam's study of Shakespeare's *Discourse* (1984) speaks of the "presence of the voice" without considering the actor responsible for it.[1] (The phrase "presence of the voice" seems somewhat ridiculous to me because it is the actor who has "presence" and not a disembodied "voice.") Professor Elam considers "the body," but only as a "sign-maker," not as something made of flesh and blood; he is content to list textual references to bodies and physical gestures and bypasses without comment the living, breathing, feeling person who is doing the speaking or making the gesture. "Speech production" is here a convenient heading for listing such textual devices for referring to an actor's art and craft as reading a letter. Similarly "units of deictic orientation," discussed in a recent study by Alessandro Serpiere, are defined by the text alone and stand well clear of the ambiguity, excitement, and pleasure of performance.[2] The gestural resources and conventions—the participation frameworks and embedded quotations— that enable Erving Goffman to describe "forms of talk" show that dialogue is like a game with various possible moves, but one that seems to be played without physical commitment.[3] All these scholars consider the speaker as a disembodied functionary, rather than as an individual human being who is alive in thought and action and involved in processes of change and chance.

The result of this new research is an old-fashioned rhetorical enumeration, tricked out in a quantity of curious categories. It is scholastic not theatrical, concerned with text and not with play. So

Professor Elam writes in the concluding section of his book:

> There is quite a distinct kind of dramatic 'dispersion' of the proverb in its citation form (the codified wording, that is, in which it is normally quoted and collected): the paraphrase containing no specific lexical clues to its own proverbial status. What is retained, rendering the transformed saying recognizable, is no longer the key word but the *kernel proposition.* And the audience's cognitive or re-cognitive task is not so much a 'filling-in' as a 'translating back.' The effect is still, however, that of a defamiliarizing estrangement of the codified proposition as such....[4]

The numerous quotation marks and parentheses and the italicization in this passage, together with its curious syntax and punctuation, show how ingeniously this new rhetorical theorizing has been applied to some few words given by Shakespeare to Orsino in the text of *Twelfth Night*. But the effort of mind needed to follow such exposition does little to further our understanding of the speech in performance. The concern here is limited to the content and organization of some words upon the page.

Any inquiry into the nature of speech in Shakespeare's plays must also consider what happens when actors assume the personages of the drama, perform their actions and speak their words. We must try to follow as this activity calls upon an individual's resources and involves him or her in a passionate or fantastic game. We should observe how a company of actors are taken out of their ordinary selves in exploration, contest, and discovery. We must notice, too, how actors are able to satisfy and amaze an audience, who will in return influence the way in which the game is played.

When we go to the theatre, we know that Macbeth will die, but neither we nor the actor can know exactly *how* he will die. We know that the pipers will "strike up" at the end of a comedy, but not how far that music will seem to resolve outstanding issues, change the behavior of the dancers, or influence the way in which we perceive the concluding action.

Performance is a complicated phenomenon and hard to study seriously. It is very tempting to conclude that performance is so out of our control that we should be content either to study the text on a page or else to enjoy, without interruption, whatever performances may please us. But I want to argue that speech, that element of performance which is most closely entwined with the smallest details of the text, does hold some clues that can be followed and help us to a greater understanding of the plays.

*

Shakespearean critics and students should observe actors at work and learn about the nature of acting. They have suffered by being confined to university departments of English where plays are never seen in performance by skilled and practiced actors.

I do not think that the variety of acting styles in evidence today or the difficulty of knowing how Elizabethan actors practiced their art should stand in the way of such inquiry. Nor should an actor's reliance on instinctive reactions cause a critic to undervalue his or her contribution to performance. A company of experienced actors in rehearsals for a Shakespeare play will show an observer how they discover each day new qualities inherent in the text and respond to demands that they had not recognized hitherto. The play seems always to move ahead of the actors' understanding, exerting its own influence more and more as the words become realized or substantiated in performance. Such an impression of progress toward a distant target could be merely an illusion, a product of the actors' need to trust the material on which they are working, but when theatre people speak of Shakespeare's directing them through his text, as they frequently do, they are scarcely aware of using a metaphor; this seems to be no less than the literal truth. As John Barton says in his *Playing Shakespeare*:

> if you want to do [Shakespeare] justice, you have to look for and follow the clues he offers. If an actor does that then he'll find that Shakespeare himself starts to direct him.[5]

When all rehearsals are done, on the first night when the whole play is performed before an audience, good actors go further and give every appearance of growing in power and subtlety, as if summoned by what unfolds before them. How does this happen? How can actors encourage it to happen? What can we learn about Shakespeare's plays from the actors' attempt to give life to the words?

Barton's book, based on a number of television programs showing the rehearsal methods of the Royal Shakespeare Company actors, is a rare attempt to describe how actors work on a text. It reveals some of the questions actors ask as they explore a play and provides some examples of how willfulness or playfulness may carry them toward sufficient confidence to stand up and perform upon a stage. It could serve as an introduction to a study of the nature of speech in Shakespeare's plays. One of its great virtues is that it raises as many questions as it seems to solve for those who had taken part in the studio rehearsals.

John Barton shows how actors can "listen" to versification and to Shakespeare's choice and arrangement of words, and how this leads on to further problems such as what words should be stressed? when should there be a pause? how should a speech or phrase be inflected? Barton encourages his actors to find what he calls the "verbal energy" for a sustained passage in *Love's Labour's Lost*, because without this supercharge it would be "hard to follow and difficult to listen to."[6] He asks each actor to "serve up the key words for the others to play off them"—as if the play were a game of tennis. They must be sure to "play with words, to give the audience the right information," and to "relish" the sounds of resonance and onomatopoeia for the same purpose.[7] Actors must not "fight shy" of rich and vivid language, even if the effort to respond leaves them, at first, breathless and bewildered. They must make the unusually demanding sounds and yet be "real": "it's a question of balance" between these two demands, as he admonishes repeatedly.

Barton's book shows actors being stretched and excited by the sheer energy needed to make these speeches their own and at the same time being exhorted to use their discretion and judgment in order to maintain close and watchful attention to small details of the text as it surges into dramatic life—and sometimes resists their hold. An army of students could find pretexts for their essays in the short compass of this very practical book.

But an exploration of "the nature of speech in Shakespeare's plays" can be taken further than this. Barton's repeated injunctions to "find the language and make his listeners feel the words"[8] are too incidental, too piecemeal, to cope with whole sentences. He pays little attention to syntax and the shape of thought. His actors can sound precious, unreal, and overheated, because they are not taught to seek out the main verb of every sentence and to organize all its words around this central activity of mind. Speech should be more than interesting and effectively colored; it should develop from the motive force or action that has formed the sentence as a whole and in a particular order. The only way to make utterance convincing is to balance its parts and find an appropriate rhythm from the needs and forces within the character in the dramatic situation as it develops throughout the play. "Relishing" words and "feeling" the language can become an almost mindless mastication.

In the television series on which his book is based, Barton was content to leave problems of character to the actor's instincts, but it is noticeable how often the actors pull him back to consider why certain words are spoken in a particular context by a particular person. Occasionally, Barton helps to make a speech sound more forceful by calling for some generalized emotional charge—as when he encourages the speaker of the Chorus in *Henry V* to be more "excited" within himself and then rewards the new rendering with "I thought the first half of that was great"[9]—but too often, in my opinion, he deals with speakers and not with characters or persons in a drama. He seems content with an actor's intellectual understanding and does not lead forward from this into the expression of a total and individual involvement in the play. He asks actors to "make the images more concrete," not to look for ways to make the words necessary to their characters in performance at the moment of utterance.

Barton takes time off from the plays to set actors working on Shakespeare's sonnets where he can avoid problems of interplay between speakers and their response to the drama's developing action. This also avoids questions about the nature of a character's involvement in words with the idiosyncrasy of a particular physical human being. But his exercises on the sonnets, with their regular form of fourteen rhymed lines, does permit him to develop the actor's ability to shape a whole speech, a task that is often missing in his other rehearsal sessions.

The Royal Shakespeare actors have to project Shakespeare's words out into the far reaches of the Stratford Theatre or the broad expanse of the Barbican Theatre in London, and this has led them, in my opinion, to simplify and exaggerate. It is important to realize that actors trained in other than the classical repertory, those used to the close scrutiny of the camera and inspired by its ability to direct attention to small signs of unspoken thoughts and sensations, can also find appropriate ways of acting Shakespeare, and they may well be more able to create characters that live intensely on the stage. I have seen a film actor, unused to Shakespeare's plays, seek to make the movements of Polonius's mind, as expressed in his convoluted prose, a part of a complete personification. The words came very slowly at first, but so did the amazing complexity of a man who was father of Ophelia and Laertes and also the chief counselor of the King. The shape and rhythms of speech governed the inner workings of the actor and his physical activity; there was no contradiction between what was heard and what was seen and sensed. The result was a character made wholly visible, palpable, true, and arresting. Polonius's speech stopped the rehearsal once the actor had achieved the connection between text and being; so strong an impression of reality had been created that the other actors in the scene were not ready to respond.

Reading the signs in a text is not enough; we need to cross over the dividing line and ask how these words can be spoken and how they can best become part of an image of fully lived experience. Experimentally, in rehearsal with trained actors, we can learn more and become skilled at reading the multitude of clues that lie implicit within it and which actors thrive upon. It is from the text that the whole play springs to life so that our study of performance will in turn lead to a fuller understanding and, perhaps, a revaluation of the most familiar plays.

*

Three brief examples will serve to indicate some of the possibilities that a study of speech may open up. The first is from *Othello*:

> Strumpet, I come.
> Forth of my heart those charms, thine eyes, are blotted;
> Thy bed, lust-stain'd, shall with lust's blood be spotted.
>
> V.1.33-36

The rhythms, syntax, and vocabulary of this soliloquy are so difficult that most directors have pity on their actor and cut it from the production script. The words are in starkest contrast to the Moor's previous utterance, which was still under control for Lodovico's sake. And the tone of his next words changes yet more surprisingly, as he is rapt in wonder and contemplates "the cause" that draws him toward murder and suicide. I have seen Paul Scofield in the pauses of rehearsals moving around and flexing his body, as he spoke these words to himself, seeking the bodily changes that could draw forth and give credibility to their emphatic, lurid, and crudely vindictive qualities, and to the syntax which piles up epithets within each line and moves from present, to past, and to future without transitional phrase. By watching the actor I realized that here the whole person of Othello passes through a dark and violent experience: it comes upon him and the audience with a sudden shock and will radically alter the way in which he approaches the final scene, when his repetitions are not violently charged and when delicacy, tenderness, and far-reaching images have repossessed his mind and made his body hesitate and remain poised above his sleeping wife.

Any one speech tends to influence others. Consider Claudius's words to Laertes, in the middle of their plotting for the assassination of

Hamlet:

> There lives within the very flame of love
> A kind of wick or snuff that will abate it
> And nothing is at a like goodness still;
> For goodness, growing to a pleurisy,
> Dies in his own too much. That we would do,
> We should do when we would; for this 'would' changes,
> And hath abatements and delays as many
> As there are tongues, are hands, are accidents;
> And then this 'should' is like a spendthrift's sigh
> That hurts by easing. But to the quick of th' ulcer:
> Hamlet comes back; what would you undertake. ...
>
> IV.7.114-24

The first ten lines of this passage insist that the breathing, rhythms, pitch, and inflections of the actor playing Claudius must all change. It seems in performance as if the thought of Gertrude has drawn Claudius off target, taking possession of his mind without his volition. He had spoken of the Queen at the beginning of the scene but despatched her from his thoughts easily enough; now, however, the structure of his thought is drawn out, the weight of sound lightens, and a new field of imagery is introduced (the same flame image that was to haunt the mind of Othello). Yet Claudius does not mention the Queen directly; and soon his thought quickens once more, as he knows he has to act alone, regardless of his pain, in order to lance the ulcer that he *can* cope with and which Laertes can recognize easily. Response to these changing demands of the text is more than a technical feat employed for the instant: the actor will make this speech credible only by preparing for it long before, by establishing a particular relationship to Gertrude in silence as well as words. This incidental passage is then capable of an impression of instinctive, private thought and of fugitive, delicate, and yet strong feeling. Claudius is forced to torture himself. We can see this in his breathing as he speaks, in the movement and changes of his eyes as he alters the object of his attention, in the relaxation and tension of his body, and in his nervous impulses as his thoughts change and seek to hide irrepressible feelings. He is suffering already, and doomed; Hamlet's final actions only complete for Claudius what has started earlier in the play.

Verbal clues to crises in performance may be very brief and easily passed over until explored in the rehearsal room. I remember Sir John

Gielgud preparing to play Prospero at the National Theatre in London and seeking the deep assurance and inner suffering required to make "Tis new to thee" and "In this last tempest" (*The Tempest*, 5.1.184 and 153) register fittingly in their context, using their precise phrasing. As his long role drew toward an end in imperfect reconciliations, Shakespeare's text could bear the great weight of feeling required by the dramatic context only after the actor had discovered, with difficulty, the appropriate means for himself, a delivery that was most delicate and softly spoken and yet reached to the back of the theatre because of the authority, poise, and timing used. Indeed the effect was richer than this, because Gielgud's Prospero seemed also to share with the audience a consciousness of the inadequacy of what was actually spoken; he was playing a part for the sake of those who knew less than he did, and he seemed to take some consoling—or some briefly diverting—pleasure in doing so. These short speeches were so immaculately phrased that the magician and rightful ruler was like a dramatist completing a play, rather than speaking his mind; and yet, at the same time, the father suffered in private and felt a quickening joy.

*

One objection to the kind of study I am recommending is that modern actors are not those Elizabethan and Jacobean actors for whom Shakespeare wrote his plays and that they bring to rehearsals many prejudices and skills which Shakespeare could not have imagined, and lack others that he took for granted. But the same argument can be leveled against any reading of the plays. No one person can reconstruct a historically accurate response, even if we could know what that might be.

Of course, any encounter with the text will be flawed and could benefit from a greater understanding of the variety of life and history of thought. But the reading that takes place in a rehearsal room has one great advantage over that of a literary student. Whatever an actor discovers must always be realized in terms of performance, and that includes a great many features of lived experience; it cannot survive as some new argument set forth in words alone. Perhaps Elizabethan actors were cruder or more eloquent, or more formalized and less lifelike, than their modern counterparts, but every actor who steps onto a stage has to bring a whole self into play and must relate what is spoken to what is there, palpably, before the audience. No actor can cheat for very long; incomplete performances, or those which have some elements at odds with others, will be recognized for what they are by audiences and by fellow actors. We need have little doubt that modern actors are responding to qualities inherent in Shakespeare's text; if they did not, they would find acting in his plays a troublesome labor and not a great pleasure.

Another objection to my argument is that rehearsals do not have comparable authority with great performances by the most famous actors from the past. We are told to study the stage history of plays to discover the undoubted nature of their theatrical life. But this is to interpose a further historical distortion between ourselves and the text. Accounts of eighteenth-century actors or even of those two or three decades before the present must all be interpreted in light of the production styles of those days and the idiosyncrasies of the star performers. Moreover the earlier performances are no longer there for us to encounter as best we may; all we can do is to read newspaper accounts that were written to make interesting copy rather than to describe performances accurately or comprehensively. We can take special note of what appealed to the crowd as well as to the more judicious critics, but that tells us only about the broader effects and, sometimes, about topical and passing enthusiasms. We can read whatever an actor or biographer has deemed fit to publish about aims and achievements, but very often these books and articles were written by way of apology or self-advertisement. Promptbooks are firmer ground for the student, but stage managers have always been concerned to record the traffic of the stage rather than the nature of performance; their reasons for noting anything were related to the smooth functioning of a complicated operation, not to the interests of an audience or future students.

The study of theatre history is useful as a corrective and stimulus. Anyone can be blind to some opportunities inherent in a text, and suggestions from the past can alert our attention. But the growing number of books that record the fortunes of plays in the theatre cannot replace the more basic and exploratory work which may be undertaken every time a play is rehearsed by skilled and experienced actors and brought to the pitch of subsequent performance. Every student of Shakespeare, of whatever experience, learning, or talents, needs access to this laboratory and to the testing ground of performance, which is also a place of entertainment. Here is where "speech" as I have defined it earlier will bridge the divide between text and theatrical understanding.

NOTES

NOTES

INTRODUCTION

1. Gordon Craig, *On the Art of the Theatre* (ed. 1957), p. 21

CHAPTER 1

1. For an informed account of the Queen's favorites, see J. E. Neale, *Queen Elizabeth* (1934)
2. A. C. Sprague, *Shakespeare and the Actors* (1948), p.140
3. Quoted W. Clark Russell, *Representative Actors* (n.d.), p.110
4. *Elizabethan Critical Essays*, ed. G. Gregory Smith (1904), i.273
5. *Ibidem*, i.160
6. Reprinted in *Shaw on Shakespeare*, ed. Edwin Wilson (1961), p.7

CHAPTER 2

1. S. L. Bethell, 'Shakespeare's Actors', *Review of English Studies*, new series, i(1950), 205
2. *Ibidem*
3. *Shakespeare and the Popular Dramatic Tradition* (1944), p.31. See also M. C. Bradbrook, *Themes and Conventions of Elizabethan Tragedy* (1935), pp. 20-1
4. Sig. B4; the italics are mine
5. John Webster, *Works*, ed. F. L. Lucas (1927), iv.43
6. F. Beaumont and J. Fletcher, *Comedies and Tragedies* (1647), Sig. f2v
7. Quoted from Sir E. K. Chambers, *The Elizabethan Stage* (1923), ii.309
8. A. Harbage, 'Elizabethan Acting', *PMLA*, liv(1939), 692; the evidence he quotes includes the verses on Burbage quoted above
9. S. L. Bethell, *op. cit.*, note 3, p. 86
10. B. L. Joseph, *Elizabethan Acting* (1951), p. 129
11. *Works*, ed. C. H. Herford and P. and E. Simpson, viii(1947),587. Jonson's editors date *Timber* between 1623 and 1635 (xi,195,213); but C. J. Sisson has shown that the work was probably composed as lecture notes while Jonson was acting as deputy for Henry Croke, the Professor of Rhetoric at Gresham College, in 1619 (*Times Literary Supplement*, 21 September 1951)
12. *The Art of English Poesie* (1599); G. Gregory Smith, *Elizabethan Critical Essays* (1904), ii.186-7
13. Cf. A. Harbage, *op. cit.*, pp.701-2; B. L. Joseph, *op. cit.*, *passim*; and S. L. Bethell, 'Shakespeare's Actors', *op. cit.*, p.202
14. Quoted from E. K. Chambers, *op. cit.*, iv. 370. There has been some argument about the validity of this evidence; see A. Harbage, *op. cit.*,

p.695 and S. L. Bethell, 'Shakespeare's Actors', *op. cit.*, pp. 200-1

15. So B. L. Joseph, *op. cit.* Even as an indication of an orator's art the books are suspect, for Bulwer himself confesses that 'I never met with any rhetorician or other, that had pictured out one of these rhetorical expressions of the hands and fingers; or met with any philologer that could exactly satisfy me in the ancient rhetorical postures of Quintilian' (*Chironomia*, p. 26; quoted from Joseph, *ibidem*, pp. 45-7)
16. B. L. Joseph, *op. cit.*, p. 141
17. *The Arcadian Rhetoric* (1588), Sig. I7v
18. 'To the Reader'; *Works*, ed. P. Vivian (1909)
19. A. Harbage, *op. cit.*, p. 690
20. B. L. Joseph, *op. cit.*, p. 146
21. *The Governor* (1531); ed. H. H. S. Croft (1880), i.124
22. *The Schoolmaster* (1570); *English Works*, ed. W. A. Wright (1904), p. 266
23. *A Defence of Poetry* (1579); ed. G. Gregory Smith, *Elizabethan Critical Essays* (1904), i.81; *Every Man Out of His Humour* (1600), III.6. 206-7; and *An Apology for Actors* (1612), Sig. Flv
24. *The Unfortunate Traveller* (1594); *W*orks, ed. R. B. McKerrow, ii(1904), 283
25. Malone Society Reprint (1909), ll. 2015-17
26. Written of *Timon of Athens*; G. Wilson Knight, *The Wheel of Fire* (1930), p. 274
27. 'To the General Reader', *Sophonisba* (1606); *Plays*, ed. H. H. Wood (1938), ii.5
28. Sir Philip Sidney, *The Defence of Poesie* (1595); *Works*, ed. A. Feuillerat (1923), iii.8
29. Dedication, *Caesar and Pompey* (1631); *Tragedies*, ed. T. M. Parrott (1910), p. 341
30. Thomas Nashe, Preface to Robert Greene's *Menaphon* (1589); *Works*, ed. R. B. McKerrow, iii(1905), 312
31. *Henslowe's Diary*, ed. R. A. Foakes and R. T. Rickert (1961), pp. 319-20
32. *Shakespeare at the Globe* (1962), p. 156

CHAPTER 3

1. Cf. W. W. Greg, *The Shakespeare First Folio* (1955), pp. 404-7
2. *Prefaces to Shakespeare*, 1st series (1927), p. xix, note
3. F. Moryson, *Shakespeare's Europe*, ed. C. Hughes (1903), p. 304
4. Cf. G. Tillotson, '*Othello* and *The Alchemist* at Oxford', *Times Literary Supplement* (20 July 1933)

CHAPTER 4

1. The New Cambridge editors emend to 'Whiter than snow upon a raven's back', commenting 'The "new" [of Q2] is Shakespeare's false start.... One cannot have *old* snow on a raven's back!'; but this is to judge a tautology by literary standards (of a restricted kind), not by dramatic standards
2. C. Stanislavski, *Building a Character*, tr. Elizabeth R. Hapgood (1950), p. 113
3. *The Drama: Addresses* (1893), pp. 40-6; my italics
4. C. Cibber, *An Apology* (ed. 1740), p. 87
5. *The Tatler*, No. 167 (1710)
6. See Chapter 2, p. 26
7. Compare Shylock's brief speeches on his exit from the Trial Scene; Chapter 6, pp. 84-5

CHAPTER 5

1. *On Dramatic Method* (ed. 1956), p. 22
2. See, for example, *The Journal of William Charles Macready*, ed. J.J. Trewin (1907) and *Henry Irving: Shakespearean*, by Alan Hughes (1981), especially pp. 27-76, 94-114, 151-60, and 240.
3. *Theatre: the Rediscovery of Style* (1960), pp. 68-9

CHAPTER 6

1. Records quoted in this chapter are taken chiefly from: F. Gentleman, *Dramatic Censor* (1770); J. T. Kirkman, *Memoirs of Macklin* (1799); *Memoirs of Charles Macklin* (1804); G. H. Lewes, *On Actors and the Art of Acting* (1875); F. W. Hawkins, *Life of Kean* (1869); J. Doran, *Their Majesties' Servants* (ed. 1897); H. H. Hillebrand, *Edmund Kean* (1933); W. Winter, *Shakespeare on the Stage* (1912); L. Irving, *Henry Irving* (1951); and A. C. Sprague, *Shakespeare and the Actors* (1944)
2. J. Boaden, *Memoirs of J. P. Kemble* (1825), i.440
3. *Lichtenberg's Visits to England*, translated Margaret L. Mare and W. H. Quarrell (1938), p. 40
4. W. Hazlitt, *Works* (ed. 1930), iv.320-4
5. R. Hole, *Essays by a Society of Gentlemen, at Exeter* (1796), p. 559
6. W. Gardiner, *The Music of Nature* (1832), pp. 48-9
7. S. B. and Marie E. Bancroft, *Mr and Mrs Bancroft* (8th ed., 1891), p. 212
8. Vandenhoff; quoted by Hillebrand, p. 346
9. *The Chronicle* (6 April 1816)

10. *The Theatre* (1879), p. 294
11. *Blackwood's Magazine* (December 1879)
12. *Daily Telegraph* (18 October 1927)
13. *Observer* (23 October and 24 December 1927)
14. *The Times* (29 April 1932)
15. *Daily Telegraph* (29 April 1932)
16. Cf. an interview in the *Observer* (3 April 1938)
17. *The Saturday Review* (30 April 1938)
18. Robert Speight, 'The 1960 Season at Stratford-Upon-Avon', *Shakespeare Quarterly*, xi(1961), 449
19. John Russell Brown, 'Three Directors', *Shakespeare Survey*, 14(1961), 135-6
20. *The Times* (30 April 1970)
21. Richard Foulkes, 'Henry Irving and Laurence Olivier as Shylock', *Theatre Notebook*, xxvii,1(1972), 33.
22. *Sunday Express* (1 May 1988)
23. *Guardian* (28 April 1988)
24. *Independent* (28 April 1988)
25. *Op. cit.* (9 June 1989)
26. *Herald Tribune* (7 June 1989)
27. *Jewish Chronicle*, *ibidem*
28. Cf. A. C. Sprague, *op. cit.* pp. 24 and 22
29. *The Times*, *ibidem*
30. Cf. *Henry V*, IV.1.99-108
31. At the time of writing *The Merchant of Venice*, the connotations of this word for Shakespeare appear to have been desolation and savagery: cf: *II Henry VI*, III.2.360; *Titus Andronicus*, III.1.54 and 94; *II Henry IV*, IV.4.137; and *Lucrece*, 1.544
32. Cf. Menenius' attempt at a similar change of subject; *Coriolanus*, IV.2.49

CHAPTER 7

1. In this chapter 'clown' indicates a kind of actor; a star, 'personality' comic. This corresponds to Elizabethan and Jacobean usage; for example, Feste, the professional fool in *Twelfth Night*, is designated 'Clown' in the speech-prefixes of the Folio text
2. *Shakespeare's Last Plays* (1951), p. 40
3. *Ellen Terry and Bernard Shaw; a Correspondence*, ed. C. St John (1949), pp. 45-6.

CHAPTER 8

1. *Stanislavski's Legacy*, edited and translated by Elizabeth Reynolds Hapgood (1958; ed. 1981), p. 11
2. Michael Redgrave, *In My Mind's Eye: an autobiography* (1983), p. 107
3. Marvin Rosenberg, *The Masks of Macbeth* (1978), p. 617. Professor Rosenberg also outlines the range of interpretations which have been recorded for this half-line

CHAPTER 10

1. See Gordon Craig's illustrations of Act I, Scene 2 and Act III, Scene 2: Plates 5-8
2. *A Life in the Theatre* (1960), pp. 58-9
3. Cf. A. C. Sprague, *Shakespeare and the Actors* (1944), pp. 147-8
4. Cf. *Building a Character* (translated 1949), Chapters 11 and 12

CHAPTER 11

1. For a convenient summary of the relationship between the staging of *The Tempest* and of court masques, see the New Arden Edition of *The Tempest*, ed. Frank Kermode (1954), Appendix E. For a general account of the influence of masques on the plays of the period, see Inga-Stina Ewbank, '"These Pretty Devices": A Study of Masques in Plays,' in *A Book of Masques*, ed. T.J.B. Spencer and Stanley Wells (1967); this also provides numerous texts and illustrations of sets and costumes. Kevin R. McNamara has argued that the masque is so central to *The Tempest* that the play was written for performance at a private theatre which resembled the Banquetting Hall at Whitehall; see 'Golden Worlds at Court: *The Tempest* and Its Masque', *Shakespeare Studies*, xix(1987), 183-202
2. See Alan Hughes, *op. cit.*, pp. 109-11

CHAPTER 12

1. See Chapter 2, p. 17
2. L. Cazamian, *The Development of English Humour* (1952), p. 302

APPENDIX i

1. *The Question of "Hamlet"* (1959). pp. 131-32

2. *Discovering Shakespeare* (1983)
3. *T. S. Eliot: A Symposium*, compiled by Richard March and Tambimuttu (1948), pp. 85-86

APPENDIX ii

1. Keir Elam, *Shakespeare's Universe of Discourse: Language-Games in the Comedies* (1984)
2. Alessandro Serpieri, "Reading the Signs: Towards a Semiotics of Shakespearean Drama," trans. Keir Elam, in *Alternative Shakespeares*, ed. John Drakakis (1985), 119-143
3. Erving Goffman, *Forms of Talk* (1981)
4. Elam, *Shakespeare's Universe of Discourse*, p. 280
5. John Barton, *Playing Shakespeare* (1984), p. 168
6. *Ibid.*, 73
7. *Ibid.*, 52
8. *Ibid.*, 86-87
9. *Ibid.*, 5-51

Index

INDEX

SHAKESCENES: SHAKESPEARE FOR TWO

The Shakespeare Scenebook

EDITED AND WITH AN INTRODUCTION BY JOHN RUSSELL BROWN

Thirty-five scenes are presented in newly edited texts, with notes which clarify meanings, topical references, puns, ambiguities, etc. Each scene has been chosen for its independent life requiring only the simplest of stage properties and the barest of spaces. A brief description of characters and situation prefaces each scene and is followed by a commentary which discusses its major acting challenges and opportunities.

paper ▮ ISBN 1-55783-049-5